I LOVE GILL SANS

I Love Type Series
Volume Five

M000087082

Published by Viction:ary

Edited & Designed by TwoPoints.Net

Eric Gill (1882-1940) did not think of himself primarily as a type designer. In his autobiography he wrote that in the field of drawing letters, he would never 'be anything but an amateur.' On his gravestone, which he devised himself, Gill described himself as a stone carver. He was, of course, many more things as well: a book designer and book illustrator; an artist who made elegant woodcuts and sensual drawings; a sharp and witty writer. Yet his typefaces — modern classics like Joanna, Perpetua, and Gill Sans — are the one aspect of his heritage that is still relevant in today's visual culture. As this book evidences, Gill Sans especially has become an ubiquitous design tool of the digital age.

Gill Sans wood type used in a contemporary piece. Concept, design and production: Flowers and Fleurons, Brighton (John Christopher)

Gill Sans is more than just a typeface: it is a meeting of cultures, an amalgam of influences as far apart as Roman stonecarving and English signpainting, renaissance calligraphy and Arts & Crafts book design. It would not have come into being without the impulses from two men that played such essential roles in Gill's life and career: Edward Johnston and Stanley Morison.

Gill's love for lettering can be traced back to his schoolboy days, when he loved making drawings of railroads — of locomotives, signals and bridges — which naturally led to (crudely) drawing type. As Gill wrote, 'locomotives have names, and these are painted on them with great care and artistry. If you're keen on engines, you collect engine names (at our school it was as popular a hobby as "stamps") and if you draw engines you cannot leave out their names.' Some years later, as a student at Chichester Technical and Art School, Gill became quite proficient in the art of lettering in the decorative style of the moment: Art Nouveau. Having moved to London at

18, he soon came to reject his earlier student work after joining the writing and lettering class given at the Central School of Arts and Crafts by Edward Johnston.

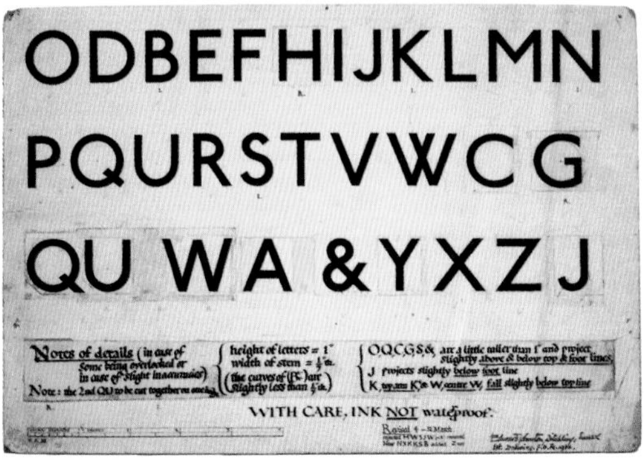

Working drawings by Edward Johnston for the 'Underground Block-letter', which would later become known as Johnston Underground, or simply Johnston.

Gill and Johnston

Meeting Johnston altered the course of Gill's life; Johnston's insights gave his work a direction and a purpose. It helped him shake off 'the art nonsense' of his Chichester days, and find an approach to calligraphy and lettering that was more direct, more honest and more precise.

Edward Johnston was largely self-taught in what was at the time considered a dead art: formal writing with a self-cut goose quill pen. He would soon become an undisputed writing master, influencing generations of calligraphers and typographers with his 1906 book *Writing & Illuminating, & Lettering*. Gill, when watching him write for the first time, felt as if struck by lightning. 'I did not know such beauty could exist. ... It was as though a secret of heaven was being revealed.' But Johnston's interest in letterforms was broader than the mediaeval and renaissance writing he revived with such conviction. When walking home one evening with Eric Gill, Johnston pointed at the simple, straightforward lettering on tradesmen's carts — capital letters done in an unadorned sans-serif style, rather bold and geometric, which Johnston and his contemporaries called 'Block-letter'. Johnston admired the clarity and unassuming craftsmanship of those alphabets; they would become a primary source of inspiration when, a decade later, he received the assignment that would result in one of the most revolutionary typefaces of the early 20th century, and the blueprint of what was to become Gill Sans.

In 1913 Johnston was approached by Frank Pick of the Underground Electric Railways Company of London (which would become London Transport in 1933), who wanted a new typeface for the public transport system: modern and functional, each of its letters 'a strong and unmistakable symbol' that would clearly stand out from the surrounding advertising. In response to Pick's specifications Johnston submitted a sans-serif, geometrically constructed alphabet whose proportions were based on the proportions of Roman monumental lettering such as the alphabet found on the famous Trajan Column. Johnston designed upper- and lowercase alphabets as well as a condensed version to be used on buses (1922); the typeface is still in use today, with the necessary modifications to guide it through the many changes in printing and typesetting technology.

Gill Sans Inlined as large size wood type for posters, Stephenson Blake, 1962

Perpetua, his first printing typeface

While Johnston was involved in the complex process of developing the Underground typeface for a variety of uses, his former student Eric Gill was gaining a firm reputation as a lettering artist, stonemason, sculptor and illustrator. When in 1924 he was approached by Stanley Morison of the Monotype company to design a printing face to be produced for the Monotype system, he politely refused, saying: 'Typography is not my line of country'. It took Morison some years of gentle persuasion to convince Gill to produce drawings for a typeface based on his stonecarving alphabet — the typeface that would become Perpetua. A strikingly contemporary roman text face, Perpetua was produced with the help of the Frenchman Charles Malin, one of the last artisan punchcutters. Morison especially admired its titling capitals, writing: 'The capitals that he did, I think, will be immortal. They'll be used as long as the Roman alphabet is ever used anywhere.'

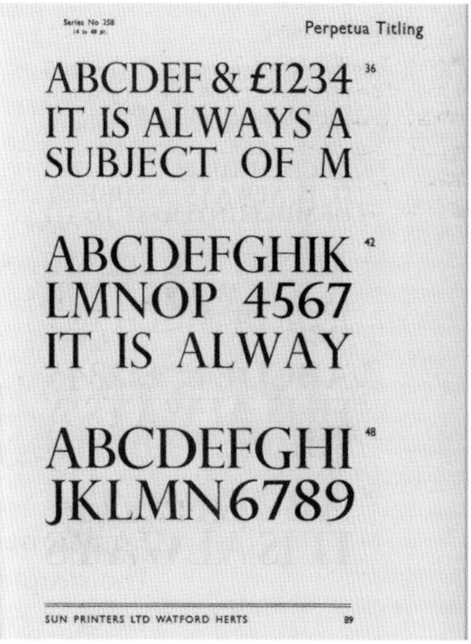

Gill's Perpetua typeface, the all-caps titling version. Stanley Morison called these capitals 'immortal'.

The first publications printed with Perpetua as a text face were published in 1928-1929, one of them being a book by Eric Gill himself. Gill's interest in type design was now aroused.

The very first drawings of what would become Gill Sans were made for Bristol bookseller Douglas Everdon, as part of a combined set of seriffed and sans alphabets. Published in 'A Book of Alphabets for Douglas Everdon drawn by Eric Gill' published in 1987 by Gill's nephew, the printer Christopher Skelton.

The making of Gill Sans

Stanley Morison soon approached Gill with a new proposal. Morison had realized that what Monotype needed to bring its type library up to date was a readable sans-serif face. German type foundries were releasing a string of geometric sans-serifs: Erbar by Jakob Erbar in 1926, Kabel by Rudolf Koch in 1927, and the most successful of all, Paul Renner's Futura in 1928. Monotype wanted to come up with a British answer to Futura — soon. And Morison believed Gill was the man for the job. One reason was that he was a letter cutter, which according to Morison made his lettering work extremely powerful: 'A cut line is very different from a drawn line... When he was cutting, he *cut*... He wasn't afraid of committing himself.' The other reason was more specific: Morison was impressed by a set of capitals that Gill had designed for a mutual friend, the bookseller Douglas Cleverdon. In 1926 Gill had sketched a few alphabets — both old-style romans and sans-serifs — for Cleverdon as suggestions for lettering for labels and placards in his new Bristol bookshop. When Cleverdon then asked Gill to paint the facia of his shop, Gill chose the 'Block-letter'. As soon as Morison saw the result, he realized the answer to Monotype's quest for a sans might lie in these capital letters. Another reason for wanting new typefaces suitable for both text and display was the launch of a new Monotype machine that was able to produce type sizes up to 72pt, the Super Caster.

Gill readily supplied complete alphabets of the upper- and lowercase and agreed, somewhat surprised by Morison's suggestion, to call the new face Gill Sans. The design owed much to Johnston's Underground alphabet, although there were many differences as well. Gill corrected many of the Underground typeface's more quirky elements — the strict Roman proportions of the capitals, its somewhat rigid monolinear character (i.e. all strokes having the same thickness), the square dots. Gill's own comments on the Johnston typeface and his departure from it are interesting, also for his strikingly modern use of the word 'fool-proof': 'The first notable attempt to work out the norm for plain letters,' wrote Gill, 'was made by Edward Johnston when he designed the sans-serif letter for the London Underground Railways. Some of these letters are not entirely satisfactory, especially when it is remembered that, for such a purpose, an alphabet should be as near as possible to "fool-proof", i.e. the forms should be measurable — nothing should be left to the imagination of the sign-writer or the enamel-plate maker. In this quality of "fool-proofness", my Monotype sans-serif face is perhaps an improvement: the letters are more strictly normal.'

g

t

a

Some of Gill Sans' more idiosyncratic letters: the compass-constructed, geometric 'g', the 't' with its triangular top; the 'a' with its strong thick-thin contrast.

Nevertheless, Gill Sans has some quirky elements as well. While the capitals are beautifully balanced, working well both as initials and in all-caps settings, the lowercase forms are plenty of surprises. The two-story 'g', with its geometric structure based on a circle and an oval, is strikingly unorthodox, as is the 't' with its triangular top; the bowl of the 'a' has a stronger thick-thin contrast than the rest of the letters seem to justify. Like its serif counterpart, Perpetua, Gill Sans comes with a hybrid italic, somewhere halfway between a calligraphic 'real' italic and a sloped roman. In the context of this rather business-like italic alphabet, a detail such as the spur on the 'p' stands out. Some typographers regard it as a flaw: too conspicuous for comfort. But of course, without these details, Gill Sans wouldn't be Gill Sans. It is these and other characteristics that lend the typeface its unique charm.

italic
"p"

Gill Sans' hybrid italic, with its rather conspicuous spurred 'p'.

The proof of a typeface is in the reading; and in that department, despite its rather unorthodox construction principles, Gill Sans does not disappoint. During its first decades, Gill Sans was recommended for advertising and display use only, especially in the UK. But in that capacity, it became a staple of British graphic design. British Rail adopted it as its corporate typeface for signage, display lettering and more. It became the default typeface for Penguin and Pelican covers, used to maximize effect in Jan Tschichold's 1949 Penguin redesign. As readers gradually got used to reading sans-serif, Gill Sans turned out to work well for body text in magazines as well as books. In the Netherlands, for instance, Gill Sans became a popular text face for non-fiction books and magazines. The Netherlands and the United Kingdom were among the countries that adopted Gill Sans for many administrative documents — notably those used by the British Post Office and the Dutch PTT. A special version called Gill Sans Schoolbook became very popular to set books for young children; in the Schoolbook version, Gill Sans' clarity of construction has been further enhanced by replacing the more complex shapes of the lowercase 'a' and 'g' by simplified single-storey variants.

When Gill Sans proved successful, Monotype capitalized on its usability for headlines by producing a vast number of derivates for display sizes — light, bold, condensed and heavy varieties; Shadowline, Inline, Cameo and Cameo Ruled versions; and the most extreme of all, Gill Sans Ultra Bold, also know as Kayo. These display versions were usually not drawn by Gill, but by anonymous workers in the Monotype Drawing Office. Surprisingly enough, in his capacity as a consultant to Monotype, Gill collaborated in the production of these rather exorbitant versions of his brainchild — typographic eccentricities one would not imagine to be compatible with Gill's rather strict typographic principles. But as Simon Loxley wrote, 'in the land of Gill, expect the unexpected.' Humor, too, is something that could be expected from Gill, witness the witty pet name he came up with for the overweight Kayo (pronounced as K-O, for 'knock-out'): Gill Sans Double Elefans.

One assignment in the last decade of his life must have pleased Gill immensely: to design the lettering of the Flying Scotsman, a locomotive of the LNER railway company, which had adopted Gill Sans as its corporate typeface. Having once admired the lettering on trains, he now created the kind of letters which, as a boy, he had merely copied.

It is this kind of job that brings to mind Gill's most famous dictum: 'Letters are things, not pictures of things.' The phrase is often misunderstood, and should be read in its context. Gill was not so much referring to letters as physical shapes, or objects, as too their autonomy — the fact that a letter is, first and foremost, itself; that as a shape, it is not referring to anything but itself. Precision is crucial: there is no such thing as an impressionist letter. Here's the complete paragraph: 'The shapes of letters do not derive their beauty from any sensual or sentimental reminiscence. No one can say that the 'O''s roundness appeals to us only because it is like that of an apple or of a girl's breast or of the full moon. We like the circle because such liking is connatural to the human mind. And no one can say lettering is not a useful trade by which you can honestly serve your fellow men and earn an honest living. Of what other trade or art are these things so palpably true? Moreover it is a precise art. You don't draw an 'A' and then stand back and say: "there, that gives you a good idea of an 'A' as seen through an autumn mist", or: "that's not a real 'A' but gives you a good effect of one." Letters are things, not pictures of things.'

Letters are things made for reading, and that is what Gill designed them for. This ultimately makes Eric Gill a functionalist; and Gill Sans, his most popular design, a very functional typeface indeed.

Jan Middendorp

Sources:

Eric Gill, *An essay on typography*. J.M. Dent & Sons, London 1931

Eric Gill, *Autobiography*. Jonathan Cape, London 1940

Simon Loxley, *Type. The Secret History of Letters*, I.B.Taurus, London/New York 2004

Fiona McCarthy, *Eric Gill. Faber and Faber*, London/Boston 1989

James Moran, *Stanley Morison. His typographic achievement*. Lund Humpries, London 1971

Stanley Morison, *A Tally of Types*, Cambridge University Press, 1973

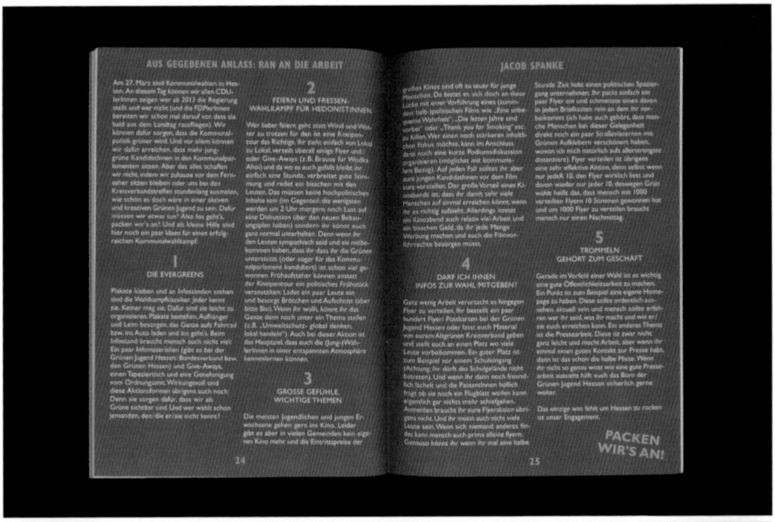

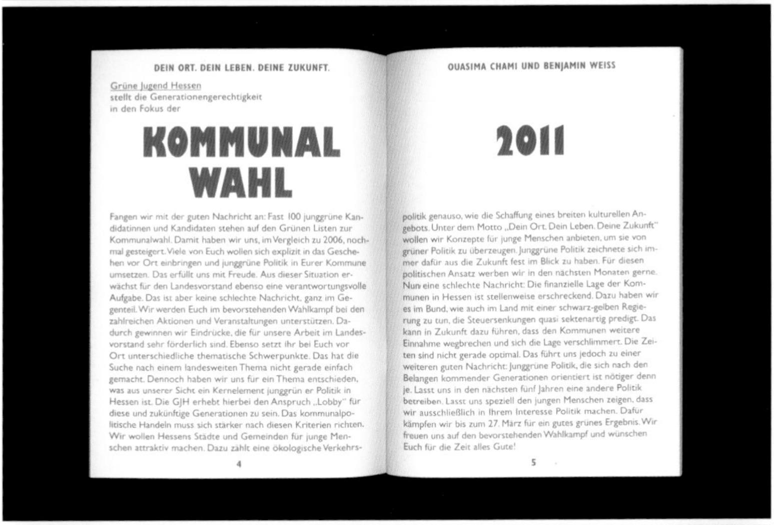
DEIN ORT. DEIN LEBEN. DEINE ZUKUNFT.

OUASIMA CHAMI UND BENJAMIN WEISS

Grüne Jugend Hessen
stellt die Generationengerechtigkeit
in den Fokus der

KOMMUNAL
WAHL

2011

Fangen wir mit der guten Nachricht an: Fast 100 junggrüne Kandidatinnen und Kandidaten stehen auf den Grünen Listen zur Kommunalwahl. Damit haben wir uns, im Vergleich zu 2006, nochmal gesteigert. Viele von Euch wollen sich explizit in das Geschehen vor Ort einbringen und junggrüne Politik in Eurer Kommune umsetzen. Das erfüllt uns mit Freude. Aus dieser Situation erwächst für den Landesvorstand ebenso eine verantwortungsvolle Aufgabe. Das ist aber keine schlechte Nachricht, ganz im Gegenteil. Wir werden Euch im bevorstehenden Wahlkampf bei den zahlreichen Aktionen und Veranstaltungen unterstützen. Dadurch gewinnen wir Eindrücke, die für unsere Arbeit im Landesvorstand sehr förderlich sind. Ebenso setzt ihr bei Euch vor Ort unterschiedliche thematische Schwerpunkte. Das hat die Suche nach einem landesweiten Thema nicht gerade einfach gemacht. Dennoch haben wir uns für ein Thema entschieden, was aus unserer Sicht ein Kernelement junggrün er Politik in Hessen ist. Die GJH erhebt hierbei den Anspruch „Lobby" für diese und zukünftige Generationen zu sein. Das kommunalpolitische Handeln muss sich stärker nach diesen Kriterien richten. Wir wollen Hessens Städte und Gemeinden für junge Menschen attraktiv machen. Dazu zählt eine ökologische Verkehrspolitik genauso, wie die Schaffung eines breiten kulturellen Angebots. Unter dem Motto „Dein Ort. Dein Leben. Deine Zukunft" wollen wir Konzepte für junge Menschen anbieten, um sie von grüner Politik zu überzeugen. Junggrüne Politik zeichnete sich immer dafür aus die Zukunft fest im Blick zu haben. Für diesen politischen Ansatz werben wir in den nächsten Monaten gerne. Nun eine schlechte Nachricht: Die finanzielle Lage der Kommunen in Hessen ist stellenweise erschreckend. Dazu haben wir es im Bund, wie auch im Land mit einer schwarz-gelben Regierung zu tun, die Steuersenkungen quasi sektenartig predigt. Das kann in Zukunft dazu führen, dass den Kommunen weitere Einnahme wegbrechen und sich die Lage verschlimmert. Die Zeiten sind nicht gerade optimal. Das führt uns jedoch zu einer weiteren guten Nachricht: Junggrüne Politik, die sich nach den Belangen kommender Generationen orientiert ist nötiger denn je. Lasst uns in den nächsten fünf Jahren eine andere Politik betreiben. Lasst uns speziell den jungen Menschen zeigen, dass wir ausschließlich in Ihrem Interesse Politik machen. Dafür kämpfen wir bis zum 27. März für ein gutes grünes Ergebnis. Wir freuen uns auf den bevorstehenden Wahlkampf und wünschen Euch für die Zeit alles Gute!

4

5

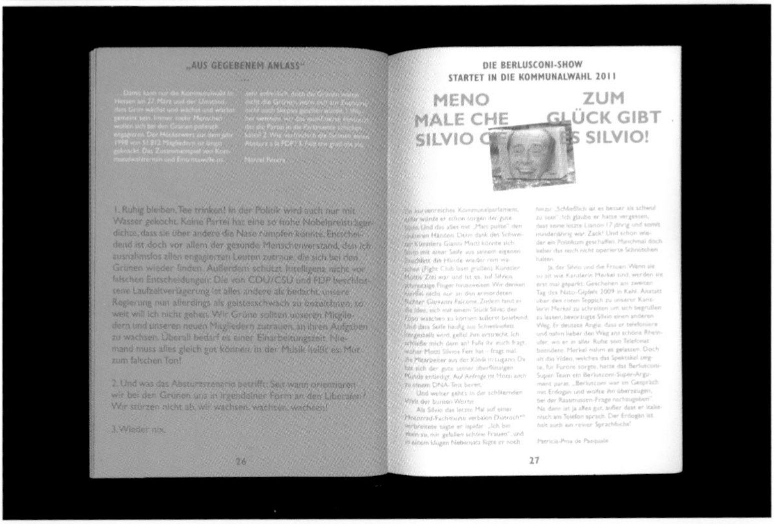
„AUS GEGEBENEM ANLASS"

Marcel Peters

1. Ruhig bleiben. Tee trinken! In der Politik wird auch nur mit Wasser gekocht. Keine Partei hat eine so hohe Nobelpreisträgerdichte, dass sie über andere die Nase rümpfen könnte. Entscheidend ist doch vor allem der gesunde Menschenverstand, den ich ausnahmslos allen engagierten Leuten zutraue, die sich bei den Grünen wieder finden. Außerdem schützt Intelligenz nicht vor falschen Entscheidungen: Die von CDU/CSU und FDP beschlossene Laufzeitverlägerung ist alles andere als bedacht, unsere Regierung nun allerdings als geistesschwach zu bezeichnen, so weit will ich nicht gehen. Wir Grüne sollten unseren Mitgliedern und unseren neuen Mitgliedern zutrauen, an ihren Aufgaben zu wachsen. Überall bedarf es einer Einarbeitungszeit. Niemand muss alles gleich gut können. In der Musik heißt es: Mut zum falschen Ton!

2. Und was das Absturzszenario betrifft: Seit wann orientieren wir bei den Grünen uns in irgendeiner Form an den Liberalen? Wir stürzen nicht ab, wir wachsen, wachsen, wachsen!

3. Wieder nix.

26

DIE BERLUSCONI-SHOW
STARTET IN DIE KOMMUNALWAHL 2011

MENO
MALE CHE
SILVIO C…

ZUM
GLÜCK GIBT
…S SILVIO!

27

Typeface in Use
Gill Sans Regular, Bold, Bold Condensed, Ultra Bold, Ultra Bold Condensed

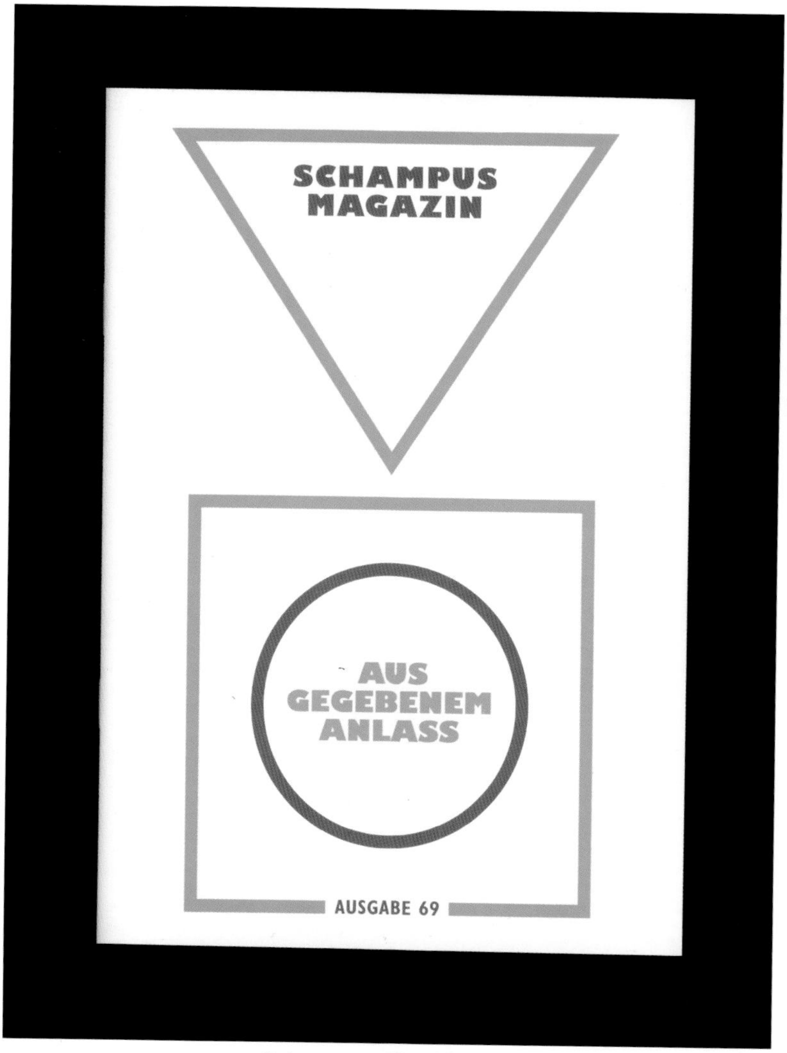

Doeller & Satter's Favorite Gill Sans Letter is "M".

Schampus Nr. 69
2011 — Editorial Design
Client Grüne Jugend Hessen
Design Doeller & Satter, Kai Bergmann

Schampus is published quarterly by the political party "Grüne Jugend Hessen".

Typeface in Use
Gill Sans MT Pro Medium

"Because it's a perfect blend between humanism and modernism."

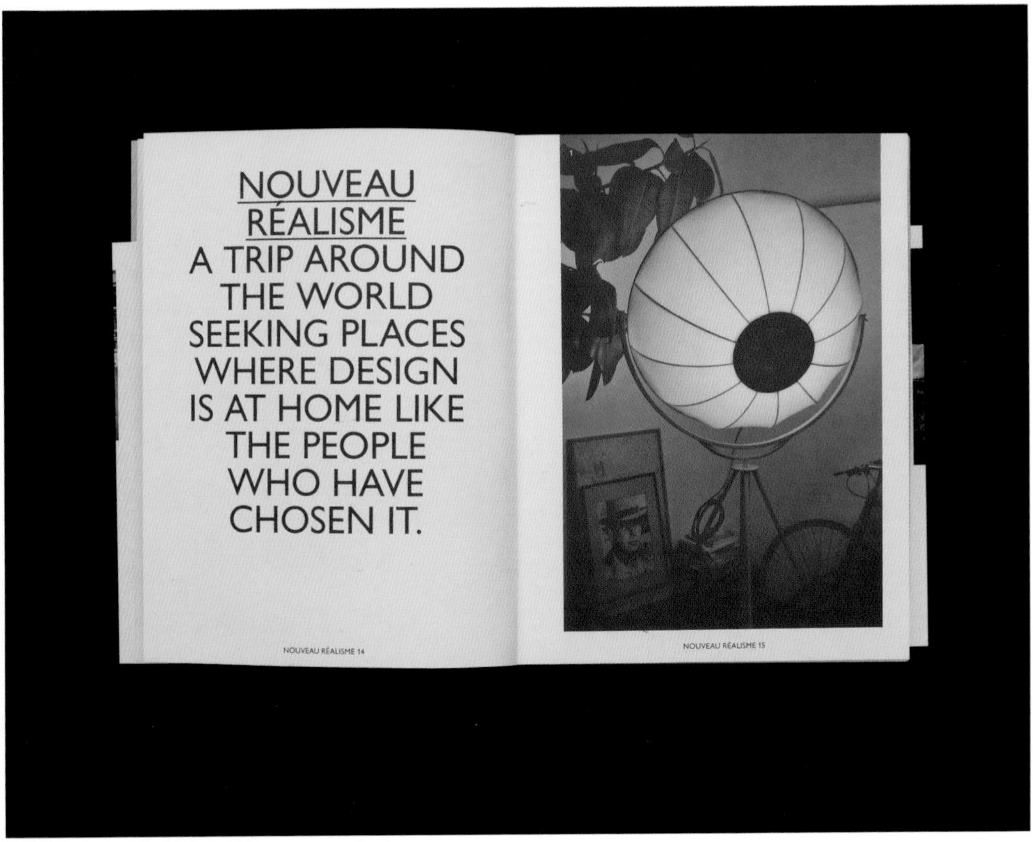

Nouveau Réalisme
2011 — Catalog
Client Pallucco
Design Tankboys (Lorenzo Mason, Marco Campardo)

We have developed an editorial project based on the idea of Nouveau Réalisme for the design firm Pallucco. This project has been realized in conjunction with the XYZ team and Tommaso Speretta. The catalog includes photos by Paul Barbera, Sean Michael Beolchini, Ailine Liefeld, Andrea Restello.

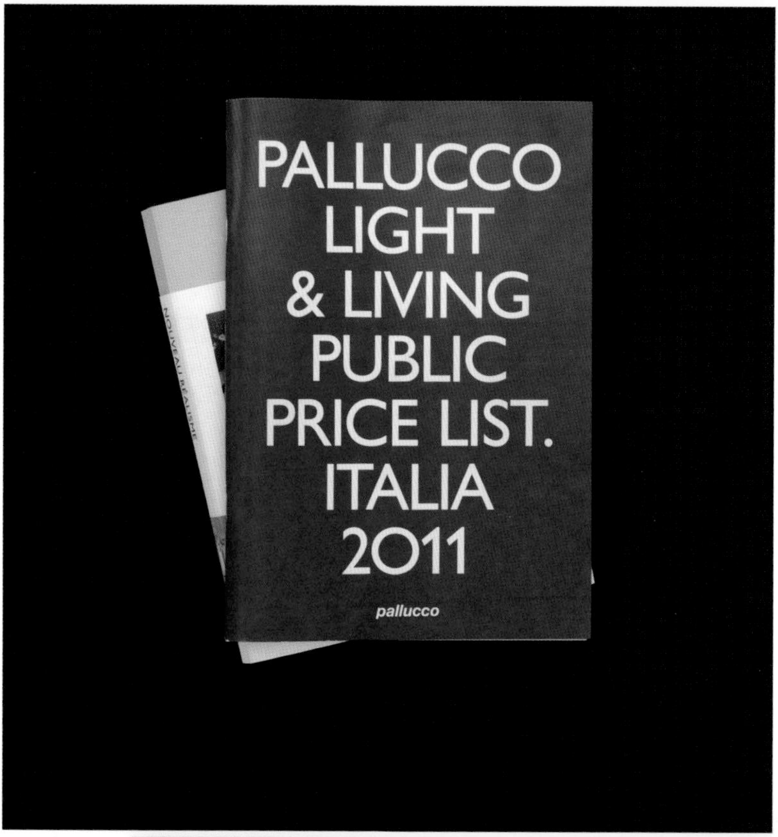
PALLUCCO
LIGHT
& LIVING
PUBLIC
PRICE LIST.
ITALIA
2011
pallucco

PALL
UCCO
NOU
VEAU
RÉALI
SME

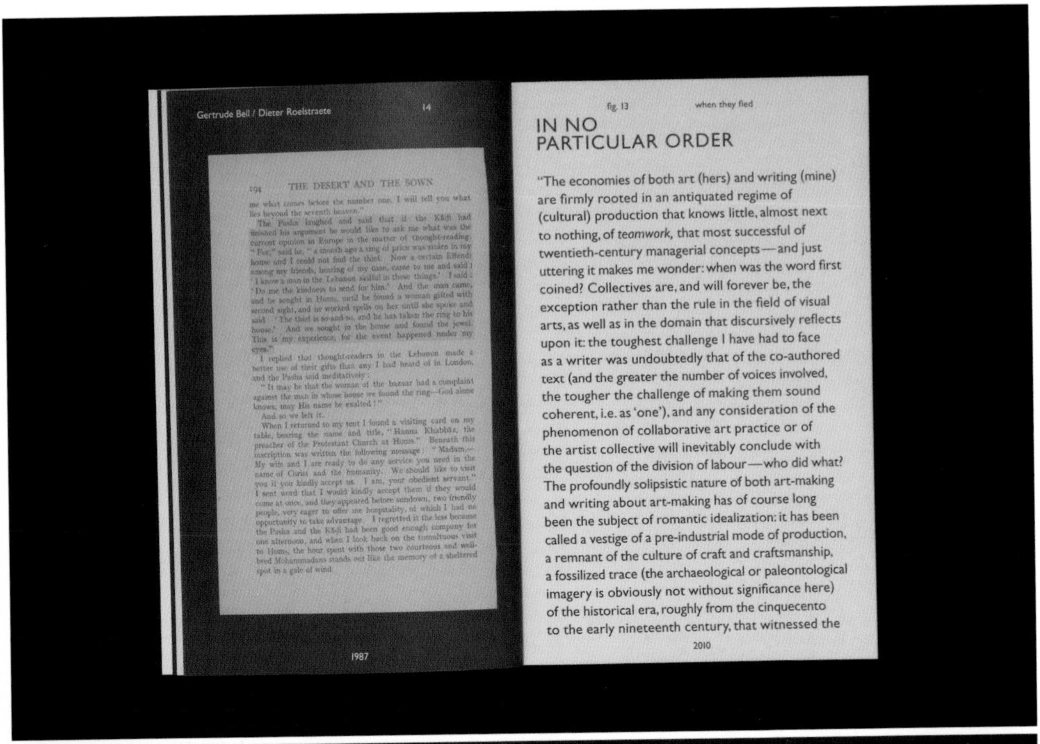

Gertrude Bell / Dieter Roelstraete 14

194 THE DESERT AND THE SOWN

me what comes before the number one. I will tell you what lies beyond the seventh heaven."

The Pasha laughed and said that if the Kādi had finished his argument he would like to ask me what was the current opinion in Europe in the matter of thought-reading. "For," said he, "a month ago a ring of price was stolen in my house and I could not find the thief. Now a certain Effendi among my friends, hearing of my case, came to me and said: 'I know a man in the Lebanon skilful in these things.' I said: 'Do me the kindness to send for him.' And the man came, and he sought in Homs, until he found a woman gifted with second sight, and he worked spells on her until she spoke and said: 'The thief is so-and-so, and he has taken the ring to his house.' And we sought in the house and found the jewel. This is my experience, for the event happened under my eyes."

I replied that thought-readers in the Lebanon made a better use of their gifts than any I had heard of in London, and the Pasha said meditatively:

"It may be that the woman of the bazaar had a complaint against the man in whose house we found the ring—God alone knows, may His name be exalted!"

And so we left it.

When I returned to my tent I found a visiting card on my table, bearing the name and title, "Hanna Khabbāz, the preacher of the Protestant Church at Homs." Beneath this inscription was written the following message: "Madam,—My wife and I are ready to do any service you need in the name of Christ and the humanity. We should like to visit you if you kindly accept us. I am, your obedient servant." I sent word that I would kindly accept them if they would come at once, and they appeared before sundown, two friendly people, very eager to offer me hospitality, of which I had no opportunity to take advantage. I regretted it the less because the Pasha and the Kādi had been good enough company for one afternoon, and when I look back on the tumultuous visit to Homs, the hour spent with those two courteous and well-bred Mohammadans stands out like the memory of a sheltered spot in a gale of wind.

1987

fig. 13 when they fled

IN NO
PARTICULAR ORDER

"The economies of both art (hers) and writing (mine) are firmly rooted in an antiquated regime of (cultural) production that knows little, almost next to nothing, of *teamwork*, that most successful of twentieth-century managerial concepts—and just uttering it makes me wonder: when was the word first coined? Collectives are, and will forever be, the exception rather than the rule in the field of visual arts, as well as in the domain that discursively reflects upon it: the toughest challenge I have had to face as a writer was undoubtedly that of the co-authored text (and the greater the number of voices involved, the tougher the challenge of making them sound coherent, i.e. as 'one'), and any consideration of the phenomenon of collaborative art practice or of the artist collective will inevitably conclude with the question of the division of labour—who did what? The profoundly solipsistic nature of both art-making and writing about art-making has of course long been the subject of romantic idealization: it has been called a vestige of a pre-industrial mode of production, a remnant of the culture of craft and craftsmanship, a fossilized trace (the archaeological or paleontological imagery is obviously not without significance here) of the historical era, roughly from the cinquecento to the early nineteenth century, that witnessed the

2010

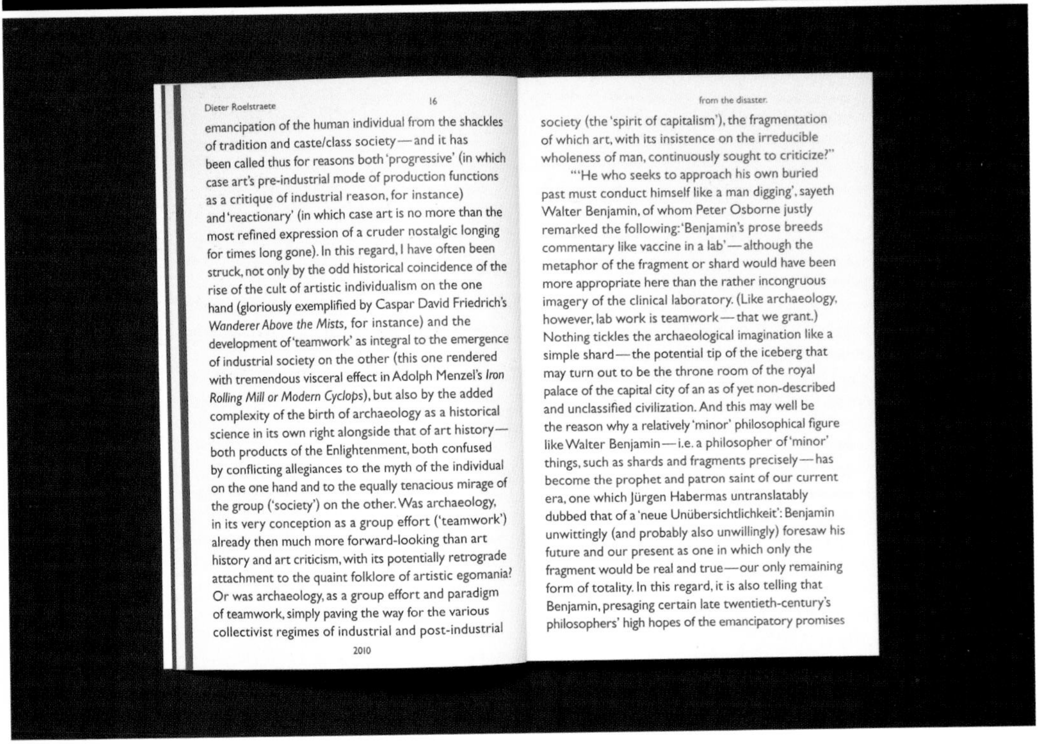

Dieter Roelstraete 16

emancipation of the human individual from the shackles of tradition and caste/class society—and it has been called thus for reasons both 'progressive' (in which case art's pre-industrial mode of production functions as a critique of industrial reason, for instance) and 'reactionary' (in which case art is no more than the most refined expression of a cruder nostalgic longing for times long gone). In this regard, I have often been struck, not only by the odd historical coincidence of the rise of the cult of artistic individualism on the one hand (gloriously exemplified by Caspar David Friedrich's *Wanderer Above the Mists*, for instance) and the development of 'teamwork' as integral to the emergence of industrial society on the other (this one rendered with tremendous visceral effect in Adolph Menzel's *Iron Rolling Mill or Modern Cyclops*), but also by the added complexity of the birth of archaeology as a historical science in its own right alongside that of art history—both products of the Enlightenment, both confused by conflicting allegiances to the myth of the individual on the one hand and to the equally tenacious mirage of the group ('society') on the other. Was archaeology, in its very conception as a group effort ('teamwork') already then much more forward-looking than art history and art criticism, with its potentially retrograde attachment to the quaint folklore of artistic egomania? Or was archaeology, as a group effort and paradigm of teamwork, simply paving the way for the various collectivist regimes of industrial and post-industrial

2010

from the disaster.

society (the 'spirit of capitalism'), the fragmentation of which art, with its insistence on the irreducible wholeness of man, continuously sought to criticize?"

"'He who seeks to approach his own buried past must conduct himself like a man digging', sayeth Walter Benjamin, of whom Peter Osborne justly remarked the following: 'Benjamin's prose breeds commentary like vaccine in a lab'—although the metaphor of the fragment or shard would have been more appropriate here than the rather incongruous imagery of the clinical laboratory. (Like archaeology, however, lab work is teamwork—that we grant.) Nothing tickles the archaeological imagination like a simple shard—the potential tip of the iceberg that may turn out to be the throne room of the royal palace of the capital city of an as of yet non-described and unclassified civilization. And this may well be the reason why a relatively 'minor' philosophical figure like Walter Benjamin—i.e. a philosopher of 'minor' things, such as shards and fragments precisely—has become the prophet and patron saint of our current era, one which Jürgen Habermas untranslatably dubbed that of a 'neue Unübersichtlichkeit': Benjamin unwittingly (and probably also unwillingly) foresaw his future and our present as one in which only the fragment would be real and true—our only remaining form of totality. In this regard, it is also telling that Benjamin, presaging certain late twentieth-century's philosophers' high hopes of the emancipatory promises

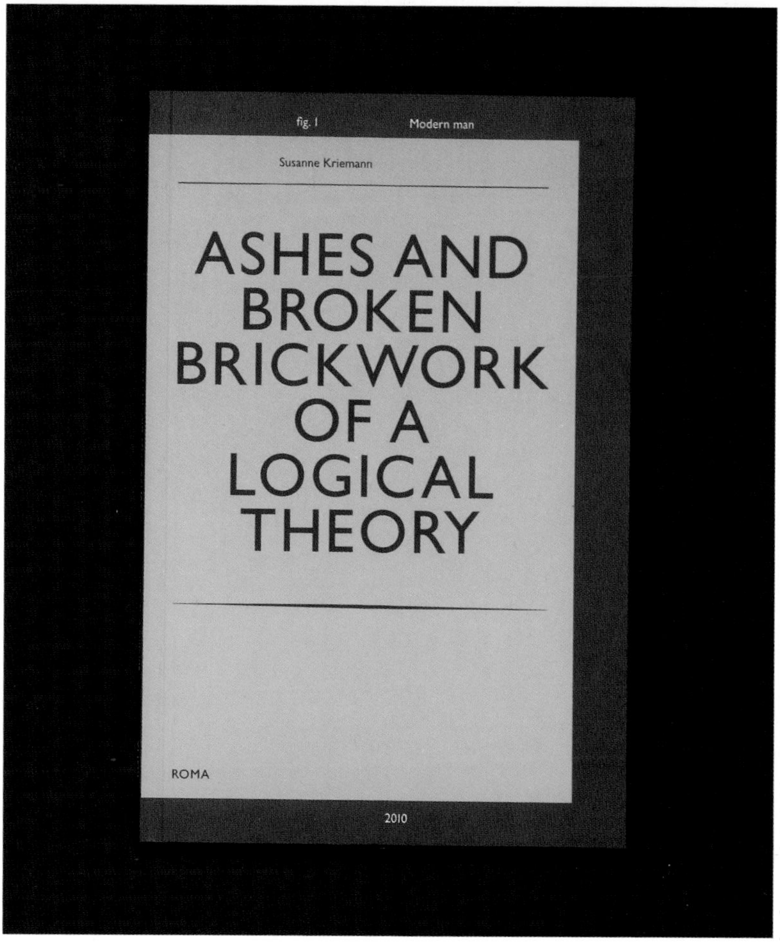

fig. 1
Modern man
Susanne Kriemann
ASHES AND BROKEN BRICKWORK OF A LOGICAL THEORY
ROMA
2010

Ashes and Broken Brickwork of a Logical Theory
2010 — Book
Client Susanne Kriemann
Design jungundwenig

This book can be read as an inventory of the trajectory that Kriemann pursued in relation to archaeology, to the artefact, to the image of the individual at work and the idea of the desert as a symbol of the modern desire to create an empty slate, a *tabula rasa*. Material from Agatha Christie's photographic archives is related to photographs that Kriemann produced of the Syrian Desert and archaeological sites in Mesopotamia.

Max Mallowan / Susanne Kriemann
30
fig. 20
fig. 21
with the supervision
1920s
2009

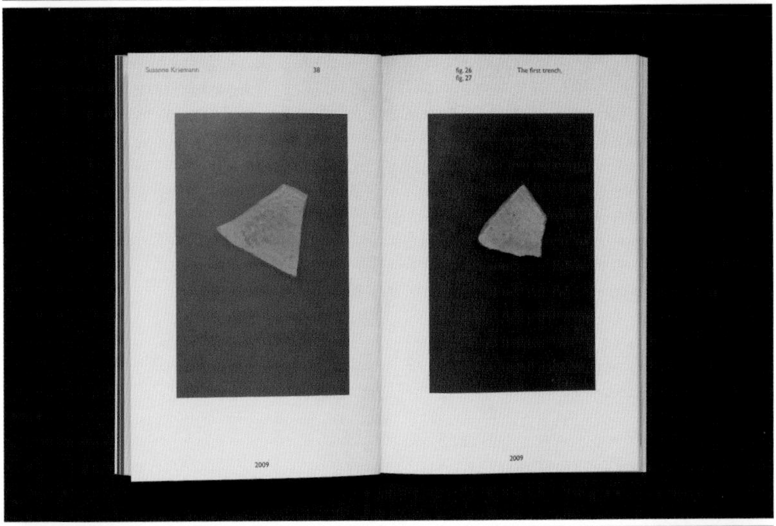
Susanne Kriemann
38
fig. 26
fig. 27
The first trench.
2009
2009

fig. 52
fig. 53
which always presented
1938

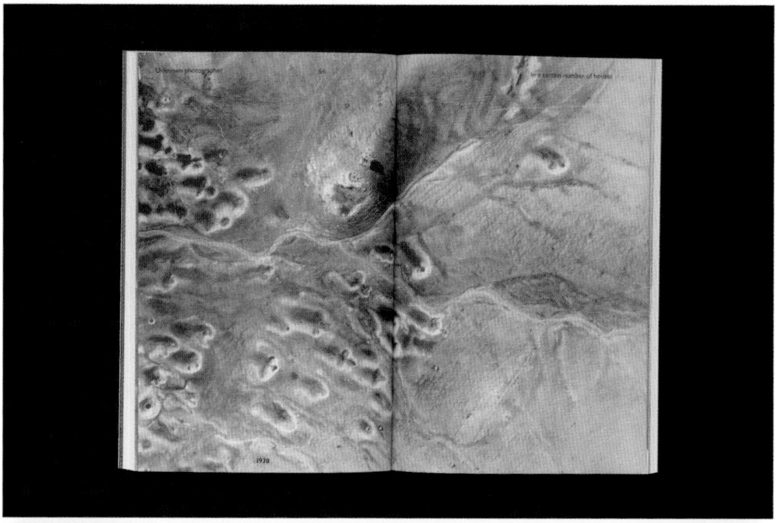

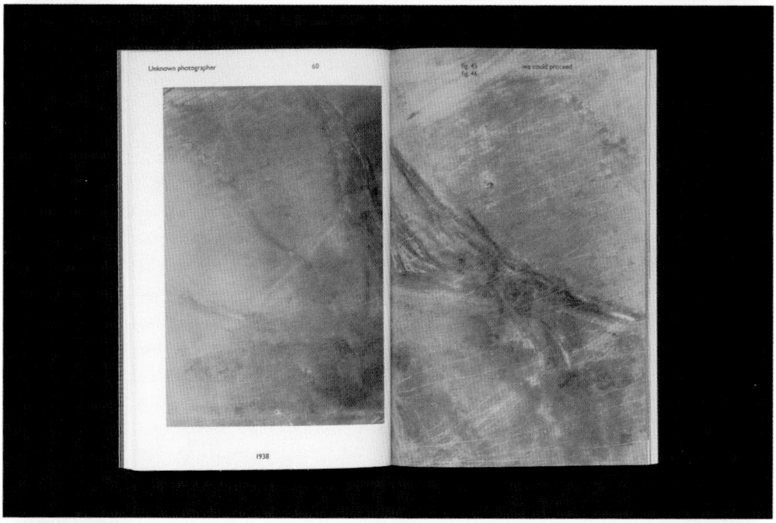
Unknown photographer
60
fig. 45
fig. 46
we could proceed
1938

90

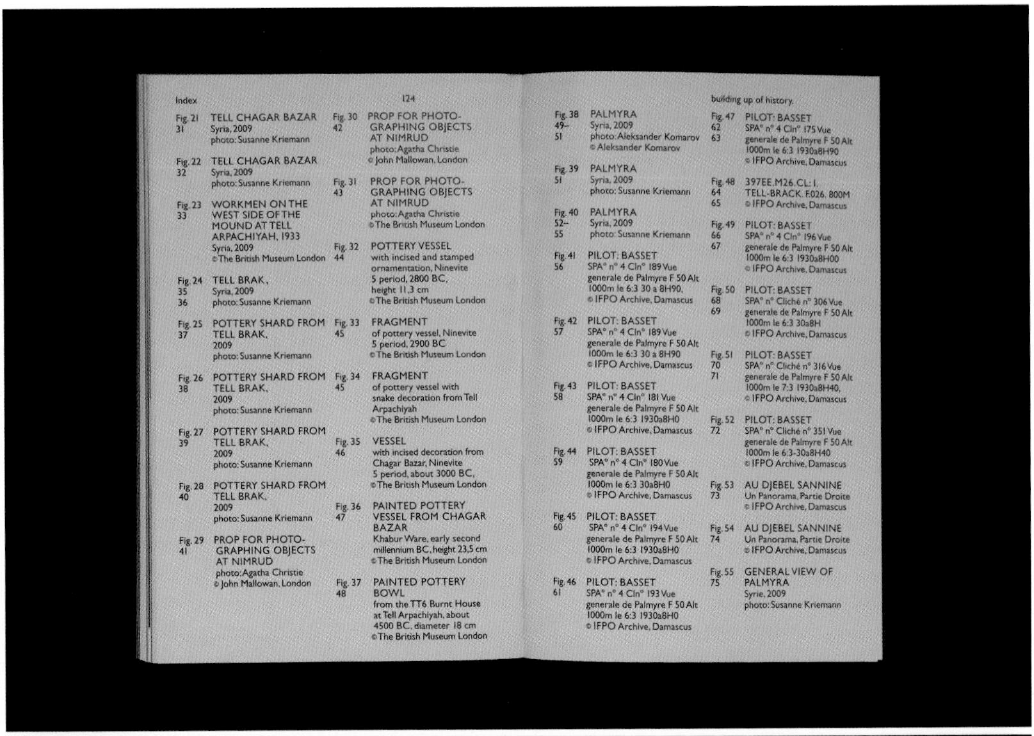

Index 124

Fig. 21 31 TELL CHAGAR BAZAR
Syria, 2009
photo: Susanne Kriemann

Fig. 22 32 TELL CHAGAR BAZAR
Syria, 2009
photo: Susanne Kriemann

Fig. 23 33 WORKMEN ON THE WEST SIDE OF THE MOUND AT TELL ARPACHIYAH, 1933
Syria, 2009
© The British Museum London

Fig. 24 35 36 TELL BRAK,
Syria, 2009
photo: Susanne Kriemann

Fig. 25 37 POTTERY SHARD FROM TELL BRAK,
2009
photo: Susanne Kriemann

Fig. 26 38 POTTERY SHARD FROM TELL BRAK,
2009
photo: Susanne Kriemann

Fig. 27 39 POTTERY SHARD FROM TELL BRAK,
2009
photo: Susanne Kriemann

Fig. 28 40 POTTERY SHARD FROM TELL BRAK,
2009
photo: Susanne Kriemann

Fig. 29 41 PROP FOR PHOTO-GRAPHING OBJECTS AT NIMRUD
photo: Agatha Christie
© John Mallowan, London

Fig. 30 42 PROP FOR PHOTO-GRAPHING OBJECTS AT NIMRUD
photo: Agatha Christie
© John Mallowan, London

Fig. 31 43 PROP FOR PHOTO-GRAPHING OBJECTS AT NIMRUD
photo: Agatha Christie
© The British Museum London

Fig. 32 44 POTTERY VESSEL
with incised and stamped ornamentation, Ninevite 5 period, 2800 BC, height 11,3 cm
© The British Museum London

Fig. 33 45 FRAGMENT
of pottery vessel, Ninevite 5 period, 2900 BC
© The British Museum London

Fig. 34 45 FRAGMENT
of pottery vessel with snake decoration from Tell Arpachiyah
© The British Museum London

Fig. 35 46 VESSEL
with incised decoration from Chagar Bazar, Ninevite 5 period, about 3000 BC,
© The British Museum London

Fig. 36 47 PAINTED POTTERY VESSEL FROM CHAGAR BAZAR
Khabur Ware, early second millennium BC, height 23,5 cm
© The British Museum London

Fig. 37 48 PAINTED POTTERY BOWL
from the TT6 Burnt House at Tell Arpachiyah, about 4500 BC, diameter 18 cm
© The British Museum London

Fig. 38 49–51 PALMYRA
Syria, 2009
photo: Aleksander Komarov
© Aleksander Komarov

Fig. 39 51 PALMYRA
Syria, 2009
photo: Susanne Kriemann

Fig. 40 52–55 PALMYRA
Syria, 2009
photo: Susanne Kriemann

Fig. 41 56 PILOT: BASSET
SPA° n° 4 Cln° 189 Vue generale de Palmyre F 50 Alt 1000m le 6:3 30 a 8H90,
© IFPO Archive, Damascus

Fig. 42 57 PILOT: BASSET
SPA° n° 4 Cln° 189 Vue generale de Palmyre F 50 Alt 1000m le 6:3 30 a 8H90
© IFPO Archive, Damascus

Fig. 43 58 PILOT: BASSET
SPA° n° 4 Cln° 181 Vue generale de Palmyre F 50 Alt 1000m le 6:3 1930a8H0
© IFPO Archive, Damascus

Fig. 44 59 PILOT: BASSET
SPA° n° 4 Cln° 180 Vue generale de Palmyre F 50 Alt 1000m le 6:3 30a8H0
© IFPO Archive, Damascus

Fig. 45 60 PILOT: BASSET
SPA° n° 4 Cln° 194 Vue generale de Palmyre F 50 Alt 1000m le 6:3 1930a8H0
© IFPO Archive, Damascus

Fig. 46 61 PILOT: BASSET
SPA° n° 4 Cln° 193 Vue generale de Palmyre F 50 Alt 1000m le 6:3 1930a8H0
© IFPO Archive, Damascus

building up of history.

Fig. 47 62 63 PILOT: BASSET
SPA° n° 4 Cln° 175 Vue generale de Palmyre F 50 Alt 1000m le 6:3 1930a8H90
© IFPO Archive, Damascus

Fig. 48 64 65 397EE.M26.CL: I. TELL-BRACK. F.026. 800M
© IFPO Archive, Damascus

Fig. 49 66 67 PILOT: BASSET
SPA° n° 4 Cln° 196 Vue generale de Palmyre F 50 Alt 1000m le 6:3 1930a8H00
© IFPO Archive, Damascus

Fig. 50 68 69 PILOT: BASSET
SPA° n° Cliché n° 306 Vue generale de Palmyre F 50 Alt 1000m le 6:3 30a8H
© IFPO Archive, Damascus

Fig. 51 70 71 PILOT: BASSET
SPA° n° Cliché n° 316 Vue generale de Palmyre F 50 Alt 1000m le 7:3 1930a8H40,
© IFPO Archive, Damascus

Fig. 52 72 PILOT: BASSET
SPA° n° Cliché n° 351 Vue generale de Palmyre F 50 Alt 1000m le 6:3-30a8H40
© IFPO Archive, Damascus

Fig. 53 73 AU DJEBEL SANNINE
Un Panorama, Partie Droite
© IFPO Archive, Damascus

Fig. 54 74 AU DJEBEL SANNINE
Un Panorama, Partie Droite
© IFPO Archive, Damascus

Fig. 55 75 GENERAL VIEW OF PALMYRA
Syrie, 2009
photo: Susanne Kriemann

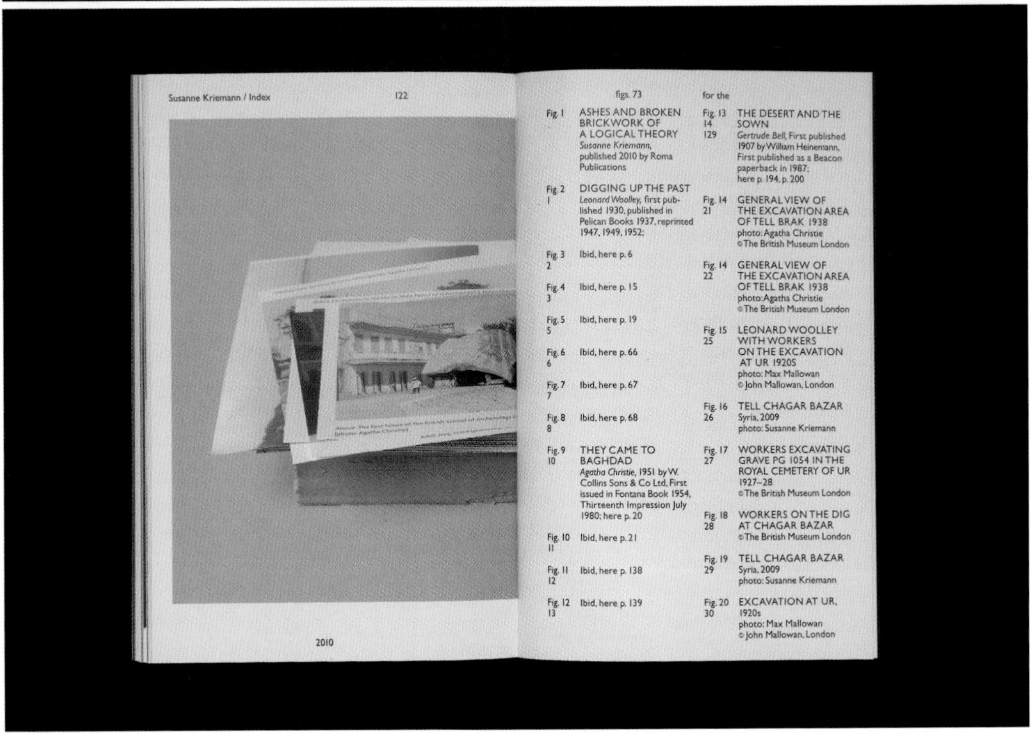

Susanne Kriemann / Index 122

2010

figs. 73 for the

Fig. 1 ASHES AND BROKEN BRICKWORK OF A LOGICAL THEORY
Susanne Kriemann, published 2010 by Roma Publications

Fig. 2 1 DIGGING UP THE PAST
Leonard Woolley, first published 1930, published in Pelican Books 1937, reprinted 1947, 1949, 1952;

Fig. 3 2 Ibid, here p. 6

Fig. 4 3 Ibid, here p. 15

Fig. 5 5 Ibid, here p. 19

Fig. 6 6 Ibid, here p. 66

Fig. 7 7 Ibid, here p. 67

Fig. 8 8 Ibid, here p. 68

Fig. 9 10 THEY CAME TO BAGHDAD
Agatha Christie, 1951 by W. Collins Sons & Co Ltd, First issued in Fontana Book 1954, Thirteenth Impression July 1980; here p. 20

Fig. 10 11 Ibid, here p. 21

Fig. 11 12 Ibid, here p. 138

Fig. 12 13 Ibid, here p. 139

Fig. 13 14 129 THE DESERT AND THE SOWN
Gertrude Bell, First published 1907 by William Heinemann, First published as a Beacon paperback in 1987; here p. 194, p. 200

Fig. 14 21 GENERAL VIEW OF THE EXCAVATION AREA OF TELL BRAK 1938
photo: Agatha Christie
© The British Museum London

Fig. 14 22 GENERAL VIEW OF THE EXCAVATION AREA OF TELL BRAK 1938
photo: Agatha Christie
© The British Museum London

Fig. 15 25 LEONARD WOOLLEY WITH WORKERS ON THE EXCAVATION AT UR 1920S
photo: Max Mallowan
© John Mallowan, London

Fig. 16 26 TELL CHAGAR BAZAR
Syria, 2009
photo: Susanne Kriemann

Fig. 17 27 WORKERS EXCAVATING GRAVE PG 1054 IN THE ROYAL CEMETERY OF UR 1927–28
© The British Museum London

Fig. 18 28 WORKERS ON THE DIG AT CHAGAR BAZAR
© The British Museum London

Fig. 19 29 TELL CHAGAR BAZAR
Syria, 2009
photo: Susanne Kriemann

Fig. 20 30 EXCAVATION AT UR, 1920s
photo: Max Mallowan
© John Mallowan, London

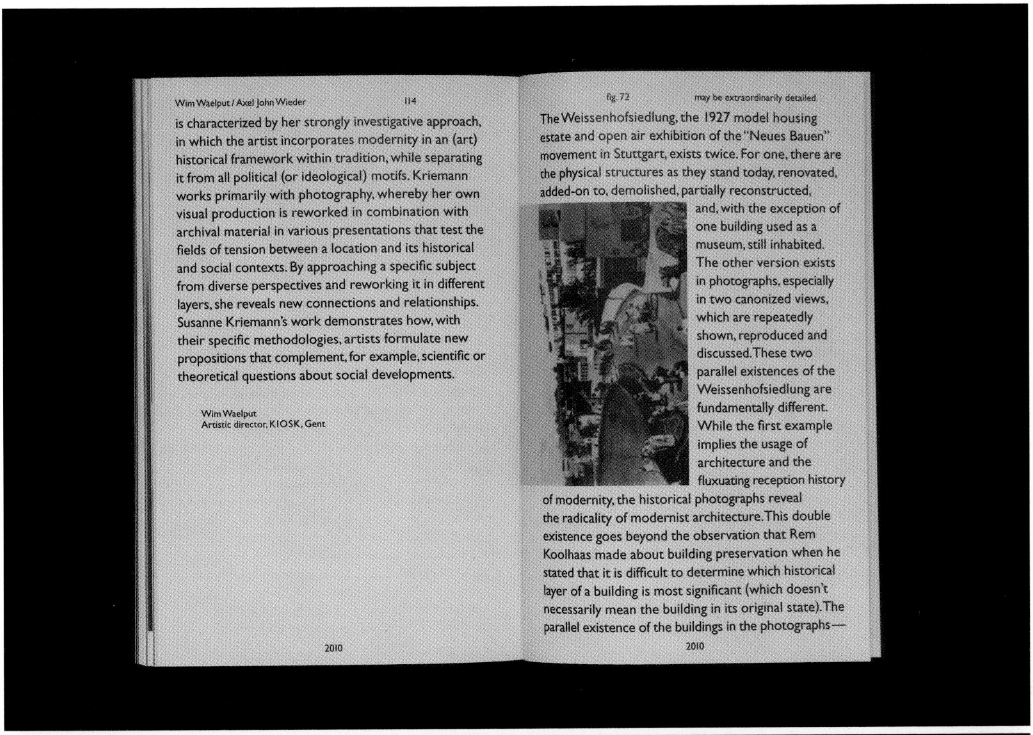

Wim Waelput / Axel John Wieder 114

is characterized by her strongly investigative approach, in which the artist incorporates modernity in an (art) historical framework within tradition, while separating it from all political (or ideological) motifs. Kriemann works primarily with photography, whereby her own visual production is reworked in combination with archival material in various presentations that test the fields of tension between a location and its historical and social contexts. By approaching a specific subject from diverse perspectives and reworking it in different layers, she reveals new connections and relationships. Susanne Kriemann's work demonstrates how, with their specific methodologies, artists formulate new propositions that complement, for example, scientific or theoretical questions about social developments.

Wim Waelput
Artistic director, KIOSK, Gent

2010

fig. 72 may be extraordinarily detailed.

The Weissenhofsiedlung, the 1927 model housing estate and open air exhibition of the "Neues Bauen" movement in Stuttgart, exists twice. For one, there are the physical structures as they stand today, renovated, added-on to, demolished, partially reconstructed, and, with the exception of one building used as a museum, still inhabited. The other version exists in photographs, especially in two canonized views, which are repeatedly shown, reproduced and discussed. These two parallel existences of the Weissenhofsiedlung are fundamentally different. While the first example implies the usage of architecture and the fluxuating reception history of modernity, the historical photographs reveal the radicality of modernist architecture. This double existence goes beyond the observation that Rem Koolhaas made about building preservation when he stated that it is difficult to determine which historical layer of a building is most significant (which doesn't necessarily mean the building in its original state). The parallel existence of the buildings in the photographs—

2010

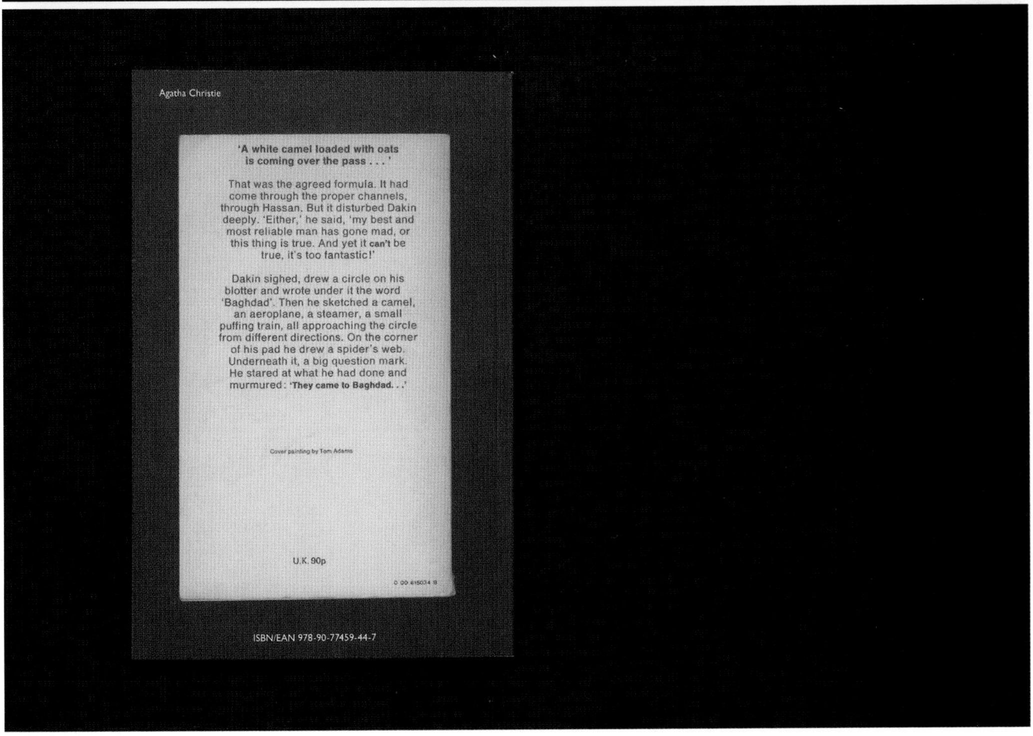

Agatha Christie

'A white camel loaded with oats is coming over the pass . . .'

That was the agreed formula. It had come through the proper channels, through Hassan. But it disturbed Dakin deeply. 'Either,' he said, 'my best and most reliable man has gone mad, or this thing is true. And yet it can't be true, it's too fantastic!'

Dakin sighed, drew a circle on his blotter and wrote under it the word 'Baghdad'. Then he sketched a camel, an aeroplane, a steamer, a small puffing train, all approaching the circle from different directions. On the corner of his pad he drew a spider's web. Underneath it, a big question mark. He stared at what he had done and murmured: **'They came to Baghdad. . .'**

Cover painting by Tom Adams

U.K. 90p

0 00 615034 8

ISBN/EAN 978-90-77459-44-7

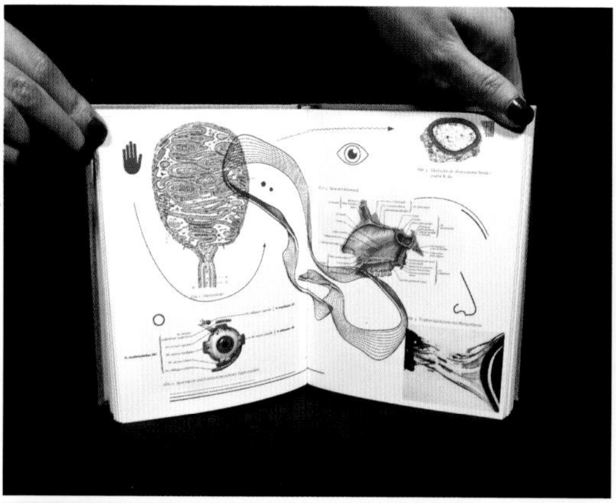

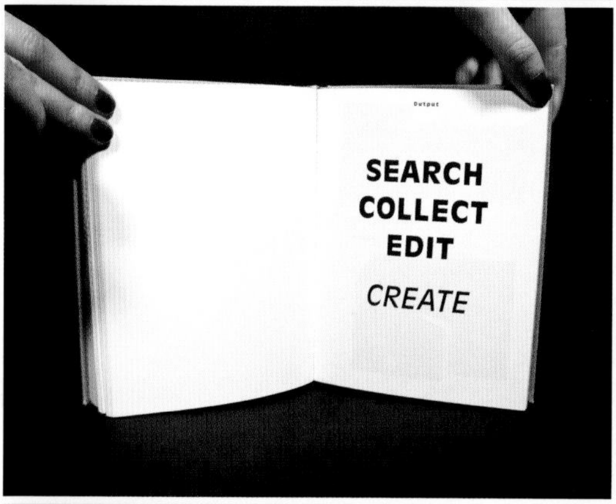

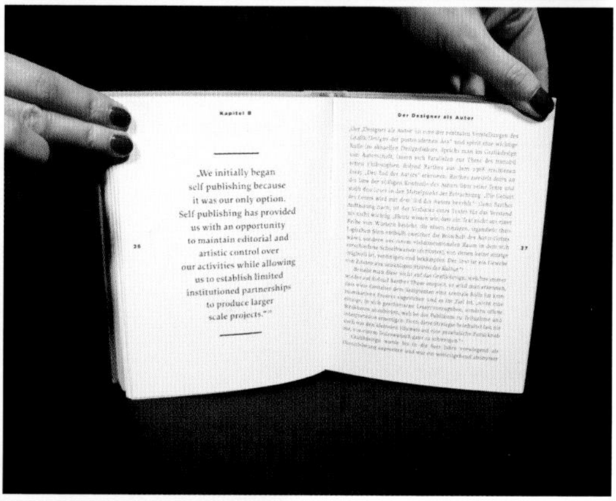

Typeface in Use
Gill Sans,
Incised 90,
Proforma CV

"I just love the strong but friendly appearance of the Gill Sans! It's like the nice guy who brings the message across."

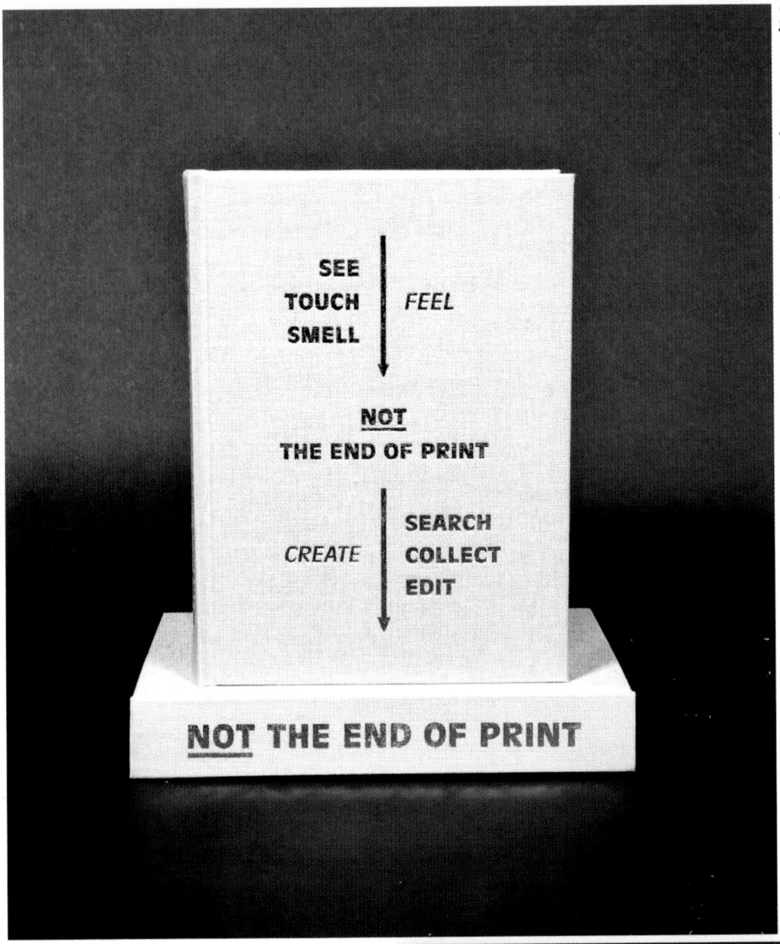

Not the end of print
2011 — Book
Client Merz Akademie, Stuttgart
Design Isabel Seiffert

Self-publishing. Designers develop and publish magazines and books in order to create a platform for self-initiated projects and experiment with their visual language. They want to be able to work autonomously and have complete control over content, purpose and message of a project. The gold which can be found on the outside and the inside of the book is a metaphor for the increased value of the print-media. In times of fast and disposable information, which is mostly spread digitally, a book seems like a decision for eternity. It becomes a valuable object.

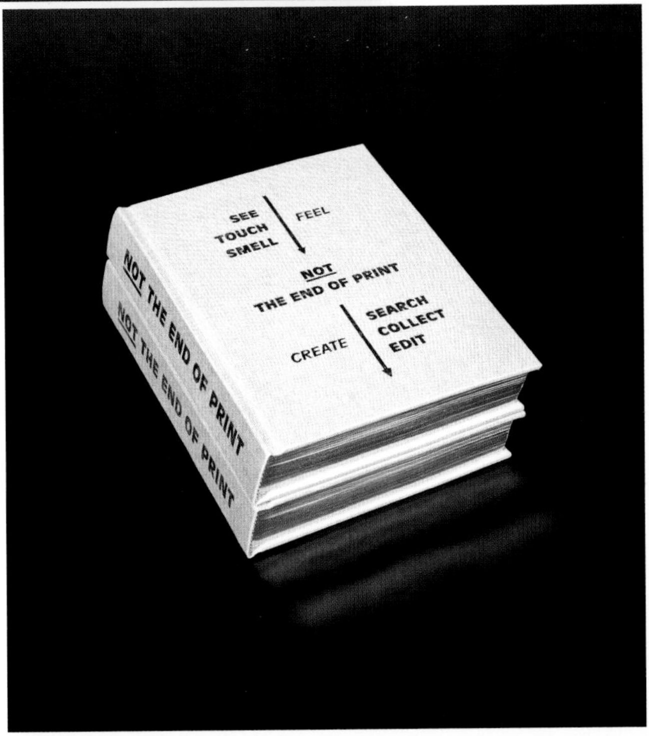

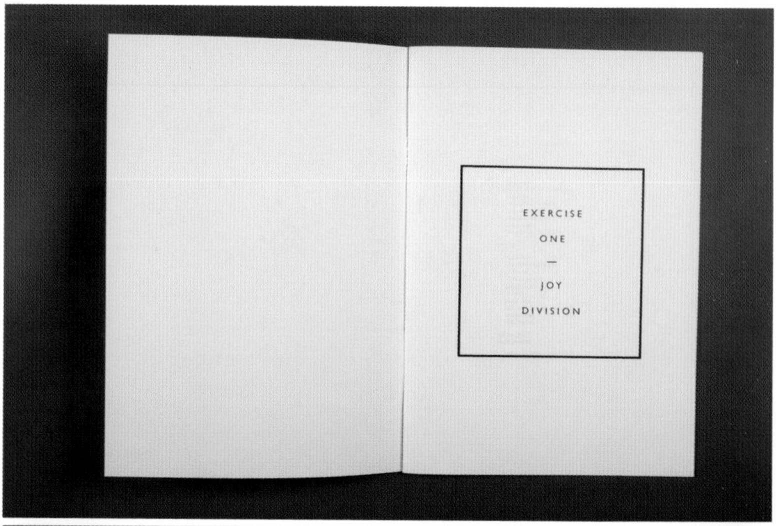
EXERCISE
ONE
—
JOY
DIVISION

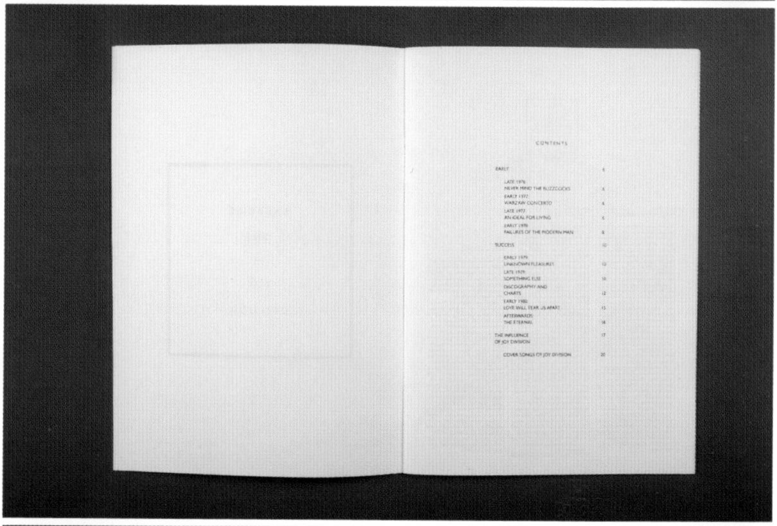
CONTENTS
EARLY
LATE 1976
NEVER MIND THE BUZZCOCKS
EARLY 1977
WARZAW CONCERTO
LATE 1977
AN IDEAL FOR LIVING
EARLY 1978
FAILURES OF THE MODERN MAN
SUCCESS
EARLY 1979
UNKNOWN PLEASURES
LATE 1979
SOMETHING ELSE
DISCOGRAPHY AND
CHARTS
EARLY 1980
LOVE WILL TEAR US APART
AFTERWARDS
THE ETERNAL
THE INFLUENCE
OF JOY DIVISION
COVER SONGS OF JOY DIVISION

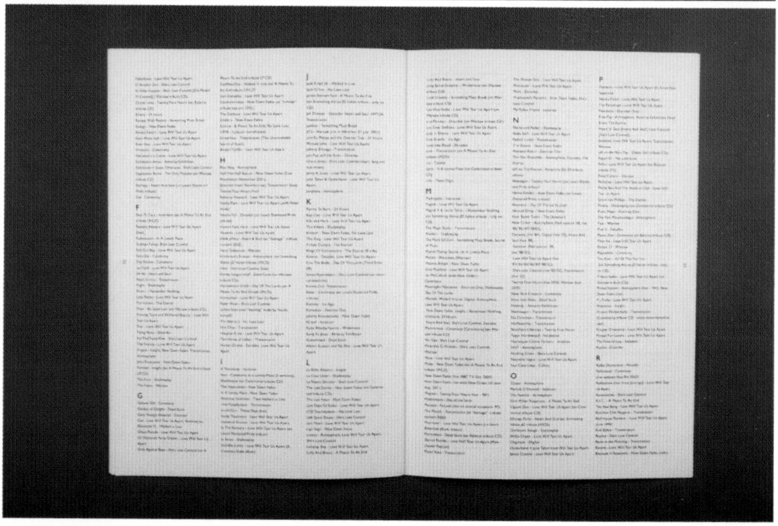

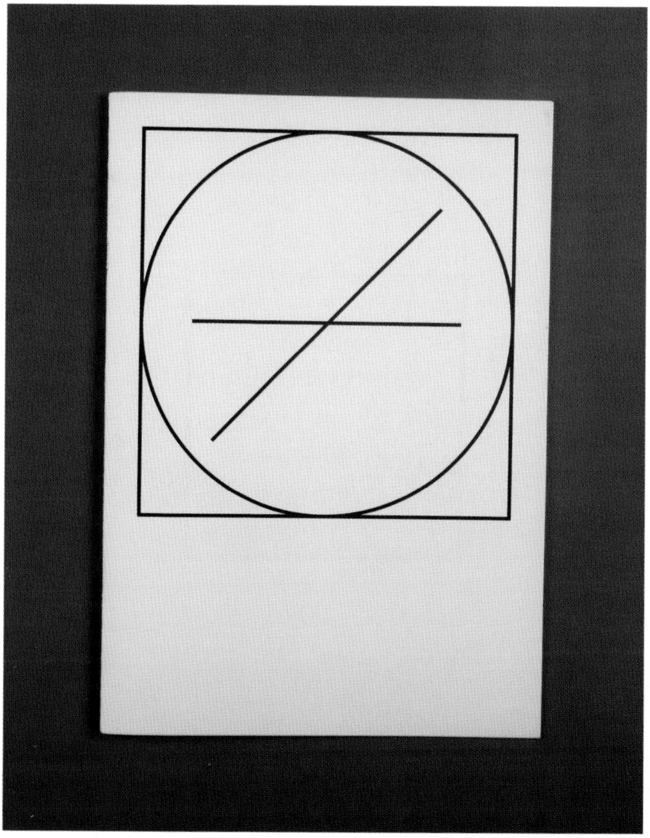

Exercise One.
Joy Division
2011 — Fanzine
Design Josep Román

Academic work consisting of a publication that shows the biography of the band from Manchester, Joy Division. The information and the data refers to concerts, tours, albums, their influences and private lives. A precise study of the band that is based on infographic material designed for the occasion, based on the original design by Peter Saville for the album *Uknown Pleasures*, where the line is the protagonist.

Typeface in Use
Gill Sans MT Pro Book, Book Italic, Medium, Heavy, Bold, Extra Bold, Bold condensed

S

Josep Román's Favorite Gill Sans Letter is "S".

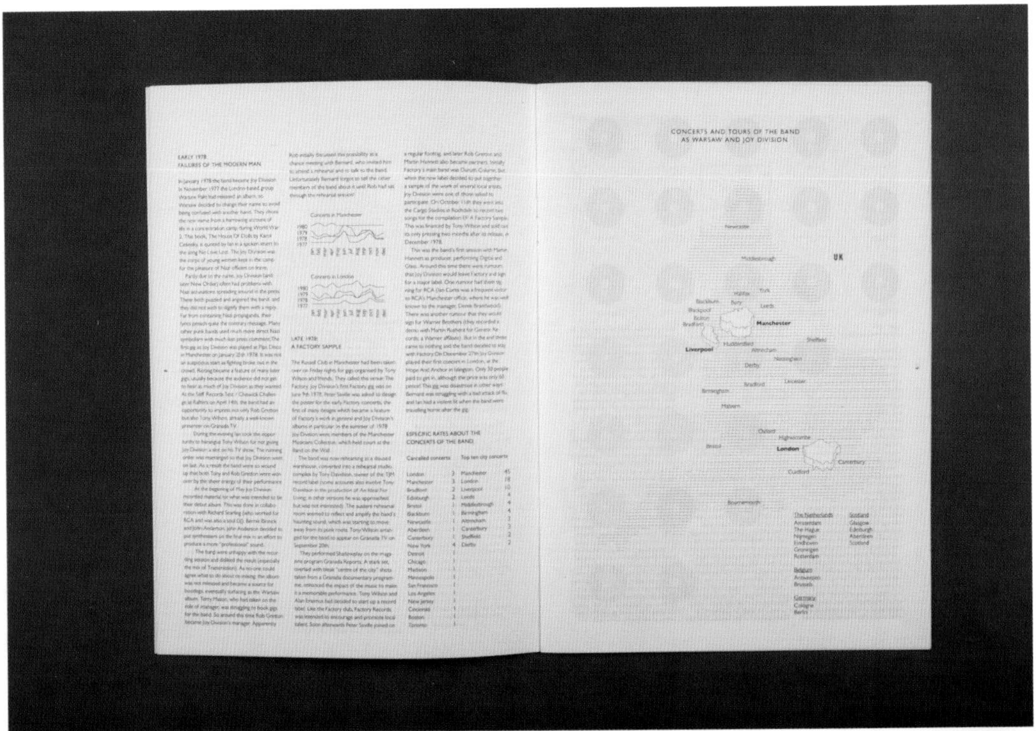
CONCERTS AND TOURS OF THE BAND
AS WARSAW AND JOY DIVISION
UK
Manchester
Liverpool
London

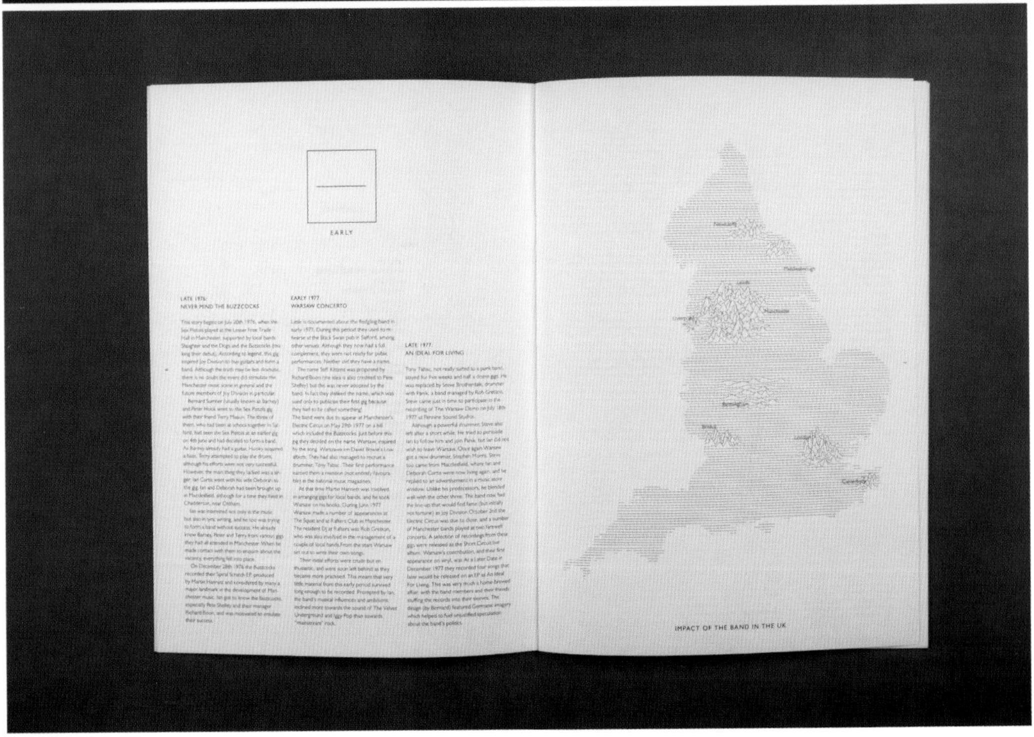
EARLY
IMPACT OF THE BAND IN THE UK

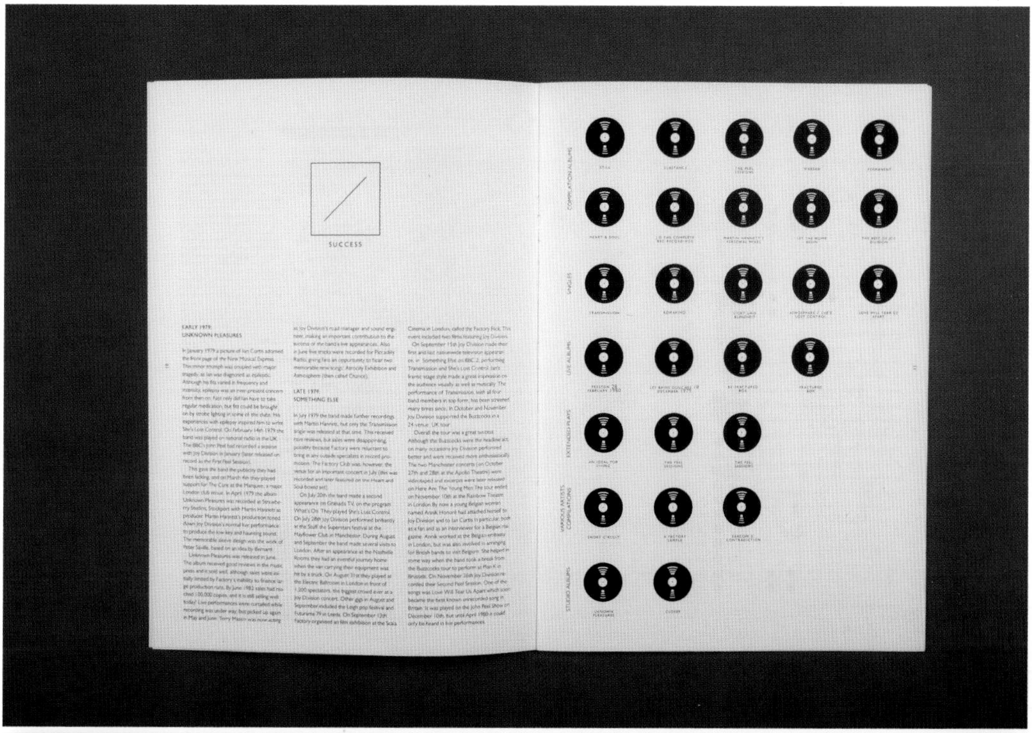
SUCCESS
EARLY 1979:
UNKNOWN PLEASURES
LATE 1979:
SOMETHING ELSE
COMPILATION ALBUMS
SINGLES
LIVE ALBUMS
EXTENDED PLAYS
VARIOUS ARTISTS COMPILATIONS
STUDIO ALBUMS

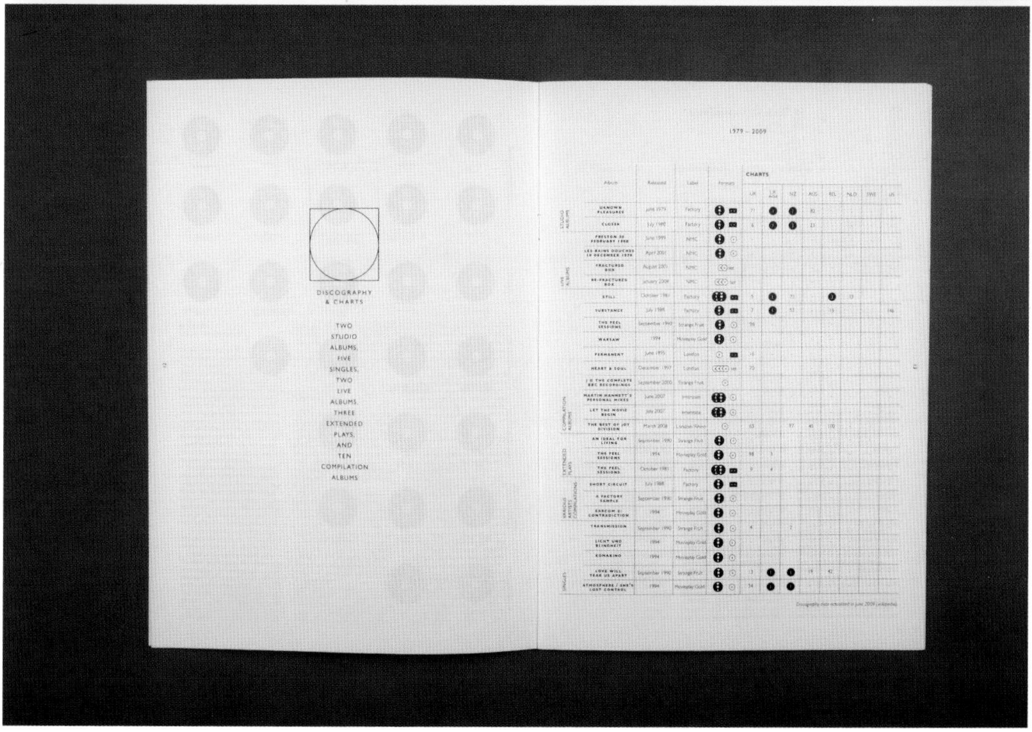
DISCOGRAPHY
& CHARTS
TWO
STUDIO
ALBUMS,
FIVE
SINGLES,
TWO
LIVE
ALBUMS,
THREE
EXTENDED
PLAYS,
AND
TEN
COMPILATION
ALBUMS
1979 – 2009
CHARTS

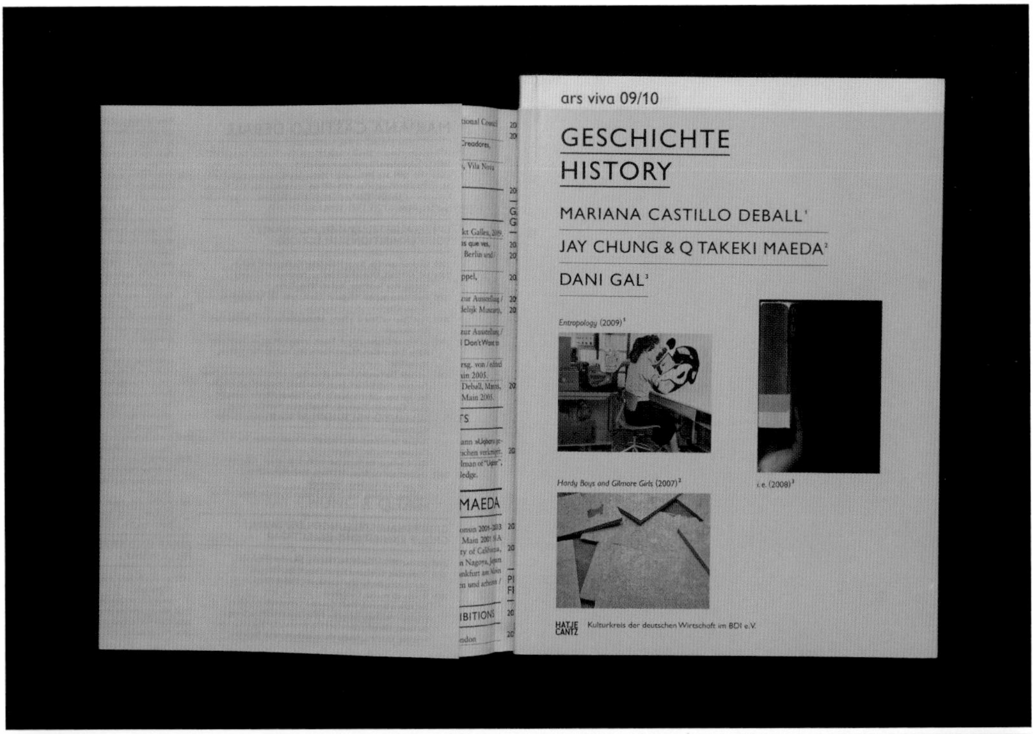
ars viva 09/10
GESCHICHTE
HISTORY
MARIANA CASTILLO DEBALL[1]
JAY CHUNG & Q TAKEKI MAEDA[2]
DANI GAL[3]
Entropology (2009)[1]
Hardy Boys and Gilmore Girls (2007)[2]
i.e. (2008)[3]
HATJE CANTZ
Kulturkreis der deutschen Wirtschaft im BDI e.V.

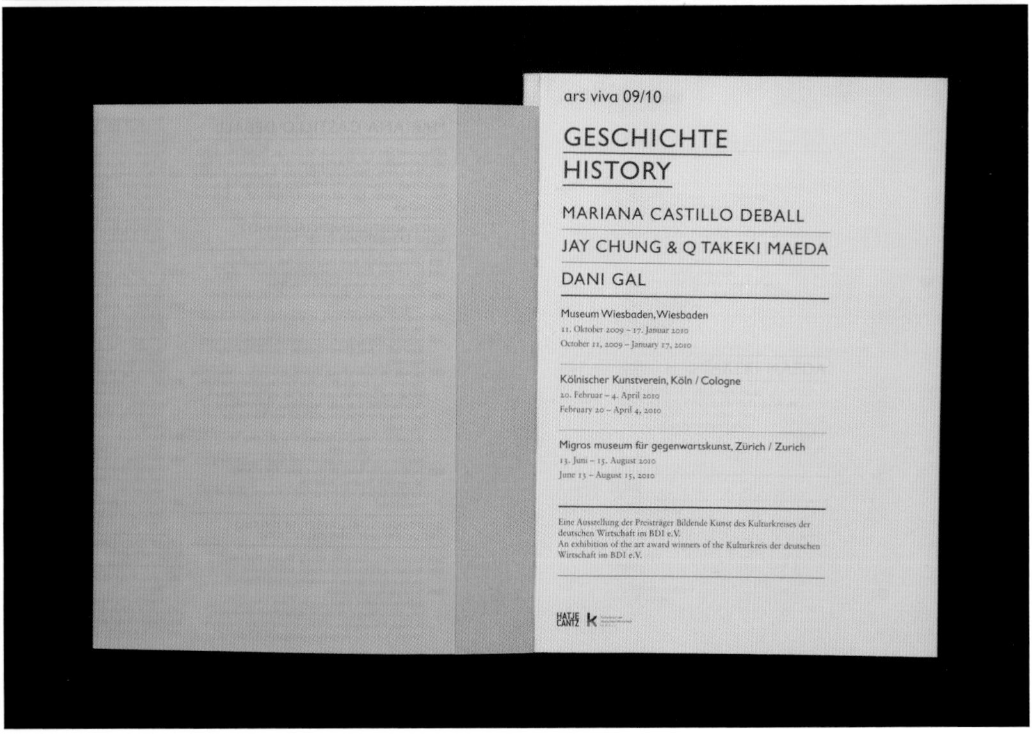
ars viva 09/10
GESCHICHTE
HISTORY
MARIANA CASTILLO DEBALL
JAY CHUNG & Q TAKEKI MAEDA
DANI GAL
Museum Wiesbaden, Wiesbaden
11. Oktober 2009 – 17. Januar 2010
October 11, 2009 – January 17, 2010
Kölnischer Kunstverein, Köln / Cologne
20. Februar – 4. April 2010
February 20 – April 4, 2010
Migros museum für gegenwartskunst, Zürich / Zurich
13. Juni – 15. August 2010
June 13 – August 15, 2010
Eine Ausstellung der Preisträger Bildende Kunst des Kulturkreises der deutschen Wirtschaft im BDI e.V.
An exhibition of the art award winners of the Kulturkreis der deutschen Wirtschaft im BDI e.V.
HATJE CANTZ

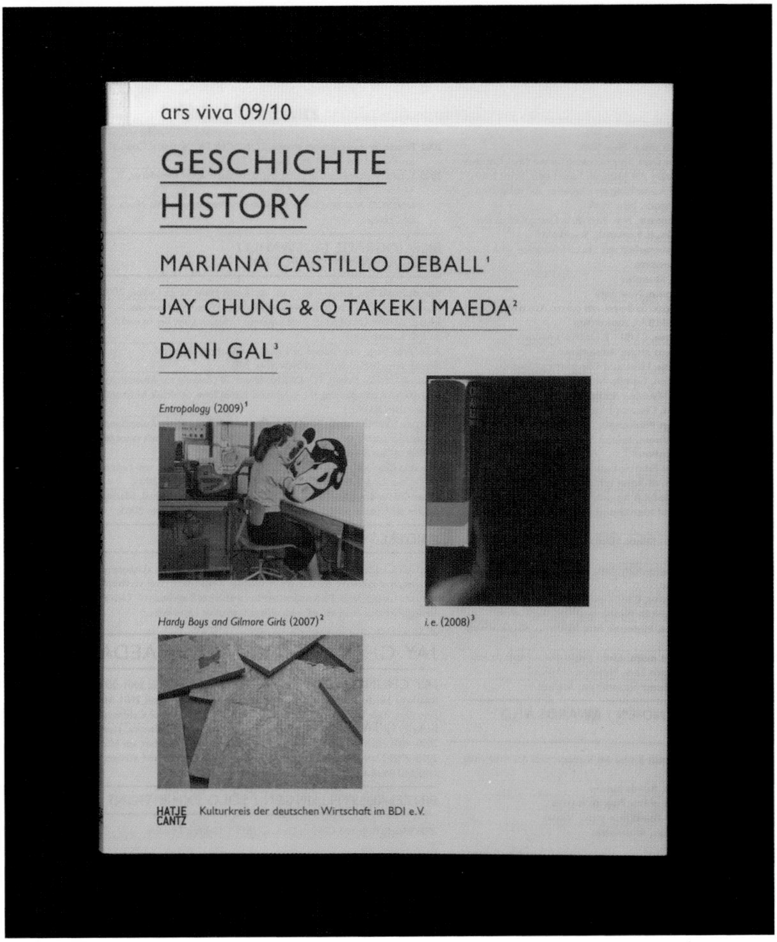

Ars Viva 09/10: Geschichte/History
2009 — Book
Client Kulturkreis der deutschen Wirtschaft
Design jungundwenig

It was under the deliberately general heading of History that the "Kulturkreis der deutschen Wirtschaft" announced this year's "Ars Viva Prize" for fine arts. Recognized for their achievements were Mexican artist Mariana Castillo Deball (*1975), the American-Japanese team of Jay Chung & Q Takeki Maeda (*1976/1977), and Israeli artist Dani Gal (*1975). The design of the catalog tries to fit the work of all three artists, who work with different techniques. As there is the imaginative polyphony of voices in the works of Mariana Castillo Deball, which she created by blending historical facts with her own fictions. Dani Gal's sound and video installations vigorously explore the construction of postwar history through media and allow the viewer to interact with them. Jay Chung's & Q Takeki Maeda's humorous treatment of the ways history are changed for today's media and consumer worlds.

Typeface in Use
Gill Sans MT Schoolbook, Sabon Roman, Gill Sans MT

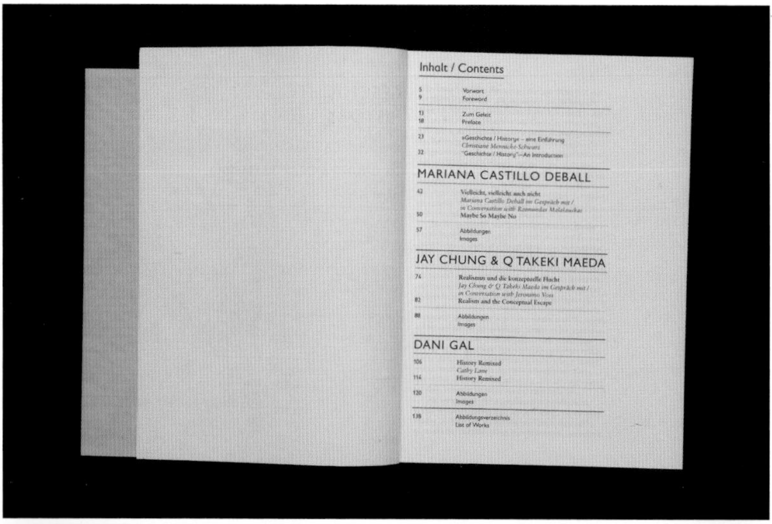

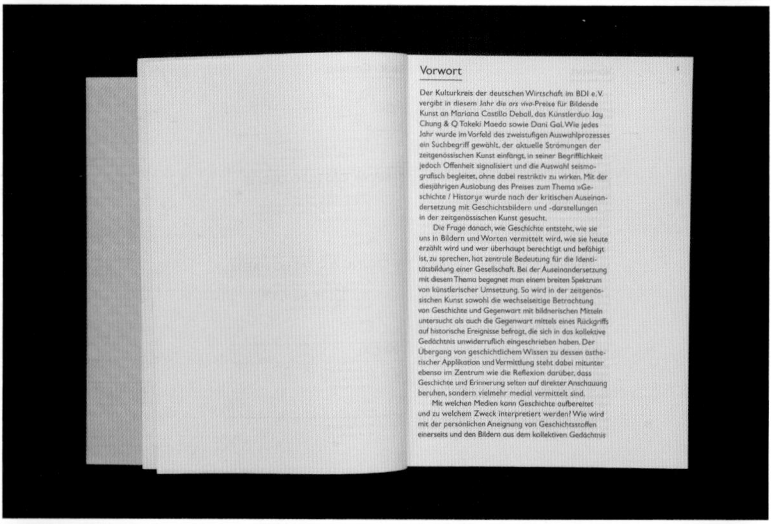

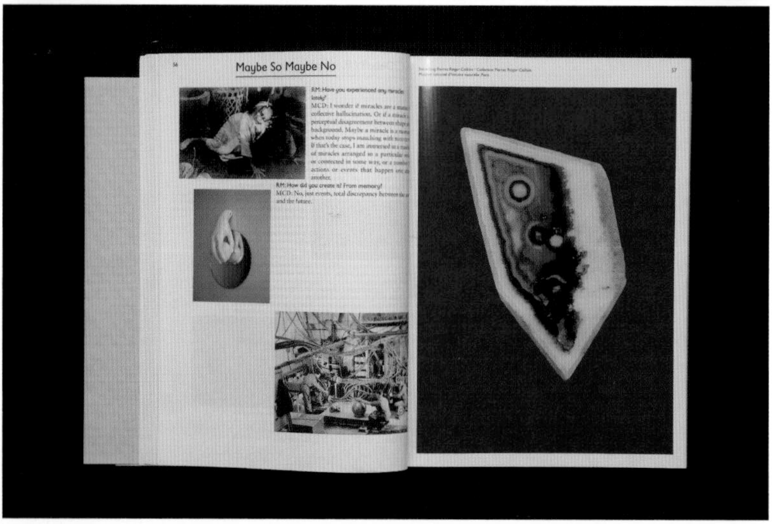

"it is a beautiful font — it's that easy."

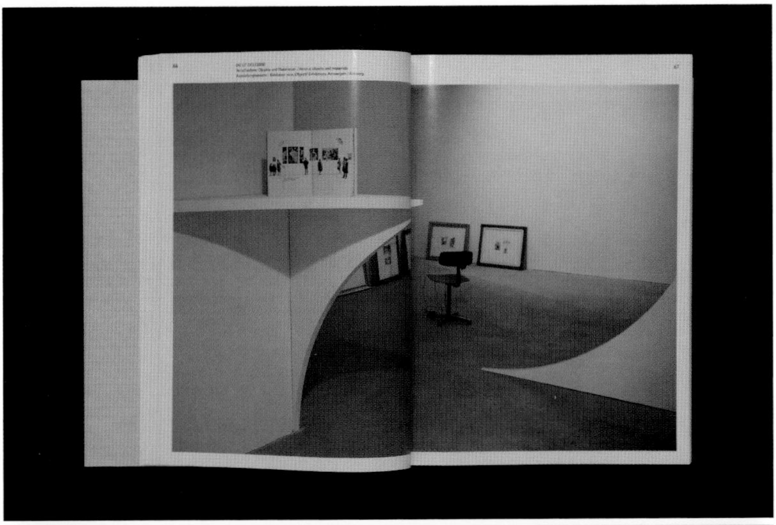

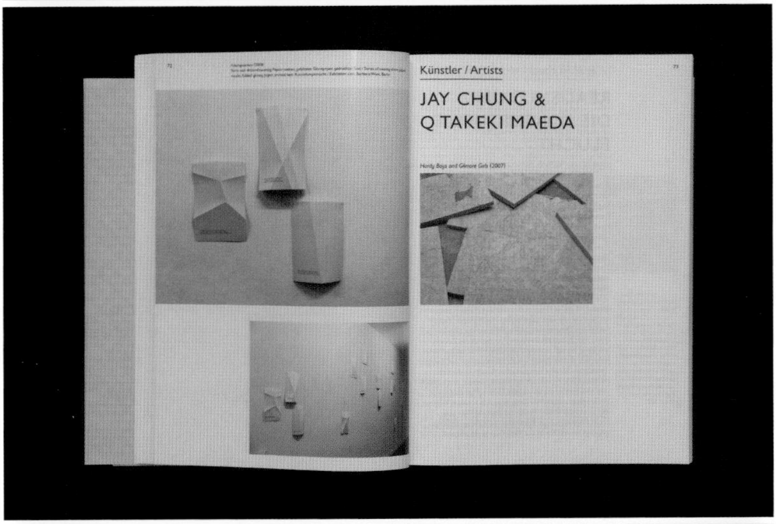

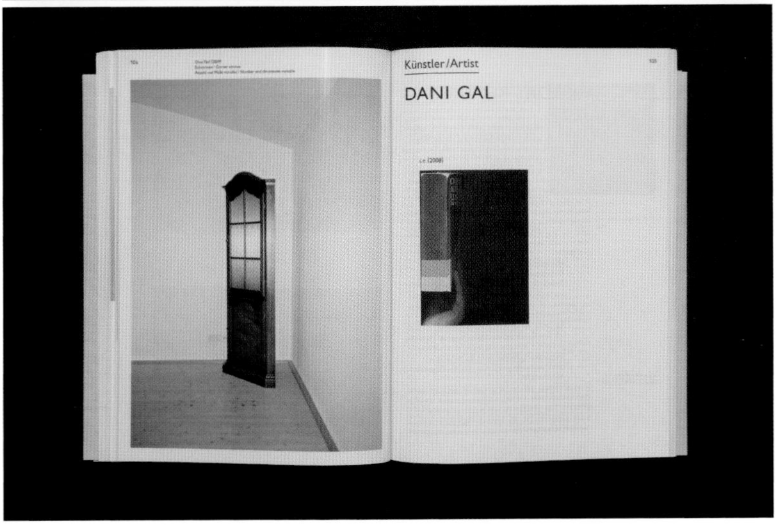

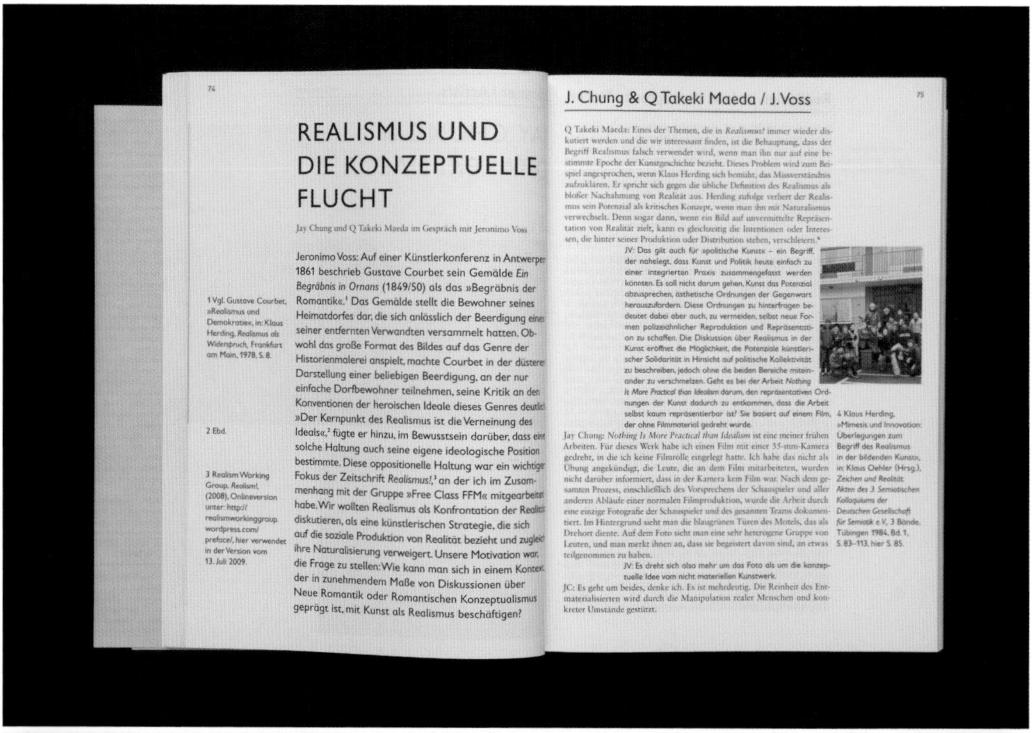

74

REALISMUS UND DIE KONZEPTUELLE FLUCHT

Jay Chung und Q Takeki Maeda im Gespräch mit Jeronimo Voss

Jeronimo Voss: Auf einer Künstlerkonferenz in Antwerpe 1861 beschrieb Gustave Courbet sein Gemälde *Ein Begräbnis in Ornans* (1849/50) als das »Begräbnis der Romantik«.[1] Das Gemälde stellt die Bewohner seines Heimatdorfes dar, die sich anlässlich der Beerdigung eines seiner entfernten Verwandten versammelt hatten. Obwohl das große Format des Bildes auf das Genre der Historienmalerei anspielt, machte Courbet in der düstere Darstellung einer beliebigen Beerdigung, an der nur einfache Dorfbewohner teilnehmen, seine Kritik an den Konventionen der heroischen Ideale dieses Genres deutlic »Der Kernpunkt des Realismus ist die Verneinung des Ideals«,[2] fügte er hinzu, im Bewusstsein darüber, dass eine solche Haltung auch seine eigene ideologische Position bestimmte. Diese oppositionelle Haltung war ein wichtige Fokus der Zeitschrift *Realismus!*,[3] an der ich im Zusammenhang mit der Gruppe »Free Class FFM« mitgearbeite habe. Wir wollten Realismus als Konfrontation der Realit diskutieren, als eine künstlerischen Strategie, die sich auf die soziale Produktion von Realität bezieht und zugleic ihre Naturalisierung verweigert. Unsere Motivation war, die Frage zu stellen: Wie kann man sich in einem Kontext der in zunehmendem Maße von Diskussionen über Neue Romantik oder Romantischen Konzeptualismus geprägt ist, mit Kunst als Realismus beschäftigen?

1 Vgl. Gustave Courbet, »Realismus und Demokratie«, in: Klaus Herding, *Realismus als Widerspruch*, Frankfurt am Main, 1978, S. 8.

2 Ebd.

3 Realism Working Group, *Realism!*, (2008), Onlineversion unter: http://realismworkinggroup.wordpress.com/preface/, hier verwendet in der Version vom 13. Juli 2009.

J. Chung & Q Takeki Maeda / J. Voss

75

Q Takeki Maeda: Eines der Themen, die in *Realismus!* immer wieder diskutiert werden und die wir interessant finden, ist die Behauptung, dass der Begriff Realismus falsch verwendet wird, wenn man ihn nur auf eine bestimmte Epoche der Kunstgeschichte bezieht. Dieses Problem wird zum Beispiel angesprochen, wenn Klaus Herding sich bemüht, das Missverständnis aufzuklären. Er spricht sich gegen die übliche Definition des Realismus als bloßer Nachahmung von Realität aus. Herding zufolge verliert der Realismus sein Potenzial als kritisches Konzept, wenn man ihn mit Naturalismus verwechselt. Denn sogar dann, wenn ein Bild auf unvermittelte Repräsentation von Realität zielt, kann es gleichzeitig die Intentionen oder Interessen, die hinter seiner Produktion oder Distribution stehen, verschleiern.[4]

JV: Das gilt auch für »politische Kunst« – ein Begriff, der nahelegt, dass Kunst und Politik heute einfach zu einer integrierten Praxis zusammengefasst werden könnten. Es soll nicht darum gehen, Kunst das Potenzial abzusprechen, ästhetische Ordnungen der Gegenwart herauszufordern. Diese Ordnungen zu hinterfragen bedeutet dabei aber auch, zu vermeiden, selbst neue Formen polizeiähnlicher Reproduktion und Repräsentation zu schaffen. Die Diskussion über Realismus in der Kunst eröffnet die Möglichkeit, die Potenziale künstlerischer Solidarität in Hinsicht auf politische Kollektivität zu beschreiben, jedoch ohne die beiden Bereiche miteinander zu verschmelzen. Geht es bei der Arbeit *Nothing Is More Practical than Idealism* darum, den repräsentativen Ordnungen der Kunst dadurch zu entkommen, dass die Arbeit selbst kaum repräsentierbar ist? Sie basiert auf einem Film, der ohne Filmmaterial gedreht wurde.

Jay Chung: *Nothing Is More Practical than Idealism* ist eine meiner frühen Arbeiten. Für dieses Werk habe ich einen Film mit einer 35-mm-Kamera gedreht, in die ich keine Filmrolle eingelegt hatte. Ich habe das nicht als Übung angekündigt, die Leute, die an dem Film mitarbeiteten, wurden nicht darüber informiert, dass in der Kamera kein Film war. Nach dem gesamten Prozess, einschließlich des Vorsprechens der Schauspieler und aller anderen Abläufe einer normalen Filmproduktion, wurde die Arbeit durch eine einzige Fotografie der Schauspieler und des gesamten Teams dokumentiert. Im Hintergrund sieht man die blaugrünen Türen des Motels, das als Drehort diente. Auf dem Foto sieht man eine sehr heterogene Gruppe von Leuten, und man merkt ihnen an, dass sie begeistert davon sind, an etwas teilgenommen zu haben.

JV: Es dreht sich also mehr um das Foto als um die konzeptuelle Idee vom nicht materiellen Kunstwerk.

JC: Es geht um beides, denke ich. Es ist mehrdeutig. Die Reinheit des Entmaterialisierten wird durch die Manipulation realer Menschen und konkreter Umstände gestützt.

4 Klaus Herding, »Mimesis und Innovation: Überlegungen zum Begriff des Realismus in der bildenden Kunst«, in: Klaus Oehler (Hrsg.), *Zeichen und Realität: Akten des 3. Semiotischen Kolloquiums der Deutschen Gesellschaft für Semiotik e.V.*, 3 Bände, Tübingen 1984, Bd. 1, S. 83–113, hier S. 85.

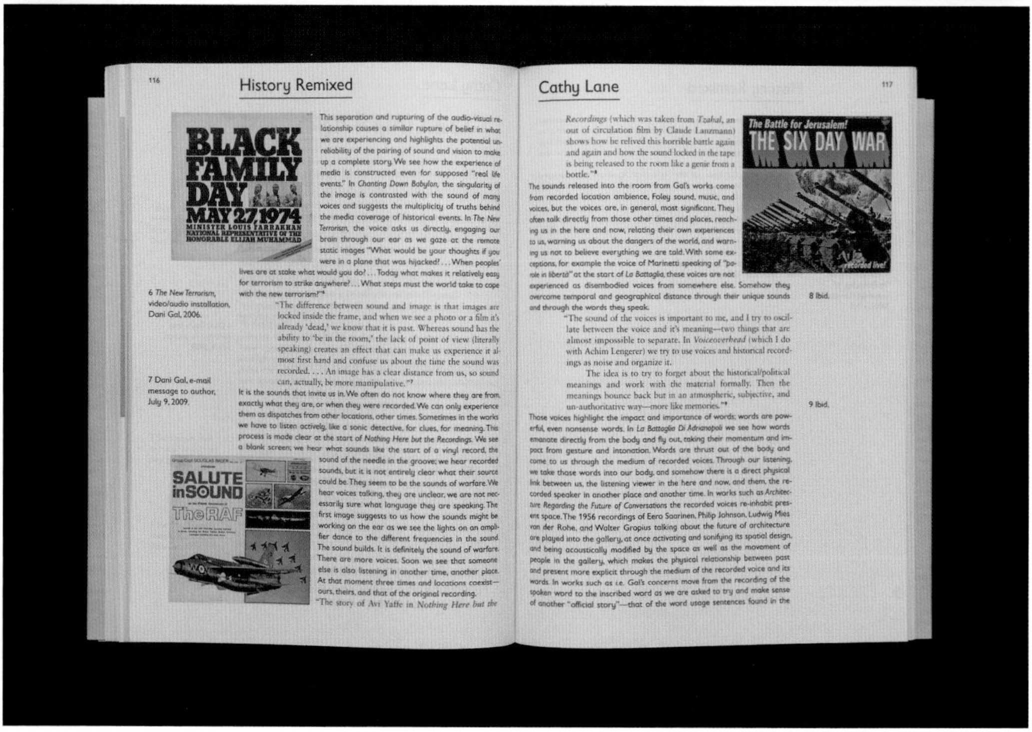

116

History Remixed

BLACK FAMILY DAY MAY 27, 1974 MINISTER LOUIS FARRAKHAN NATIONAL REPRESENTATIVE OF THE HONORABLE ELIJAH MUHAMMAD

This separation and rupturing of the audio-visual relationship causes a similar rupture of belief in what we are experiencing and highlights the potential unreliability of the pairing of sound and vision to make up a complete story. We see how the experience of media is constructed even for supposed "real life events." In *Chanting Down Babylon*, the singularity of the image is contrasted with the sound of many voices and suggests the multiplicity of truths behind the media coverage of historical events. In *The New Terrorism*, the voice asks us directly, engaging our brain through our ear as we gaze at the remote static images "What would be your thoughts if you were in a plane that was hijacked? ... When peoples' lives are at stake what would you do? ... Today what makes it relatively easy for terrorism to strike anywhere? ... What steps must the world take to cope with the new terrorism?"[6]

"The difference between sound and image is that images are locked inside the frame, and when we see a photo or a film it's already 'dead,' we know that it is past. Whereas sound has the ability to 'be in the room,' the lack of point of view (literally speaking) creates an effect that can make us experience it almost first hand and confuse us about the time the sound was recorded. ... An image has a clear distance from us, so sound can, actually, be more manipulative."[7]

It is the sounds that invite us in. We often do not know where they are from, exactly what they are, or when they were recorded. We can only experience them as dispatches from other locations, other times. Sometimes in the works we have to listen actively, like a sonic detective, for clues, for meaning. This process is made clear at the start of *Nothing Here but the Recordings*. We see a blank screen; we hear what sounds like the start of a vinyl record, the sound of the needle in the groove; we hear recorded sounds, but it is not entirely clear what their source could be. They seem to be the sounds of warfare. We hear voices talking, they are unclear, we are not necessarily sure what language they are speaking. The first image suggests to us how the sounds might be working on the ear as we see the lights on an amplifier dance to the different frequencies in the sound. The sound builds. It is definitely the sound of warfare. There are more voices. Soon we see that someone else is also listening in another time, another place. At that moment three times and locations coexist—ours, theirs, and that of the original recording.

"The story of Avi Yaffe in *Nothing Here but the*

SALUTE in SOUND The RAF

6 *The New Terrorism*, video/audio installation, Dani Gal, 2006.

7 Dani Gal, e-mail message to author, July 9, 2009.

Cathy Lane

117

The Battle for Jerusalem! THE SIX DAY WAR recorded live!

Recordings (which was taken from *Tzahal*, an out of circulation film by Claude Lanzmann) shows how he relived this horrible battle again and again and how the sound locked in the tape is being released to the room like a genie from a bottle."[8]

The sounds released into the room from Gal's works come from recorded location ambience, Foley sound, music, and voices, but the voices are, in general, most significant. They often talk directly from those other times and places, reaching us in the here and now, relating their own experiences to us, warning us about the dangers of the world, and warning us not to believe everything we are told. With some exceptions, for example the voice of Marinetti speaking of "*parole in libertà*" at the start of *La Battaglia*, these voices are not experienced as disembodied voices from somewhere else. Somehow they overcome temporal and geographical distance through their unique sounds and through the words they speak.

"The sound of the voices is important to me, and I try to oscillate between the voice and it's meaning—two things that are almost impossible to separate. In *Voiceoverhead* (which I do with Achim Lengerer) we try to use voices and historical recordings as noise and organize it.

The idea is to try to forget about the historical/political meanings and work with the material formally. Then the meanings bounce back but in an atmospheric, subjective, and un-authoritative way—more like memories."[9]

Those voices highlight the impact and importance of words: words are powerful, even nonsense words. In *La Battaglia Di Adrianopoli* we see how words emanate directly from the body and fly out, taking their momentum and impact from gesture and intonation. Words are thrust out of the body and come to us through the medium of recorded voices. Through our listening, we take those words into our body, and somehow there is a direct physical link between us, the listening viewer in the here and now, and them, the recorded speaker in another place and another time. In works such as *Architecture Regarding the Future of Conversations* the recorded voices re-inhabit present space. The 1956 recordings of Eero Saarinen, Philip Johnson, Ludwig Mies van der Rohe, and Walter Gropius talking about the future of architecture are played into the gallery, at once activating and sonifying its spatial design, and being acoustically modified by the space as well as the movement of people in the gallery, which makes the physical relationship between past and present more explicit through the medium of the recorded voice and its words. In works such as *i.e.* Gal's concerns move from the recording of the spoken word to the inscribed word as we are asked to try and make sense of another "official story"—that of the word usage sentences found in the

8 Ibid.

9 Ibid.

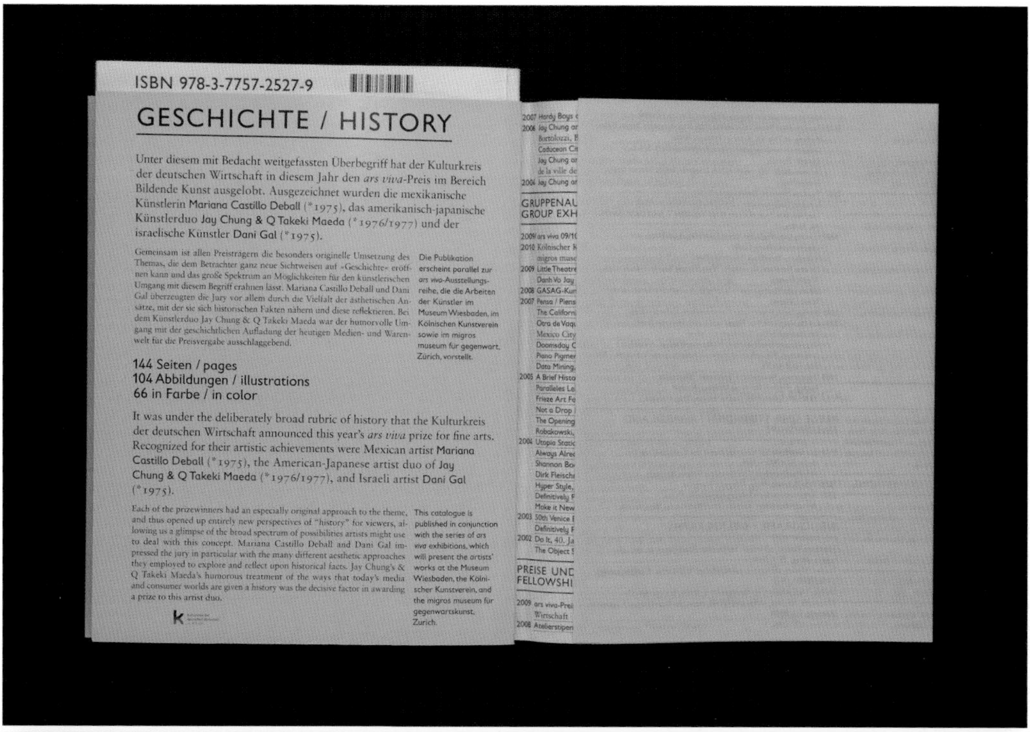
ISBN 978-3-7757-2527-9
GESCHICHTE / HISTORY
Unter diesem mit Bedacht weitgefassten Überbegriff hat der Kulturkreis der deutschen Wirtschaft in diesem Jahr den ars viva-Preis im Bereich Bildende Kunst ausgelobt. Ausgezeichnet wurden die mexikanische Künstlerin Mariana Castillo Deball (*1975), das amerikanisch-japanische Künstlerduo Jay Chung & Q Takeki Maeda (*1976/1977) und der israelische Künstler Dani Gal (*1975).
Gemeinsam ist allen Preisträgern die besonders originelle Umsetzung des Themas, die dem Betrachter ganz neue Sichtweisen auf »Geschichte« eröffnen kann und das große Spektrum an Möglichkeiten für den künstlerischen Umgang mit diesem Begriff erahnen lässt. Mariana Castillo Deball und Dani Gal überzeugten die Jury vor allem durch die Vielfalt der ästhetischen Ansätze, mit der sie sich historischen Fakten nähern und diese reflektieren. Bei dem Künstlerduo Jay Chung & Q Takeki Maeda war der humorvolle Umgang mit der geschichtlichen Aufladung der heutigen Medien- und Warenwelt für die Preisvergabe ausschlaggebend.
Die Publikation erscheint parallel zur ars viva-Ausstellungsreihe, die die Arbeiten der Künstler im Museum Wiesbaden, im Kölnischen Kunstverein sowie im migros museum für gegenwart, Zürich, vorstellt.
144 Seiten / pages
104 Abbildungen / illustrations
66 in Farbe / in color
It was under the deliberately broad rubric of history that the Kulturkreis der deutschen Wirtschaft announced this year's ars viva prize for fine arts. Recognized for their artistic achievements were Mexican artist Mariana Castillo Deball (*1975), the American-Japanese artist duo of Jay Chung & Q Takeki Maeda (*1976/1977), and Israeli artist Dani Gal (*1975).
Each of the prizewinners had an especially original approach to the theme, and thus opened up entirely new perspectives of "history" for viewers, allowing us a glimpse of the broad spectrum of possibilities artists might use to deal with this concept. Mariana Castillo Deball and Dani Gal impressed the jury in particular with the many different aesthetic approaches they employed to explore and reflect upon historical facts. Jay Chung's & Q Takeki Maeda's humorous treatment of the ways that today's media and consumer worlds are given a history was the decisive factor in awarding a prize to this artist duo.
This catalogue is published in conjunction with the series of ars viva exhibitions, which will present the artists' works at the Museum Wiesbaden, the Kölnischer Kunstverein, and the migros museum für gegenwartskunst, Zurich.

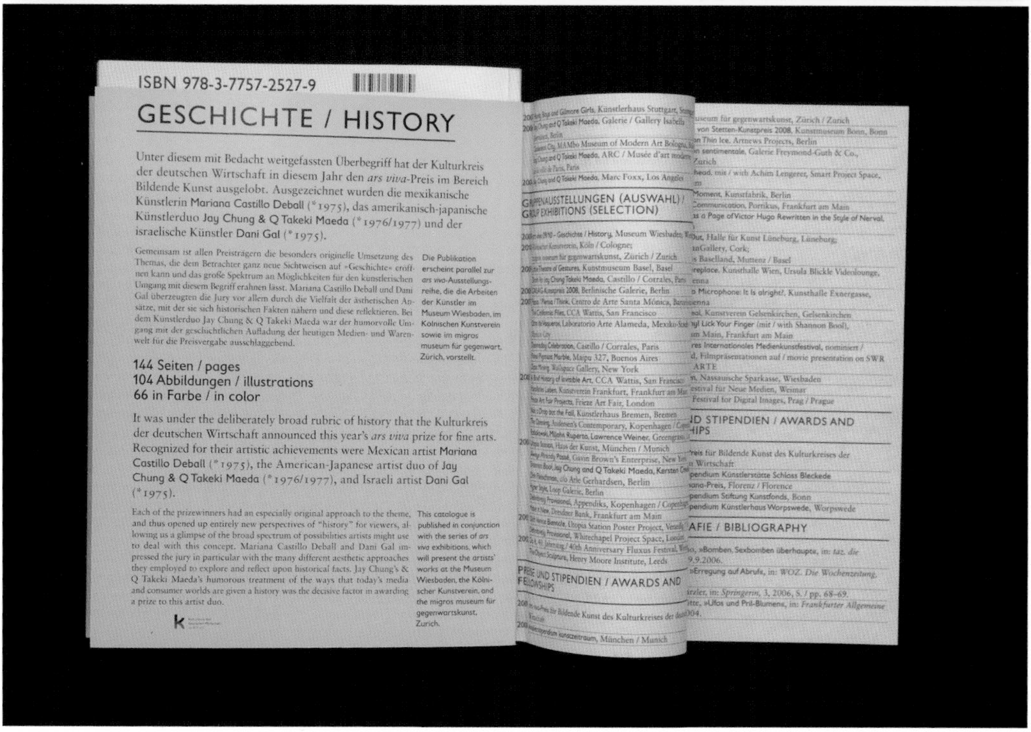
ISBN 978-3-7757-2527-9
GESCHICHTE / HISTORY
GRUPPENAUSSTELLUNGEN (AUSWAHL) / GROUP EXHIBITIONS (SELECTION)
PREISE UND STIPENDIEN / AWARDS AND FELLOWSHIPS
BIBLIOGRAFIE / BIBLIOGRAPHY

3327 Division Street
Los Angeles, CA 90065

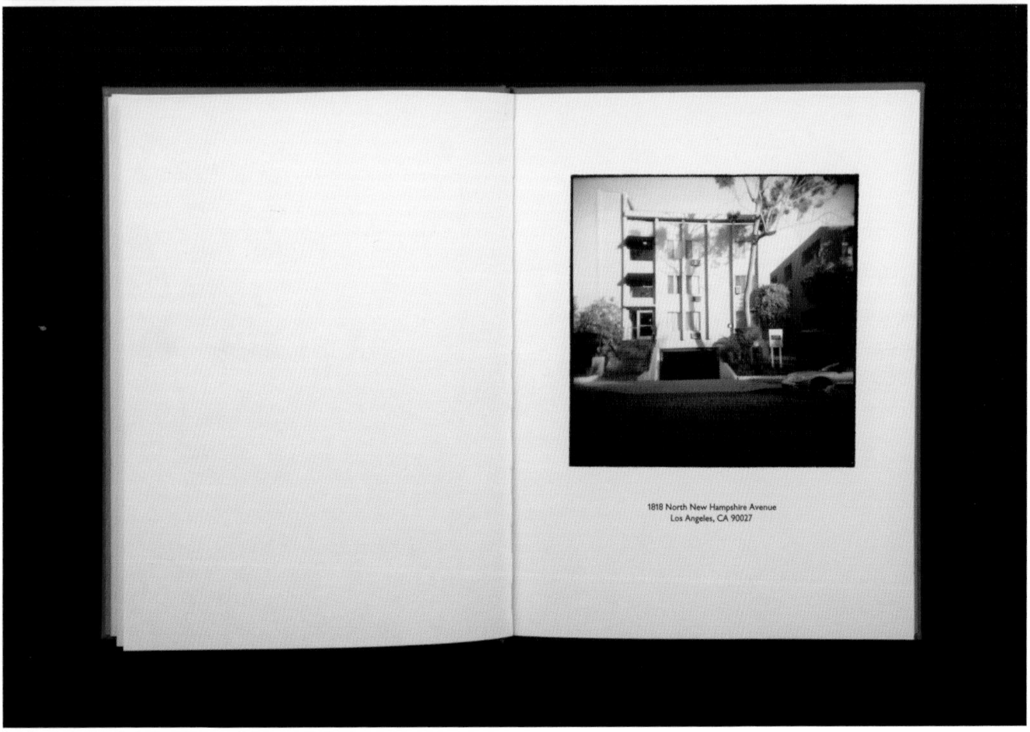
1818 North New Hampshire Avenue
Los Angeles, CA 90027

Various Studios & Homes Inhabited by Ed Ruscha
2008 — Book
Design Chris Svensson

"Most of the aesthetic decisions in the Ruscha book were made by me imagining what Ruscha wouldn't have done, or what 'felt' the least Ruscha. Gill Sans's 'Englishness' just seemed to work for me in this context."

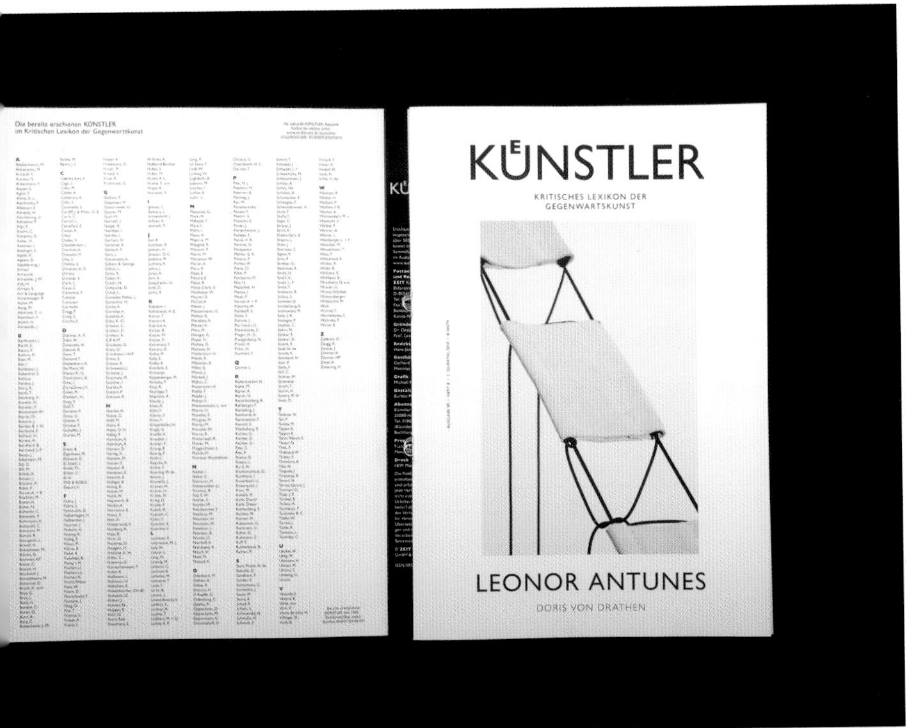
Die bereits erschienen KÜNSTLER
im Kritischen Lexikon der Gegenwartskunst
KÜNSTLER
KRITISCHES LEXIKON DER
GEGENWARTSKUNST
LEONOR ANTUNES
DORIS VON DRATHEN

KÜNSTLER
KRITISCHES LEXIKON DER
GEGENWARTSKUNST
HERMANN PITZ
THOMAS WULFFEN

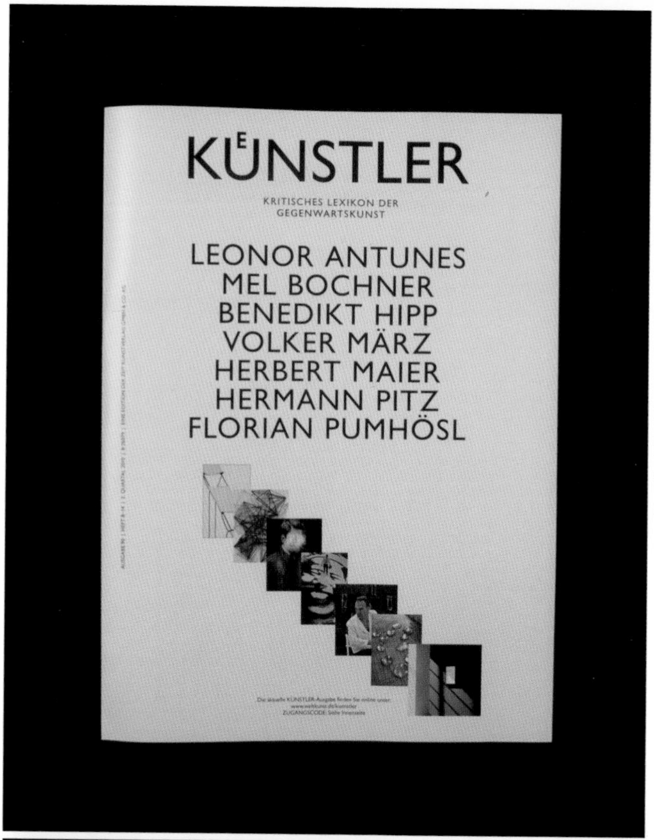

Kuenstler — Kritisches Lexikon der Gegenwartskunst
2010 — Booklet
Client Zeit Kunstverlag
Design Bureau Mirko Borsche

Four times a year KUENSTLER offers high-quality and elaborate 20-page monographs on seven artists each time. The monographs can be taken out as individual books and can be collected like an encyclopedia.

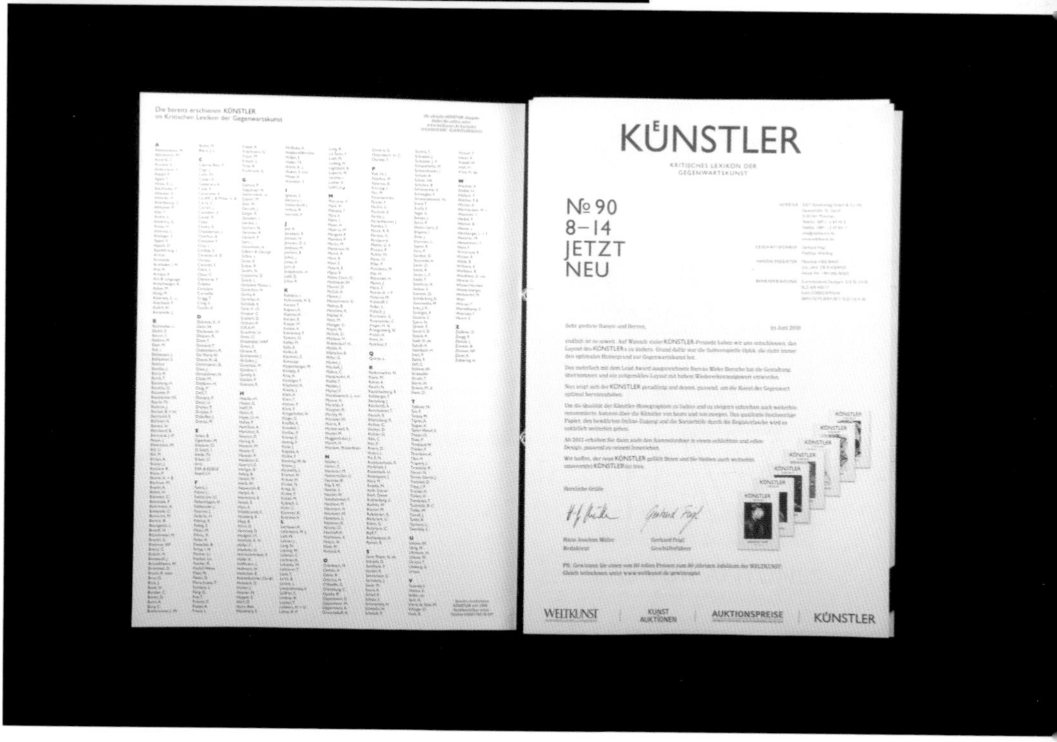

KÜNSTLER
KRITISCHES LEXIKON DER GEGENWARTSKUNST
FLORIAN PUMHÖSL
STEPHAN MAIER

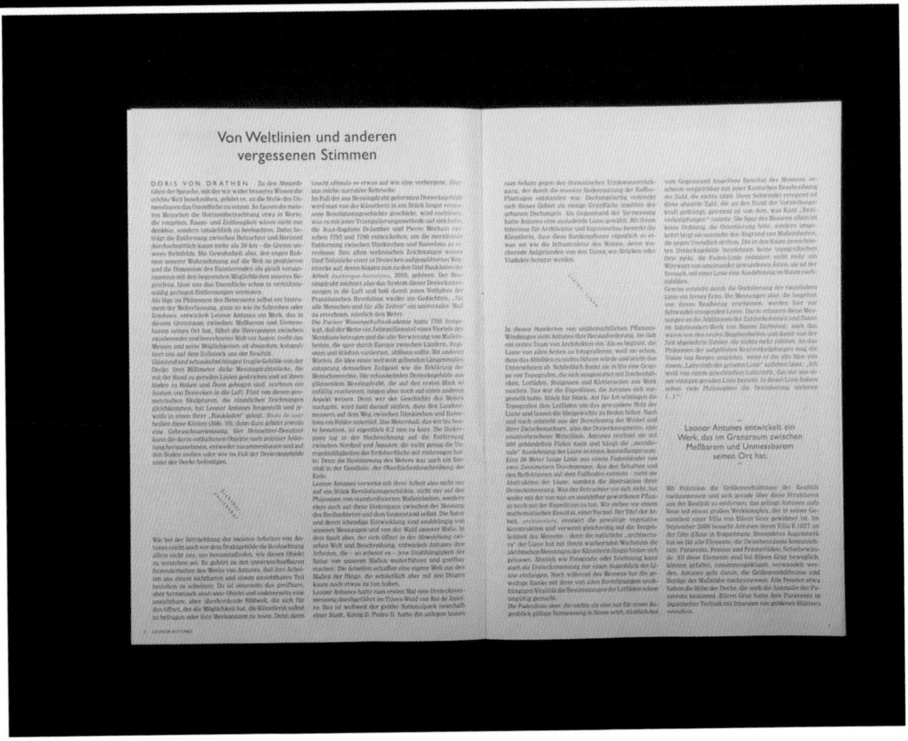
Von Weltlinien und anderen vergessenen Stimmen
Leonor Antunes entwickelt ein Werk, das im Grenzraum zwischen Meßbarem und Unmessbarem seinen Ort hat.

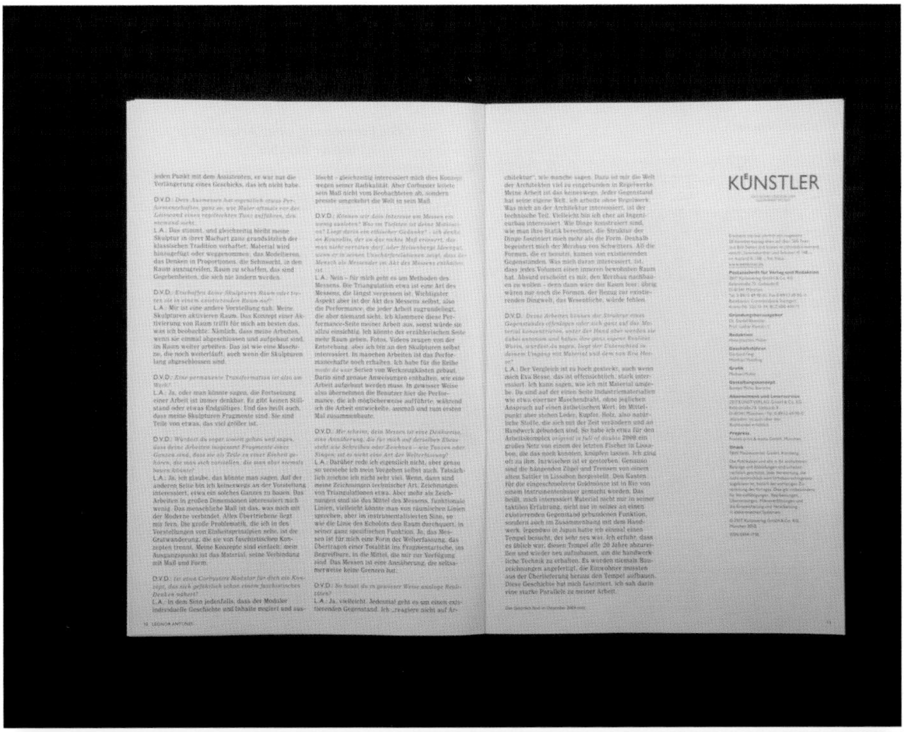
KÜNSTLER
10 LEONOR ANTUNES

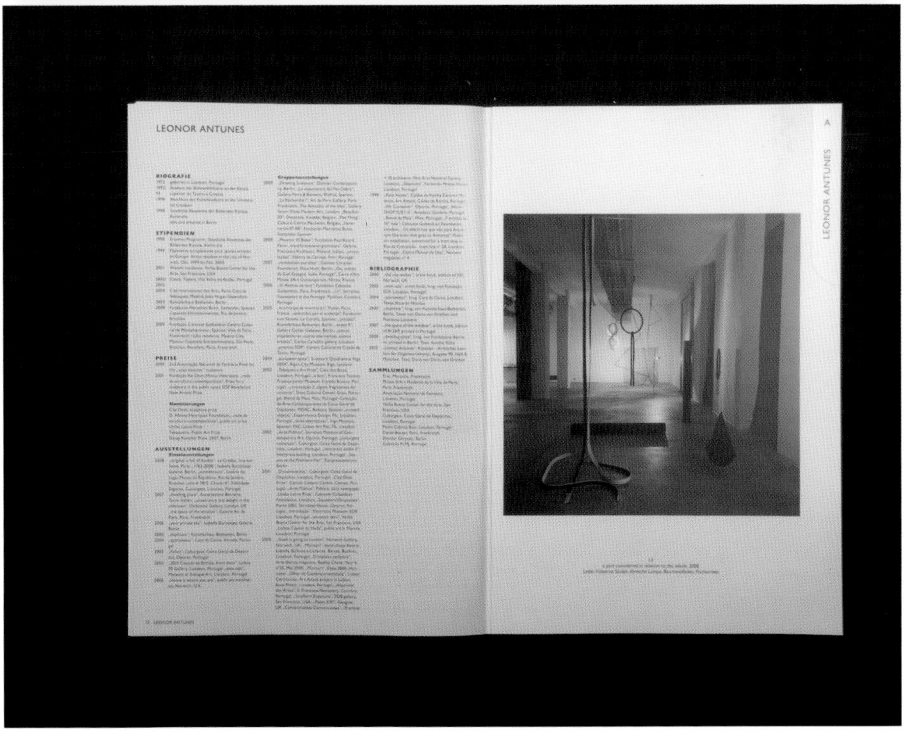
LEONOR ANTUNES
BIOGRAFIE
STIPENDIEN
PREISE
AUSSTELLUNGEN
BIBLIOGRAPHIE
SAMMLUNGEN
LEONOR ANTUNES
12 LEONOR ANTUNES

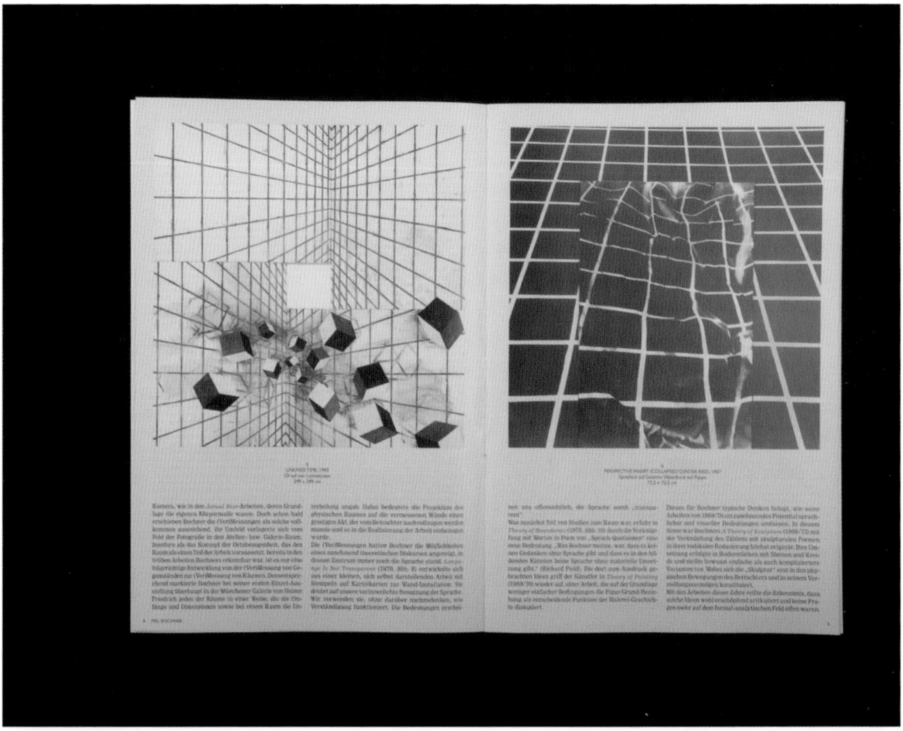

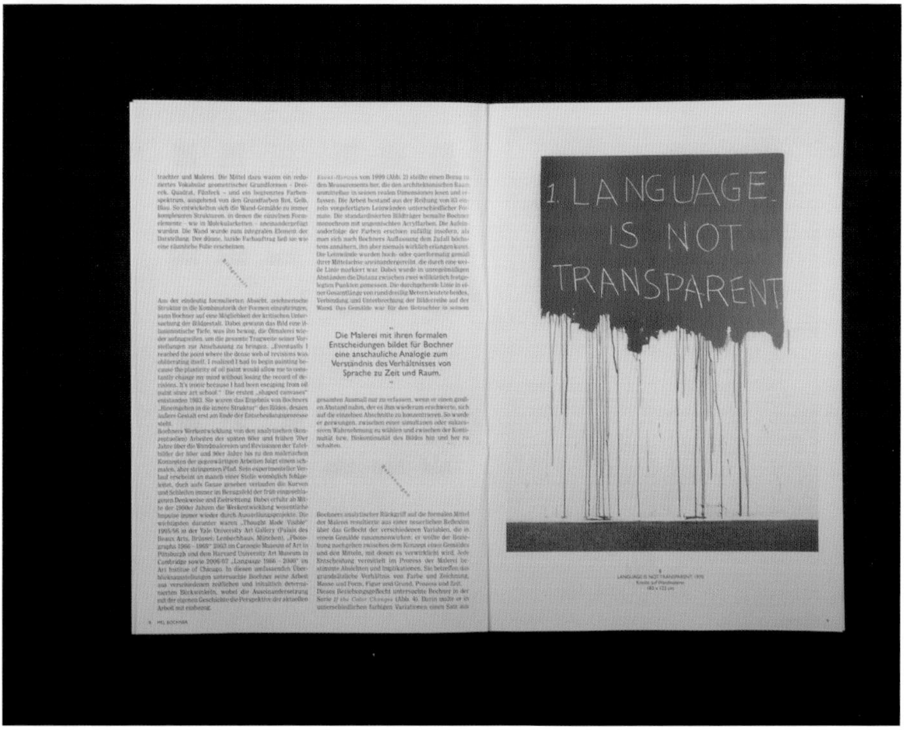
Die Malerei mit ihren formalen Entscheidungen bildet für Bochner eine anschauliche Analogie zum Verständnis des Verhältnisses von Sprache zu Zeit und Raum.
1. LANGUAGE IS NOT TRANSPARENT

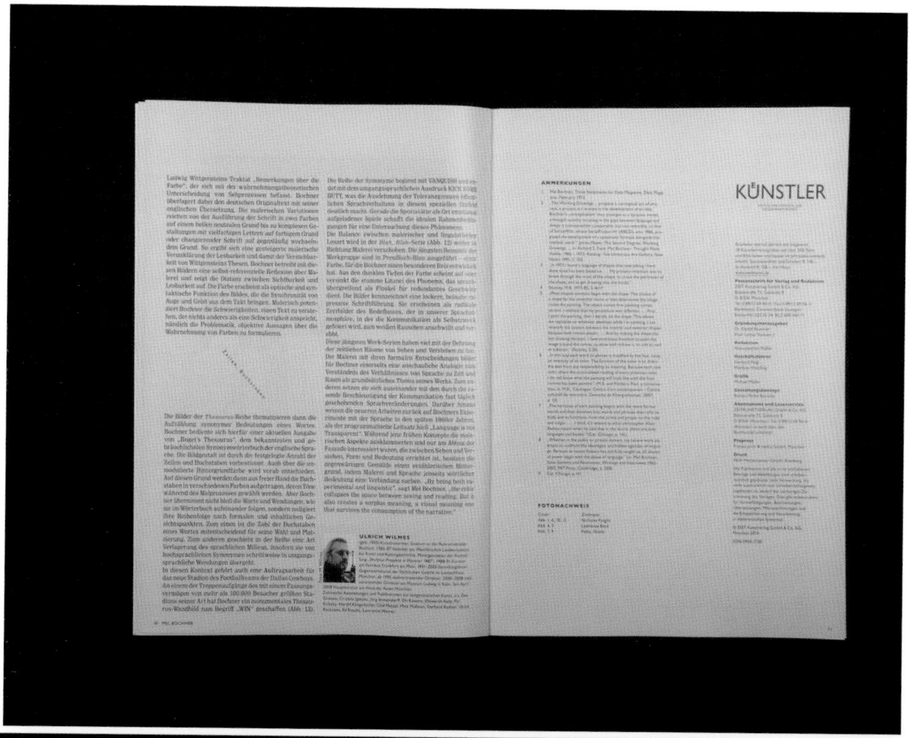
ANMERKUNGEN
FOTONACHWEIS
ULRICH WILMES
KÜNSTLER

BENEDIKT HIPP
„Man spricht meinen Bildern oft Surreales zu, was aber nicht ganz stimmt. Vielmehr gehe ich in meiner Arbeit Grundfragen nach, Urformen und Strukturen und somit den Fragen, an denen alle Stränge von Wissenschaft, Philosophie und Theologie oder Spiritualität zusammenlaufen."

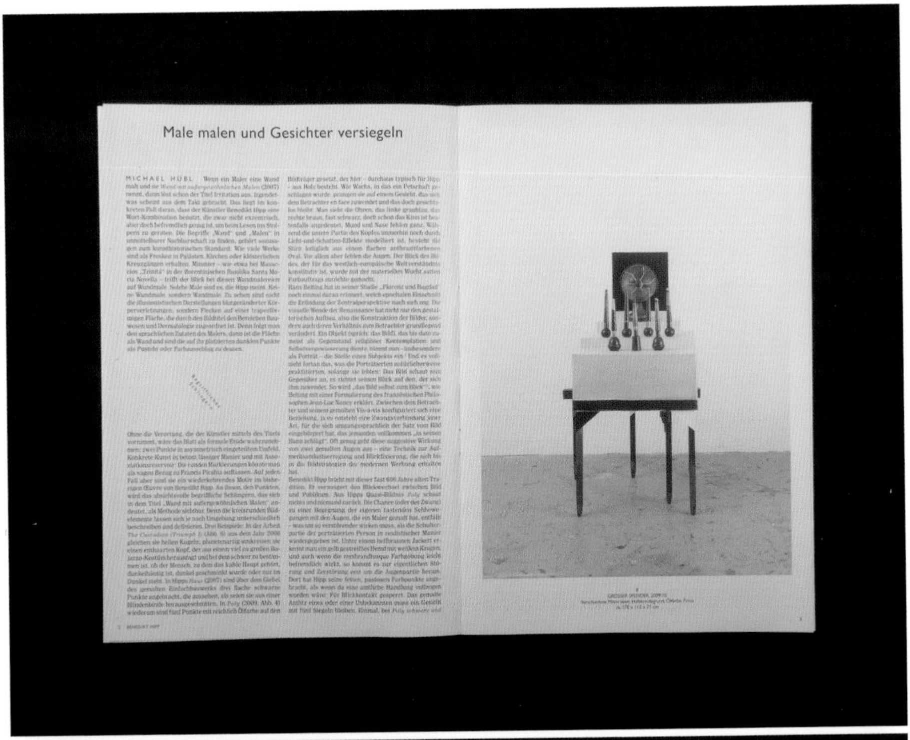
Male malen und Gesichter versiegeln
MICHAEL HÜBL

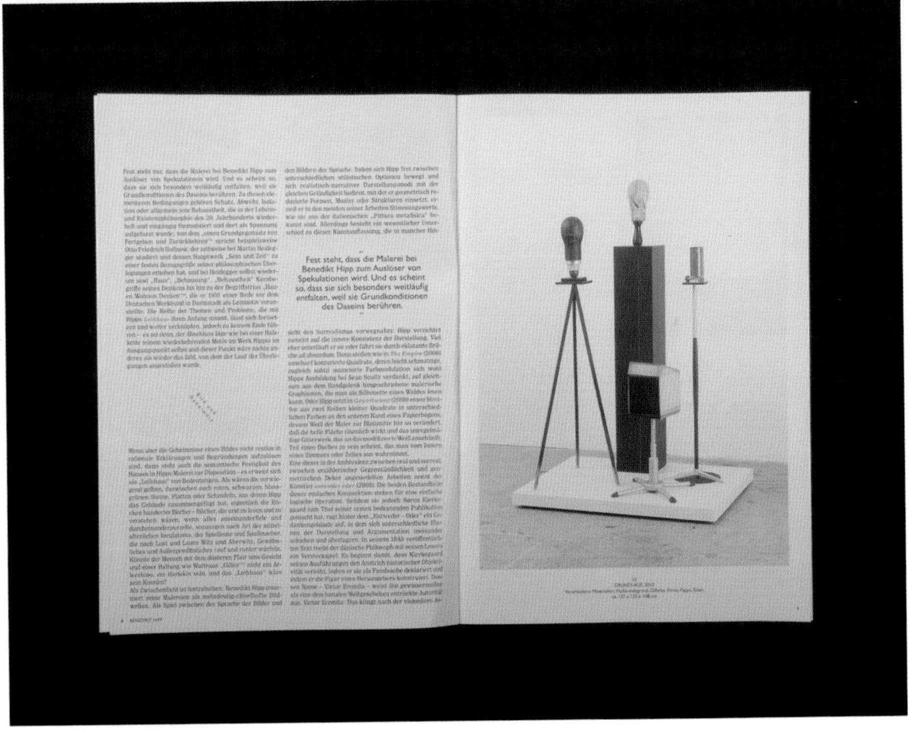
Fest steht, dass die Malerei bei Benedikt Hipp zum Auslöser von Spekulationen wird. Und es scheint so, dass sie sich besonders weitläufig entfalten, weil sie Grundkonditionen des Daseins berühren.

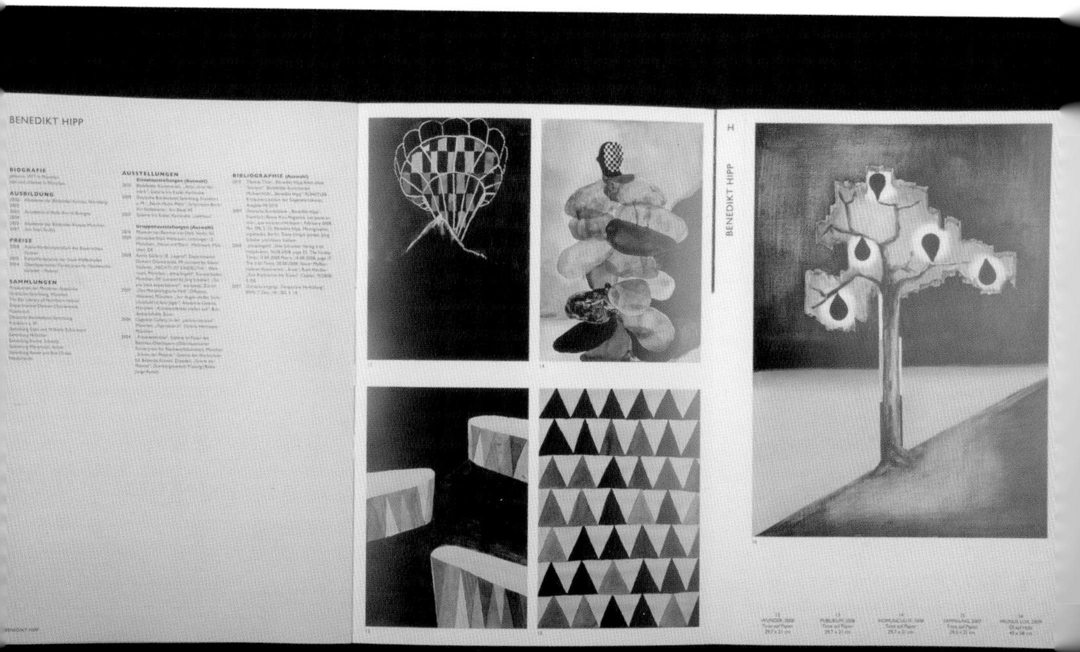
BENEDIKT HIPP
BIOGRAFIE
AUSBILDUNG
PREISE
SAMMLUNGEN
AUSSTELLUNGEN
Einzelausstellungen (Auswahl)
Gruppenausstellungen (Auswahl)
BIBLIOGRAPHIE (Auswahl)
BENEDIKT HIPP
H

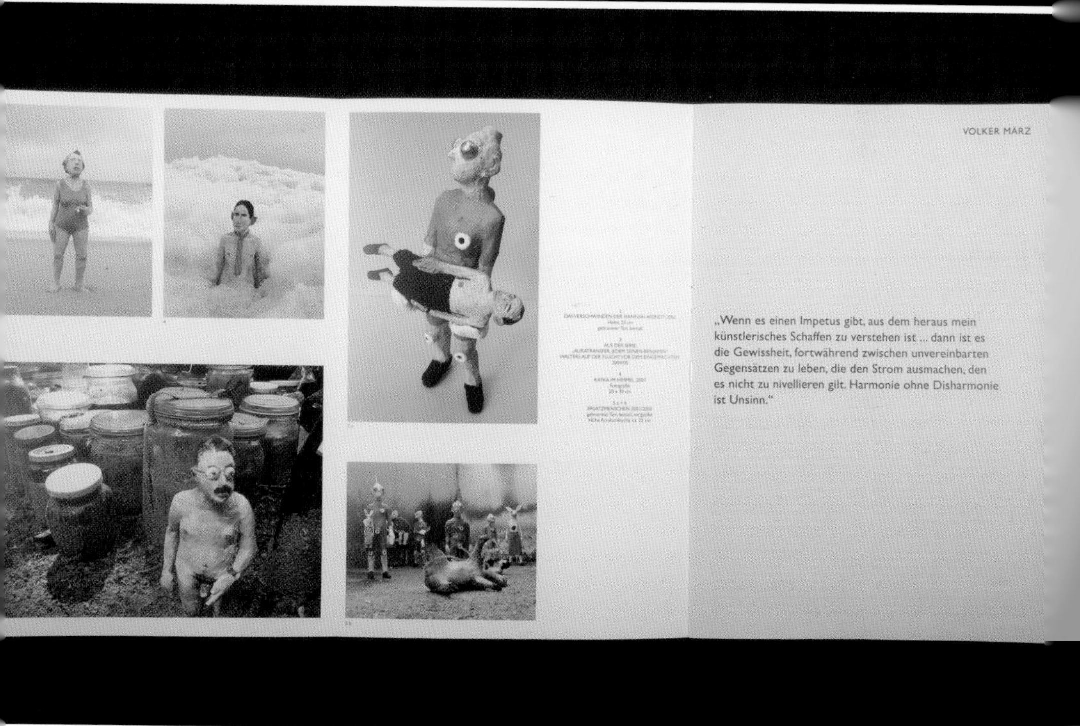
VOLKER MARZ
„Wenn es einen Impetus gibt, aus dem heraus mein künstlerisches Schaffen zu verstehen ist ... dann ist es die Gewissheit, fortwährend zwischen unvereinbarten Gegensätzen zu leben, die den Strom ausmachen, den es nicht zu nivellieren gilt. Harmonie ohne Disharmonie ist Unsinn."

Lonely Boy Mag (No. A-2 Boys & Their Cars)
2011 — Book
Client Little Brown Mushroom
Design Jenny Tondera
Photography Peter Davidson, Todd Hido, Alec Soth, Chad States

This is the second issue of photographer Alec Soth's "Lonely Boy Mag" series. The series is based on Lenny Burtman fetish magazines of the 1950s. My challenge as the designer was to allude to those playful publications while creating a piece that feels contemporary and direct, as Alec and I didn't want the featured photographers' work to be overshadowed by overly designed spreads. I selected a combination of typefaces that harken back to vintage fetish magazines, but aimed to use them in a fresh way — a 2011 take on trendy mid-century typography. Gill Sans Shadow Std was my starting point.

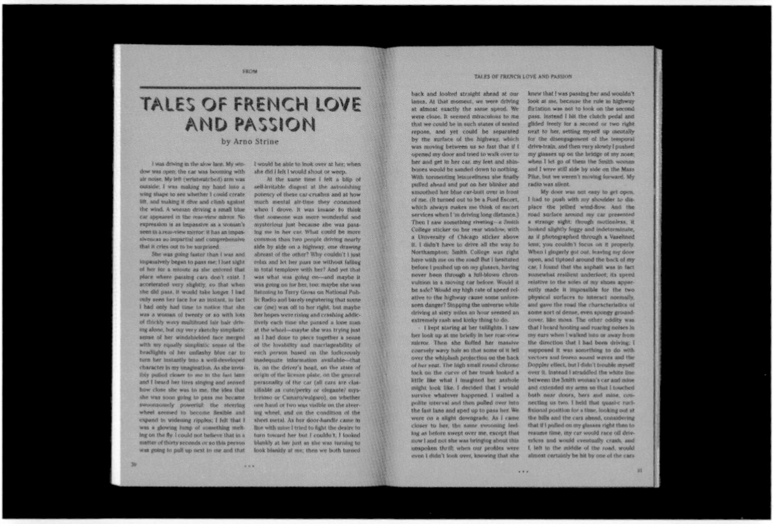

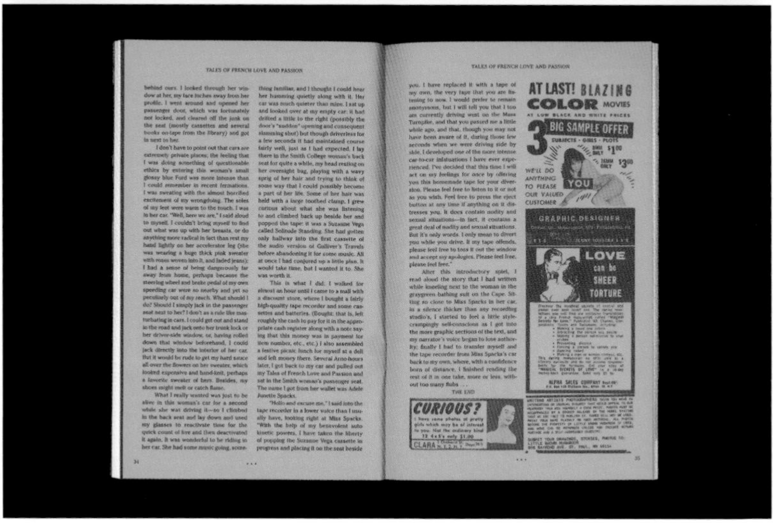

C

Jenny Tondera's Favorite Gill Sans Letter is "C".

Typeface in Use
Gill Sans Shadow Std, Shadowed Std Light, Std Bold

"This project was the first time I've used Gill Sans. I actually disliked the typeface until I studied abroad at the University of Brighton in Brighton, UK — where Eric Gill was born. Gill Sans was much more prevalent in every-day life in England — from street signage to bits of ephemera found at the local charity shop — and the typeface grew on me."

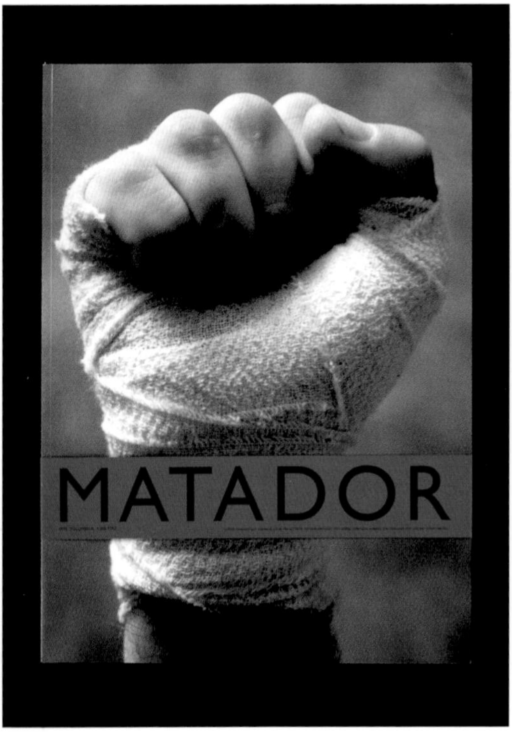

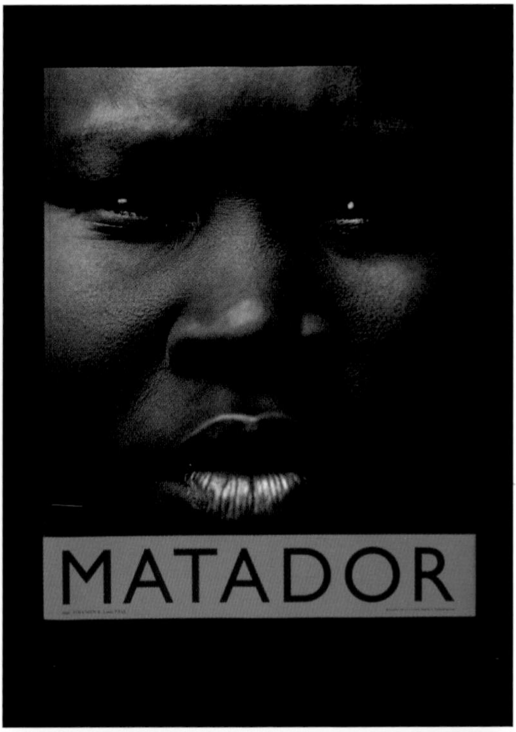

Matador Volume A
1995-2002 — Editorial Design
Client La Fabrica, Madrid, Spain
Design Fernando Gutiérrez
Photography James A. Fox

International annual magazine about Culture, Ideas and Trends

"I selected this font because it's timeless, a perfect balance of the modern and the classic. These values seemed to me to capture perfectly the spirit of the Matador project and where we wanted to position it. Gill Sans is an elegant sans serif font that has endured and will be very difficult to improve upon."

MATADOR

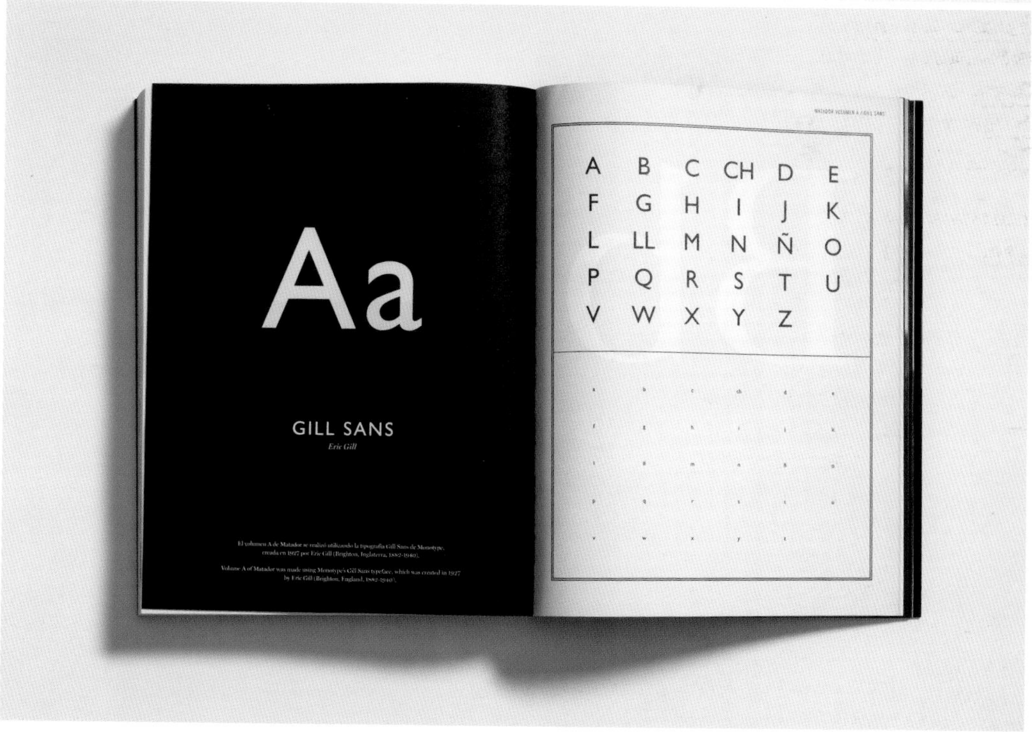
Aa
GILL SANS
Eric Gill
El volumen A de Matador se realizó utilizando la tipografía Gill Sans de Monotype, creada en 1927 por Eric Gill (Brighton, Inglaterra, 1882-1940).
Volume A of Matador was made using Monotype's Gill Sans typeface, which was created in 1927 by Eric Gill (Brighton, England, 1882-1940).
A B C CH D E
F G H I J K
L LL M N Ñ O
P Q R S T U
V W X Y Z

K

Meiré und Meiré's Favorite Gill Sans Letter is "K".

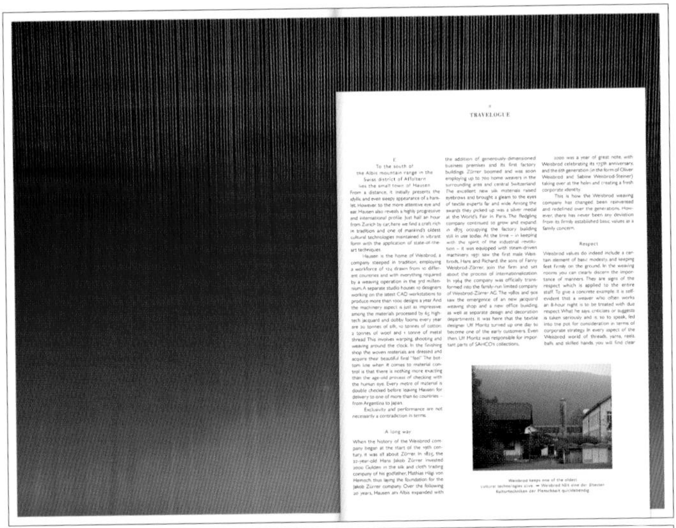

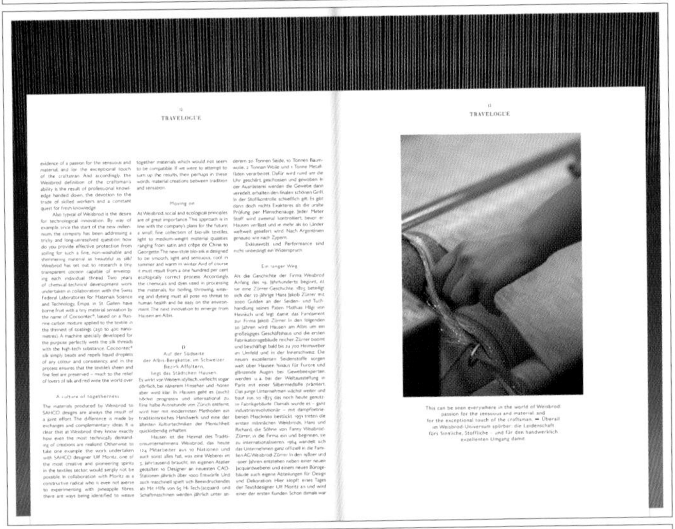

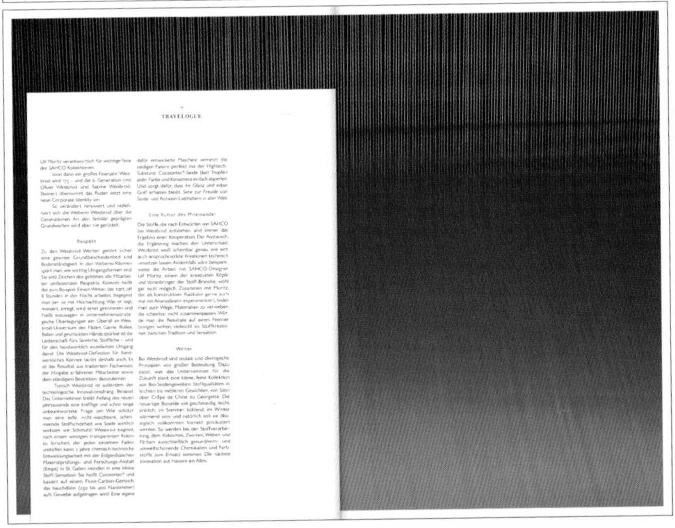

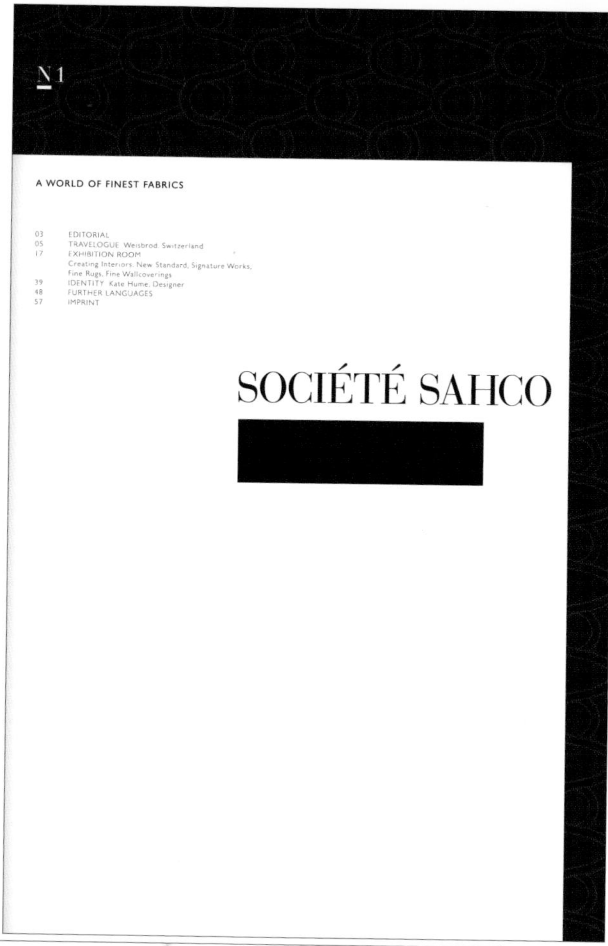

SOCIÉTÉ SAHCO
2011 — Corporate Identity, Magazine
Client SAHCO
Design Meiré und Meiré

The Société SAHCO magazine reflects both the spirit of the exclusive textiles producer and the new brand architecture developed by Meiré und Meiré. The reports, interviews and sophisticated photo spreads allow you to experience, touch and see the delicate world of SAHCO.

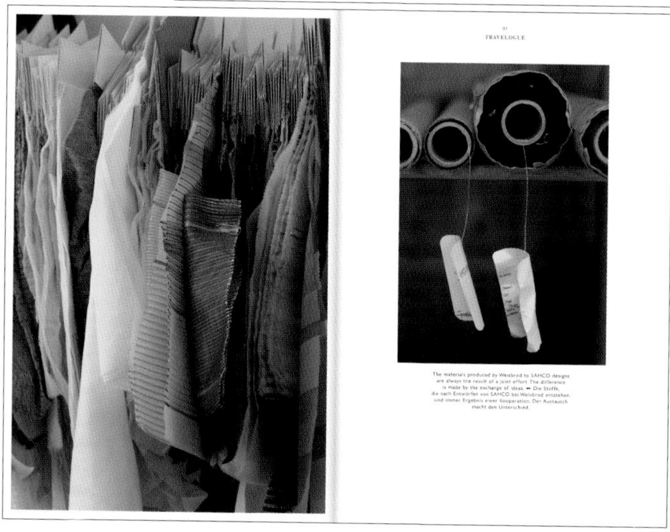

Typeface in Use
Gill Sans Light

"It is classic and clean and works very well in combination with the used Bodoni typeface"

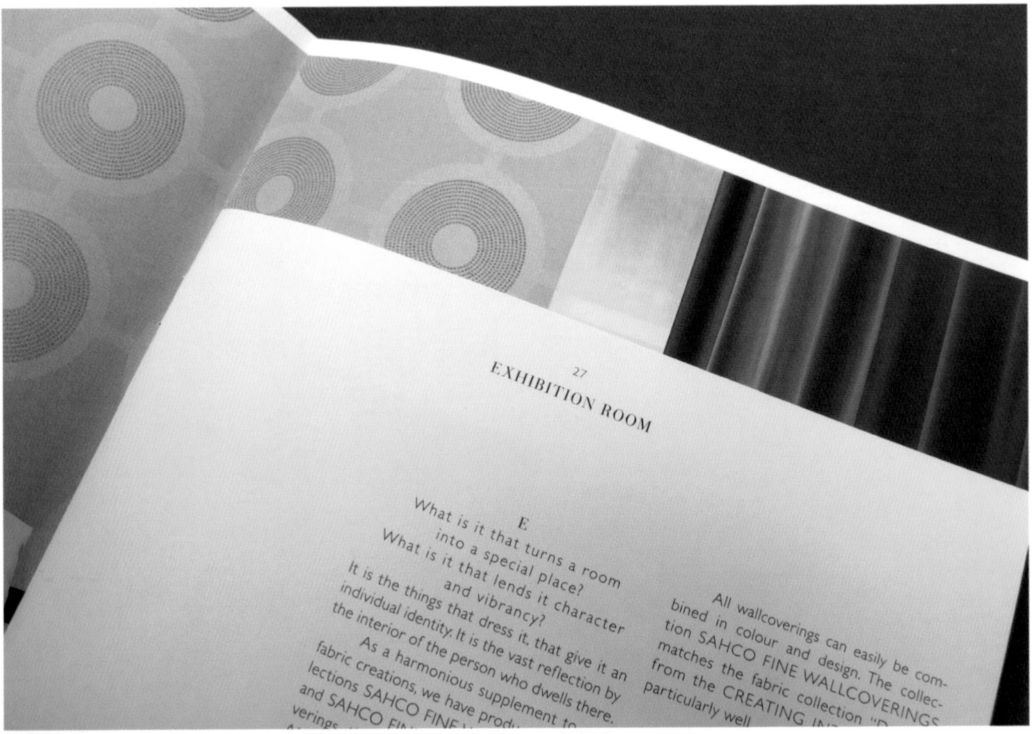
27
EXHIBITION ROOM
E
What is it that turns a room
into a special place?
What is it that lends it character
and vibrancy?
It is the things that dress it, that give it an
individual identity. It is the vast reflection by
the interior of the person who dwells there.
As a harmonious supplement
fabric creations, we have
lections SAHCO
and SAHCO
All wallcoverings can easily be combined in colour and design. The collection SAHCO FINE WALLCOVERINGS
matches the fabric collection
from the CREATING
particularly well

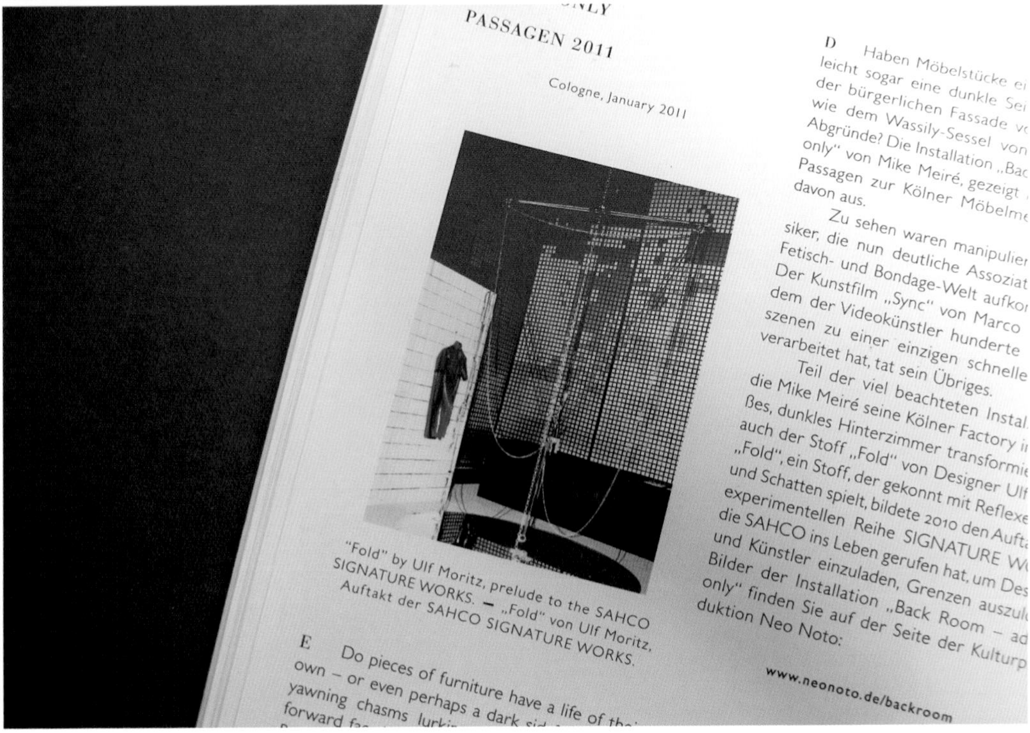
PASSAGEN 2011
Cologne, January 2011
"Fold" by Ulf Moritz, prelude to the SAHCO
SIGNATURE WORKS. – „Fold" von Ulf Moritz,
Auftakt der SAHCO SIGNATURE WORKS.
E Do pieces of furniture have a life of
own – or even perhaps a dark
yawning chasms
forward
D Haben Möbelstücke
leicht sogar eine dunkle
der bürgerlichen Fassade
wie dem Wassily-Sessel
Abgründe? Die Installation
only" von Mike Meiré, gezeigt
Passagen zur Kölner
davon aus.
Zu sehen waren
siker, die nun deutliche
Fetisch- und Bondage-Welt
Der Kunstfilm „Sync" von Marco
dem der Videokünstler hunderte
szenen zu einer einzigen
verarbeitet hat, tat sein Übriges.
Teil der viel beachteten
die Mike Meiré seine Kölner Factory
ßes, dunkles Hinterzimmer
auch der Stoff „Fold" von Designer
„Fold", ein Stoff, der gekonnt mit
und Schatten spielt, bildete 2010 den
experimentellen Reihe SIGNATURE
die SAHCO ins Leben gerufen hat, um
und Künstler einzuladen, Grenzen
Bilder der Installation „Back Room –
only" finden Sie auf der Seite der
duktion Neo Noto:
www.neonoto.de/backroom

N1
N2
A WORLD OF FINEST FABRICS
03
05
17
39
48
57
EDITORIAL
TRAVELOGUE Weisbrod, Switzerland
EXHIBITION ROOM
Creating Interiors, New Standard, Signature
Fine Rugs, Fine Wallcoverings
IDENTITY Kate Hume, Designer
FURTHER LANGUAGES
IMPRINT
03
04
14
34
46
EDITORIAL
REVIEW

N1
A WORLD OF FINEST FABRICS

ZEIT MAGAZIN
DAS INTERNET verwandelt DIE MODEWELT.
HEUTE ist sie TRANSPARENTER denn je

ZEIT MAGAZIN
KENNEN WIR
UNS NICHT VON
FACEBOOK?

DAS MODEHEFT 8

ÄRA DER TRANSPARENZ

Nichts beeinflusst die Mode heute so sehr wie das Internet. Schauen werden dort live übertragen. Mode wird über Onlineportale gekauft. Unzählige Blogger tauschen sich über Outfits aus und schaffen selbst neue Stile. Nie war Mode uns näher, nie war ihr Werden transparenter. Sie ist zur Kultursprache einer Generation geworden. In diesem Heft verraten Fotografen und Blogger, wie sie Mode mitgestalten – und das Model Christina Kruse zeigt die neuen Sommerkollektionen

WIR VERMISSEN ALEXANDER MCQUEEN

Am 10. Februar starb der Designer Alexander McQueen viel zu früh im Alter von 40 Jahren in London. Er war einer der wegweisenden Modemacher unserer Zeit. Seine letzte, visionäre Show in Paris hat uns zu diesem Spezial inspiriert. Wir widmen ihm dieses Heft

TITELFOTOS UND FOTO INHALT RALPH MECKE STYLING MARKUS EBNER TITEL I DREITEILIGES KOSTÜM AUS SPITZE VON DOLCE & GABBANA
TITEL 2 NEGLIGÉ MIT SCHMETTERLINGS-APPLIKATIONEN VON NINA RICCI INHALT PAILLETTEN-MINIKLEID MIT CAMOUFLAGE-EFFEKT VON BALMAIN

5

Fashion Issue No. 08
2010 — Magazine
Client Zeit
Design Bureau Mirko Borsche

UNTERWEGS MIT JUERGEN TELLER (17)

Die Ausstrahlung von Vivienne Westwood, 68

LONDON

Ich habe zurzeit eine Show im Consortium von Dijon und wollte dafür unbedingt neue Fotos machen. Ich kenne die Designerin Vivienne Westwood schon lange, und seit drei Jahren arbeiten wir zusammen an ihren Werbekampagnen. Ich war schon immer begeistert von ihr und ihrem Aussehen, ihrem Mut und ihrer Haltung, auch in politischen Fragen. Sie ist eigentlich überhaupt nicht an Fotografie interessiert, aber als ich sie fragte, ob wir Aktaufnahmen machen wollen, vertraute sie mir völlig und fand die Idee, das gerade jetzt, im Alter von 68 Jahren, zu machen, sehr schön. (Es gibt übrigens noch mehr, offenere Fotos aus der Serie.) Ich bin begeistert, wie kokett und jugendlich und sexuell attraktiv Vivienne auf den Bildern aussieht – und genau das alles ist sie ja auch.

UNTERWEGS MIT JUERGEN TELLER (29)

Nachts und nackt im Louvre

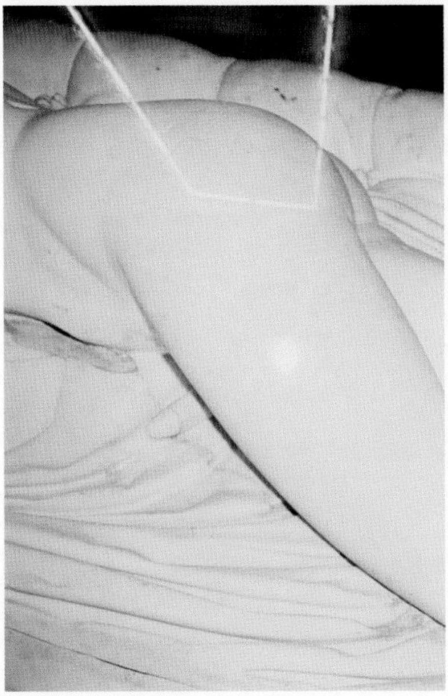

PARIS

Ein Freund von mir, Thomas Lenthal, der Herausgeber des Magazins *Paradis*, fragte mich einmal am Telefon, ob ich im Louvre Nacktaufnahmen machen wollte und wen ich denn dafür im Sinn hätte. Erstaunt sagte ich, dass es doch wahrscheinlich völlig unmöglich sei, im Louvre Nacktaufnahmen zu machen, legte auf und machte mir keine Gedanken mehr. Zwei Tage später rief Thomas wieder an und fragte noch mal, wen ich denn mitnehmen wollte. Ich sagte: »Im Ernst?« Ich wollte die Schauspielerin Charlotte Rampling und das Model Raquel Zimmermann mitnehmen.
Beide konnten nicht Nein sagen zur Möglichkeit, eine Nacht lang nackt im Louvre vor der *Mona Lisa* zu stehen. Ich war wahnsinnig nervös, machte mir technische Sorgen und auch darüber Gedanken, endlich mal Charlotte nackt zu sehen – und nicht nur immer sie mich, wie bei früheren Fotos.
Ich nahm meine Frau mit, um mir und Charlotte zu helfen. Dieses Bild ist in dieser Nacht entstanden, es ist ein Detail einer wundervollen Skulptur von einem Hermaphroditen.

7

Juergen Tellers weekly column
2010 — Magazine
Client Zeit
Design Bureau Mirko Borsche

UNTERWEGS MIT JUERGEN TELLER (20)

Stalagmiten und Stalaktiten

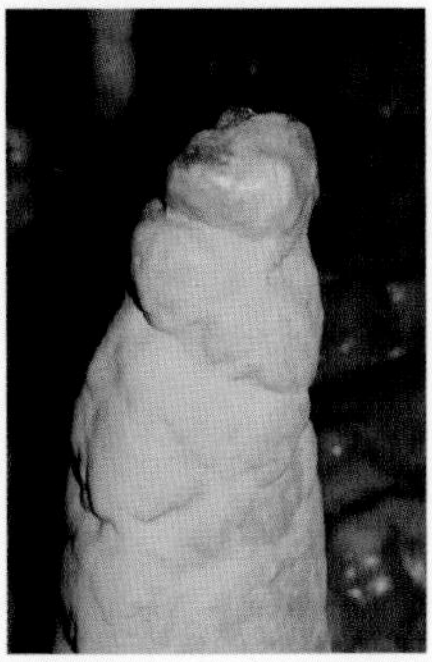

FRÄNKISCHE SCHWEIZ

Meine Mutter kam auf die Idee, als ich mit meiner Tochter Lola zu Besuch bei ihr war, mal wieder zu den Höhlen in der fränkischen Schweiz zu fahren. Die hatte ich völlig vergessen. Bin früher öfter mit dem Moped, Freundin und Schlafsack hinten drauf, am Wochenende zu den kleineren Höhlen gefahren und habe dort übernachtet. Lola staunte über die Dinger, die von oben und von unten auf einen zukamen. Wie damals, man fühlte sich stark.

8

"Gill Sans & Gill Sans Ultra Bold are like the Arnold Schwarzenegger and Danny Devito of fonts."

Karen Dalton "Katie Cruel"

Known as a great interpreter of choice material, Karen Dalton has an effect on people — her timeless, aching, blues-soaked, Native American spirit inspired both Dylan & The Band's "Katie's Been Gone" (on The Basement Tapes) and Nick Cave's "When I First Came To Town" (from Henry's Dream).

lightintheattic.net

Bill Quick "Take Me Away"

Spaniard Bill Quick released the ultra-rare Maravillosa Gente in 1972, an amalgam of psychedelic pop and folk. The sun-baked album was virtually unheard outside the Spanish psych scene, but has slowly gained the popularity it deserves.

guerssen.com

Gill Sans Regular,
Ultra Bold

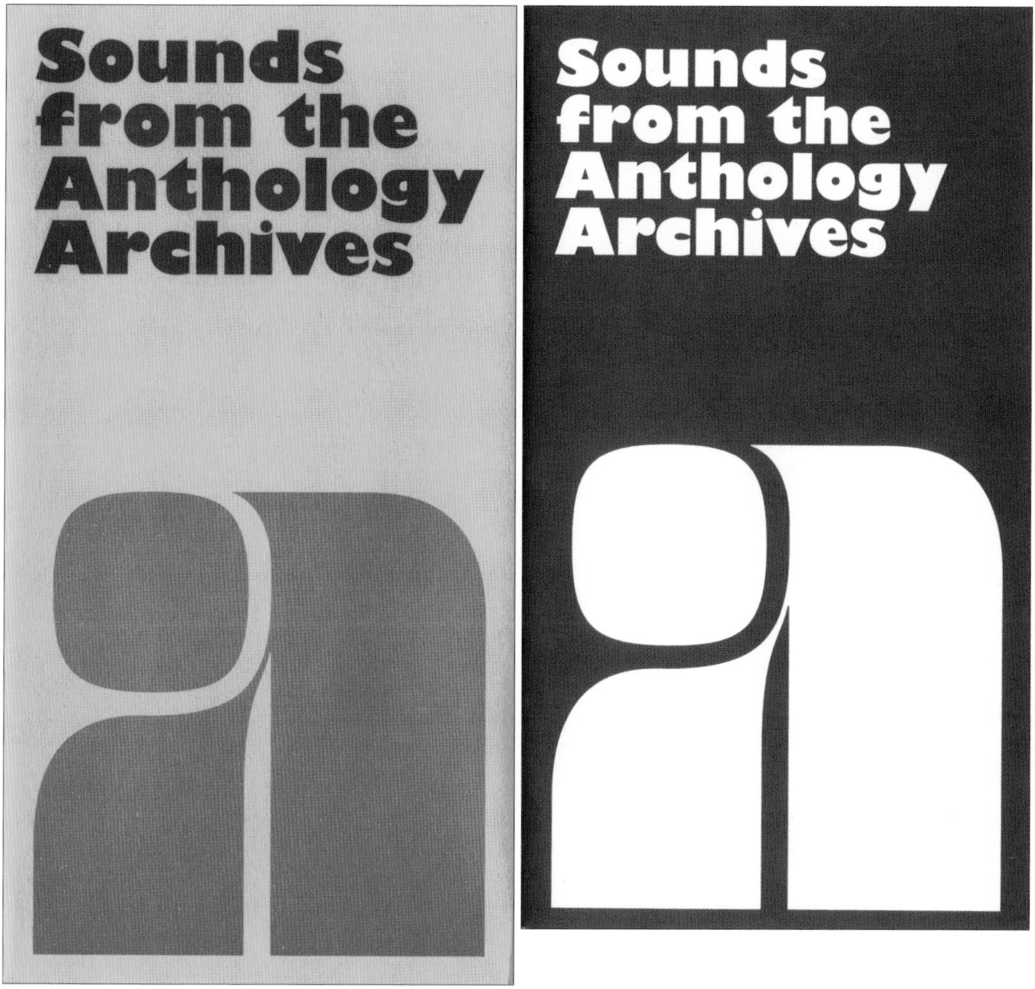

Sounds from the Anthology Archives
2009 — Digital Music Packaging
Client Viva Radio
Design Will Work for Good

e

Will Work for Good's Favorite Gill Sans Letter is "e".

GREAT LOVES
JAMES BALDWIN
GIOVANNI'S ROOM

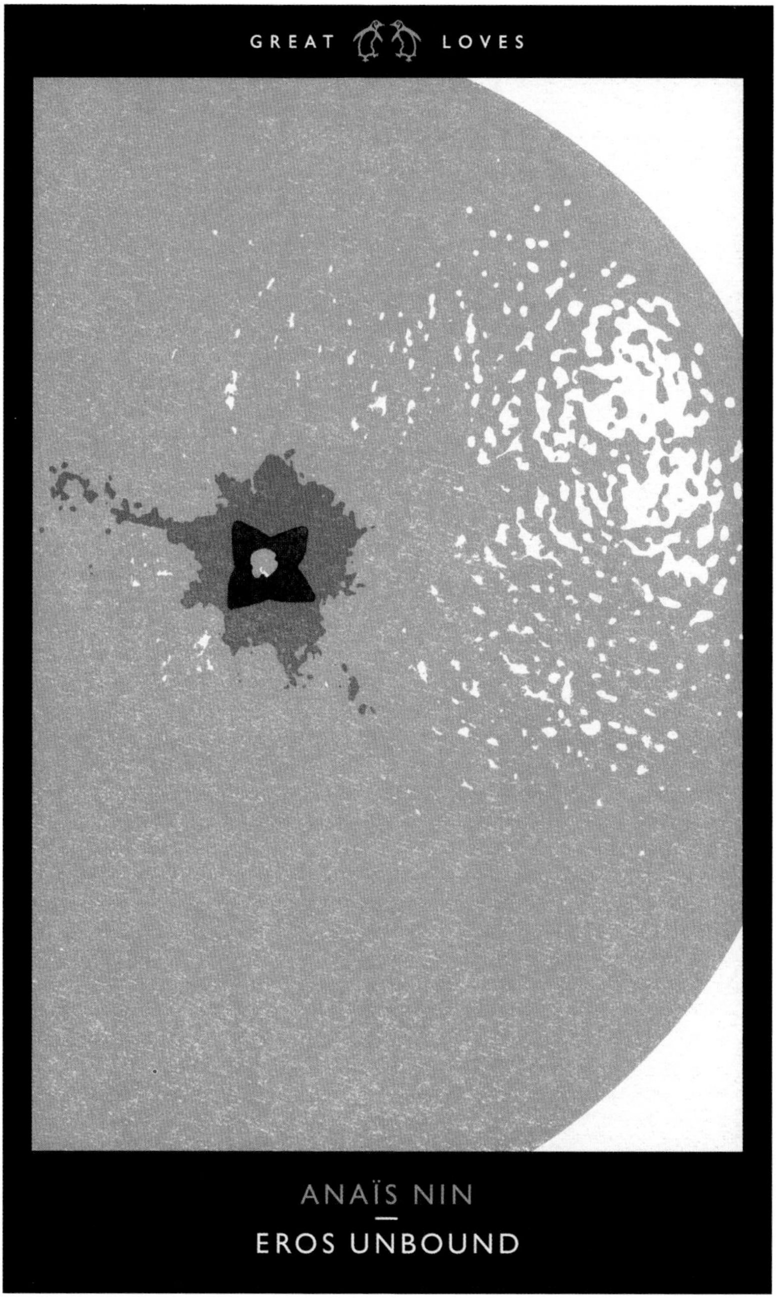

Great Loves
2007 — Book Covers
Client Penguin Books
Design David Pearson, Victoria Sawdon

For this series of paperbacks, botany was chosen as the central theme to depict love in all its varied forms.

GREAT LOVES
IVAN TURGENEV
FIRST LOVE

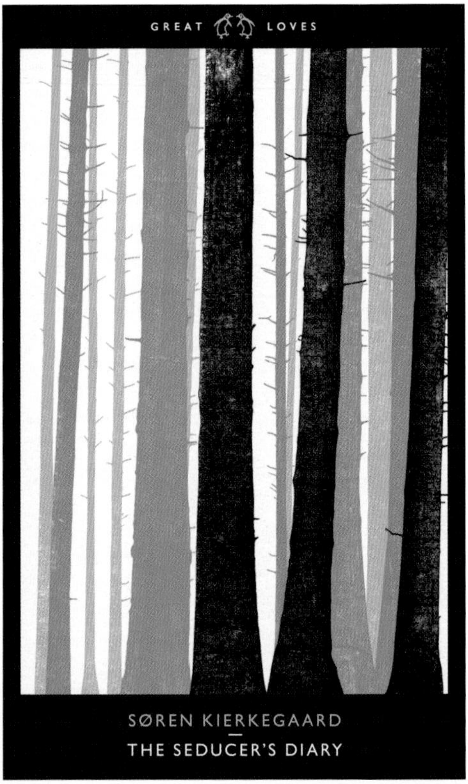
GREAT LOVES
SØREN KIERKEGAARD
THE SEDUCER'S DIARY

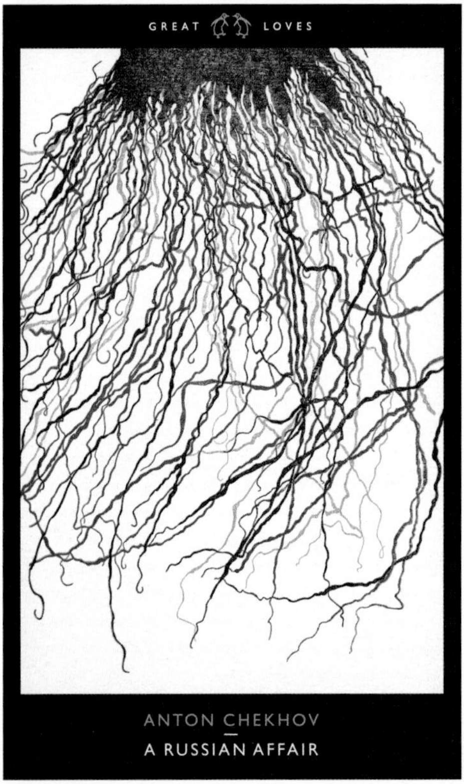
GREAT LOVES
ANTON CHEKHOV
A RUSSIAN AFFAIR

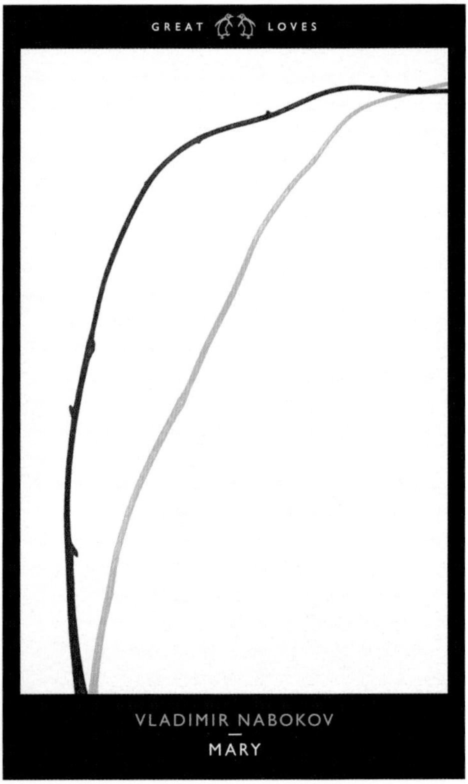
GREAT LOVES
VLADIMIR NABOKOV
MARY

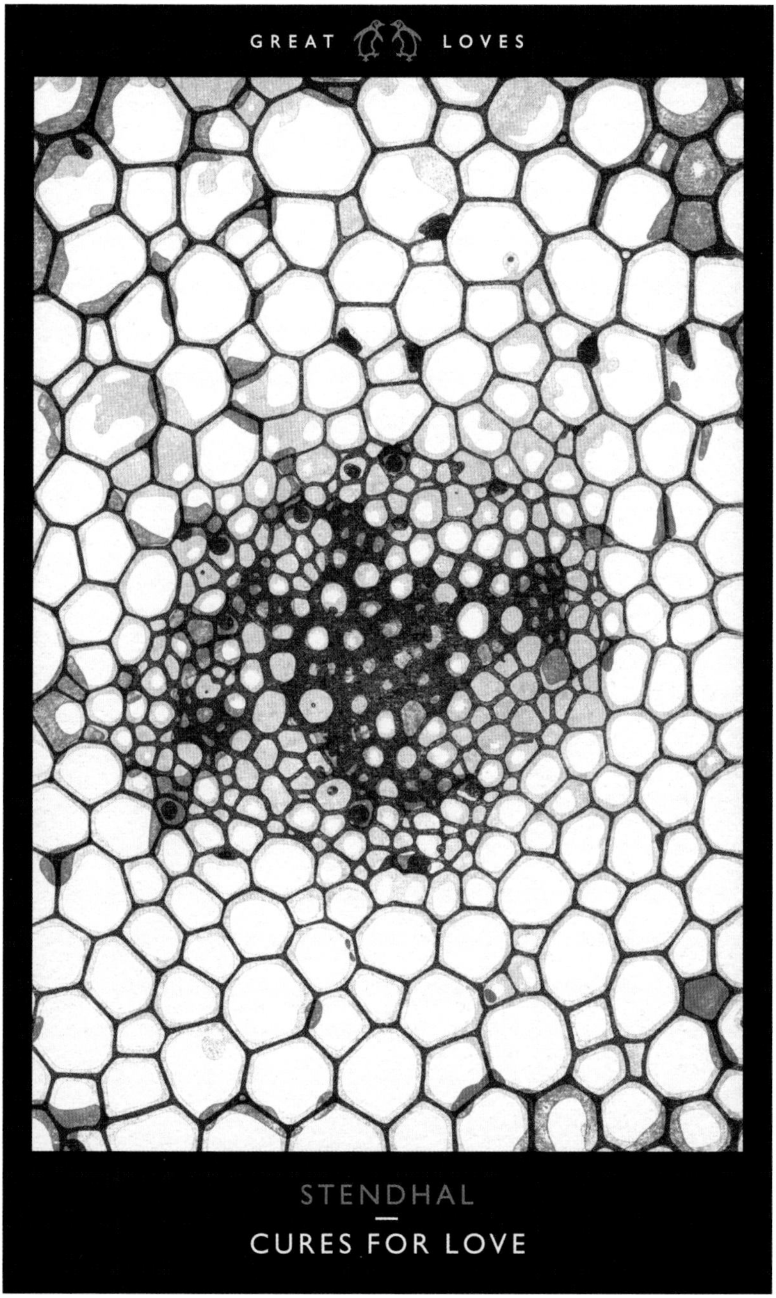

R

David Pearson's Favorite Gill Sans Letter is "R".

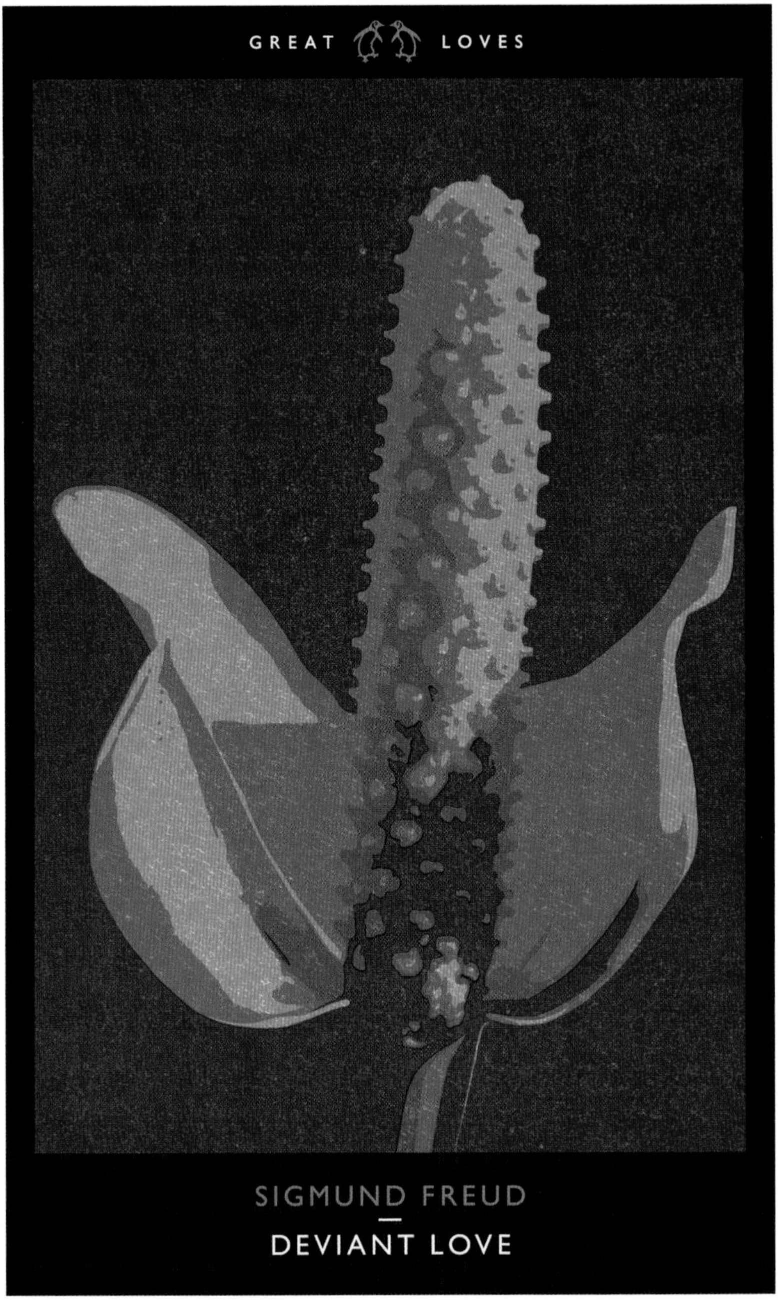
GREAT LOVES
SIGMUND FREUD
DEVIANT LOVE

"Gill Sans was chosen as it was robust enough to use at small sizes, neutral enough to use alongside ever-changing imagery and yet characterful enough to avoid appearing monotonous across multiple titles."

VANILLA
CUPCAKE
KITCHEN

VANILLA
CUPCAKE
KITCHEN

VANILLA
CUPCAKE
KITCHEN

Typeface in Use
Johnston ITC Std, Gill Sans

C

Family's Favorite Gill Sans Letter is "C".

Vanilla Cupcake Kitchen
2010 — Branding, Print, Online Presence
Client Vanilla Cupcake Kitchen
Design Family (Daniel Westwood)

We were approached by the small bakery in early 2010, to produce and develop a strong brand identity that would set them apart from the ever-growing competition of the cupcake marketplace. Once the brand identity was finalized, accompanying printed collateral and an online presence were also created.

"We wanted a strong, clean typeface and the circular forms of the font were so symmetrical it felt right within the round stencil shape of the ident"

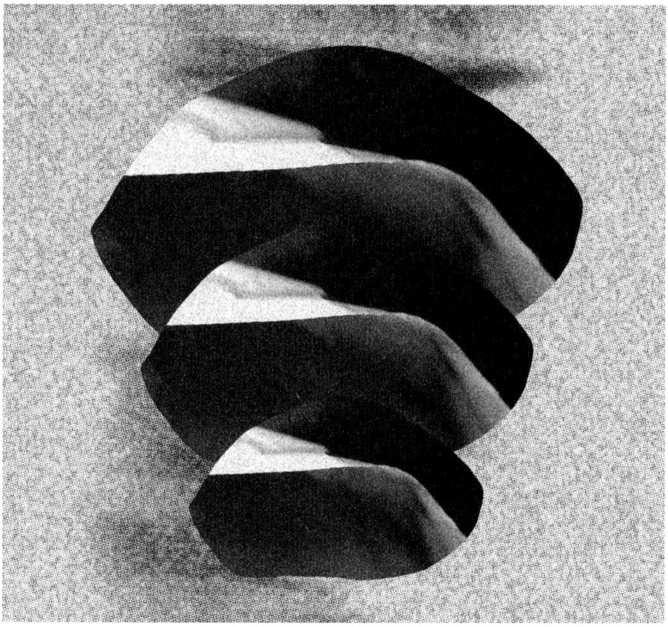

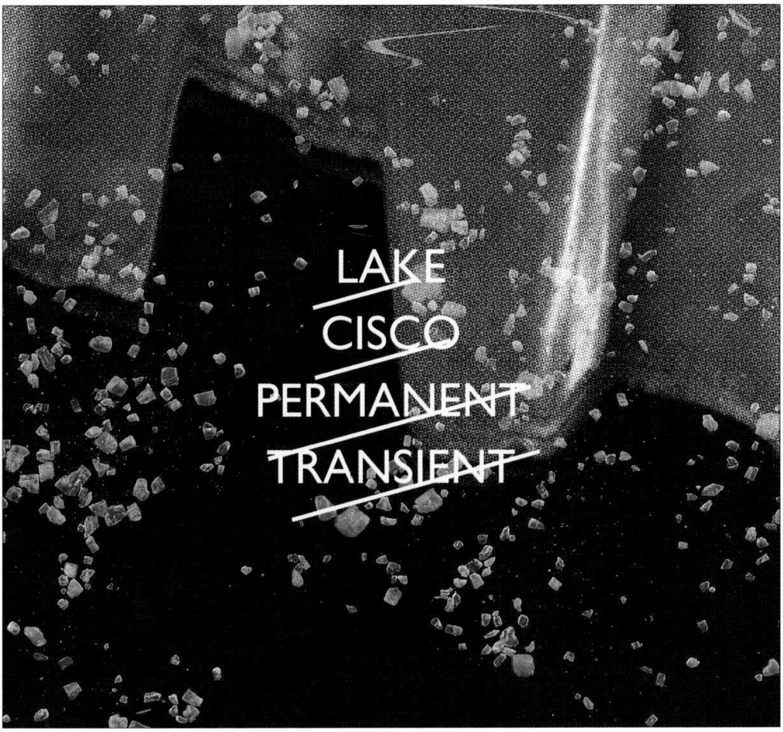

Lake Cisco — ermanent Transient
2011 — Music Album Design
Client Lake Cisco
Design Estudio Ritxi Ostáriz

Art direction and design for the album "Permanent Transient" by the German prog-indie band Lake Cisco.

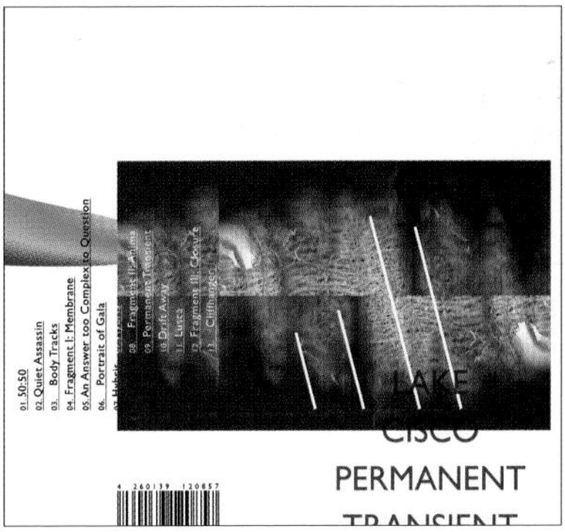

Typeface in Use
Gill Sans

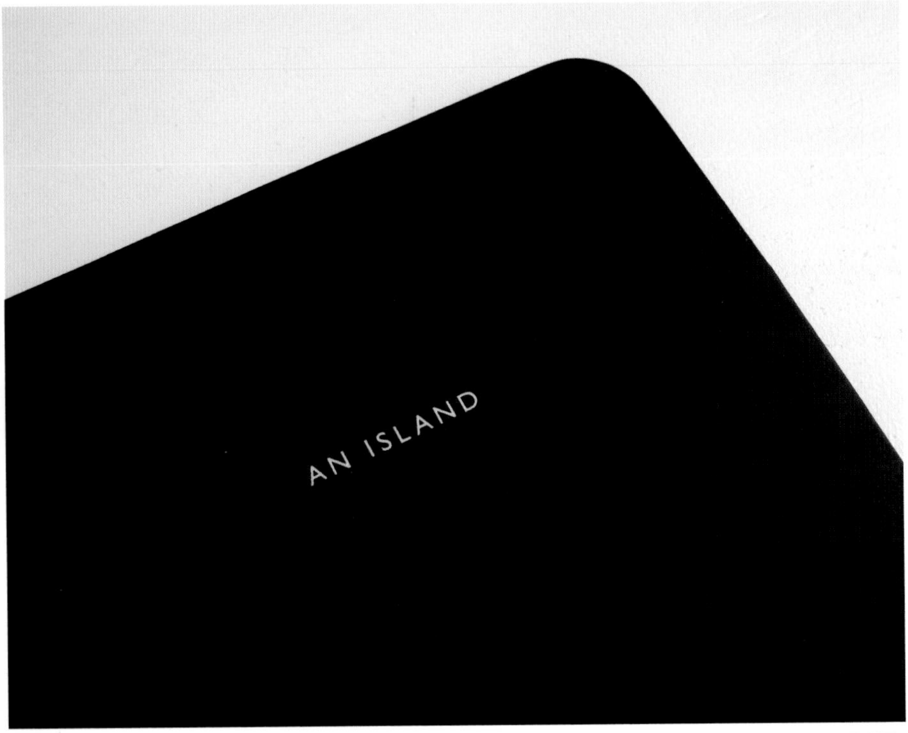

"It's simple and beautiful, good old Gill Sans!"

An Island
2011 — Poster, DVD Packaging
Client Efterklang, Rumraket, 4AD, Vincent Moon
Design Hvass&Hannibal (Nan Na Hvass)
Photography Antje Taiga Jandrig

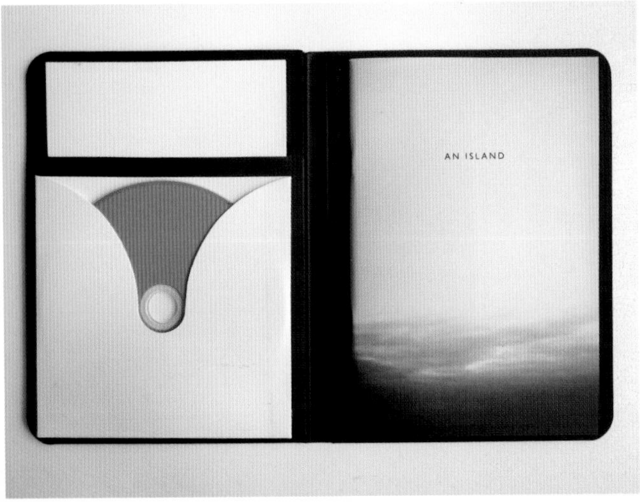

Limited edition DVD package for Efterklang and Vincent Moon's collaboration, the beautiful 50-minute music documentary, *An Island*, which was filmed in 2010 on Als in the South of Denmark. We had the package specially designed and custom made for this release, and it was carefully printed and assembled by Stumptown Printers in Portland, Oregon. It's printed on recycled paper with vegetable based inks. The outer cover is printed on their beautiful old letterpress machines and the package includes a set of litho printed postcards and a booklet full of photos. It's a limited edition of 5000, numbered.

The poster uses an analog photo from the island Als, where the movie was filmed.

EFTERKLANG
presents
AN ISLAND
a film by
VINCENT MOON
A film by VINCENT MOON & EFTERKLANG / Images by VINCENT MOON
Sounds by EFTERKLANG featuring NIKLAS ANTONSON, HEATHER W. BRODERICK, PETER BRODERICK & FREDERIK TEIGE
Recordings by ANDERS BOLL & NILS FRAHM / Film Editing by LUCAS ARCHAMBAULT & VINCENT MOON
Audio Mixing by MADS BRAUER & NILS FRAHM / Still Photography by ANTJE TAIGA JANDRIG / Titles & Design by HVASS&HANNIBAL
Produced by RASMUS STOLBERG, RUMRAKET & TEMPORARY AREAS
rumraket
4AD
LEAF
WWW.ANISLAND.CC

Typeface in Use
Gill Sans Ultra Bold, Brush script, Avenir

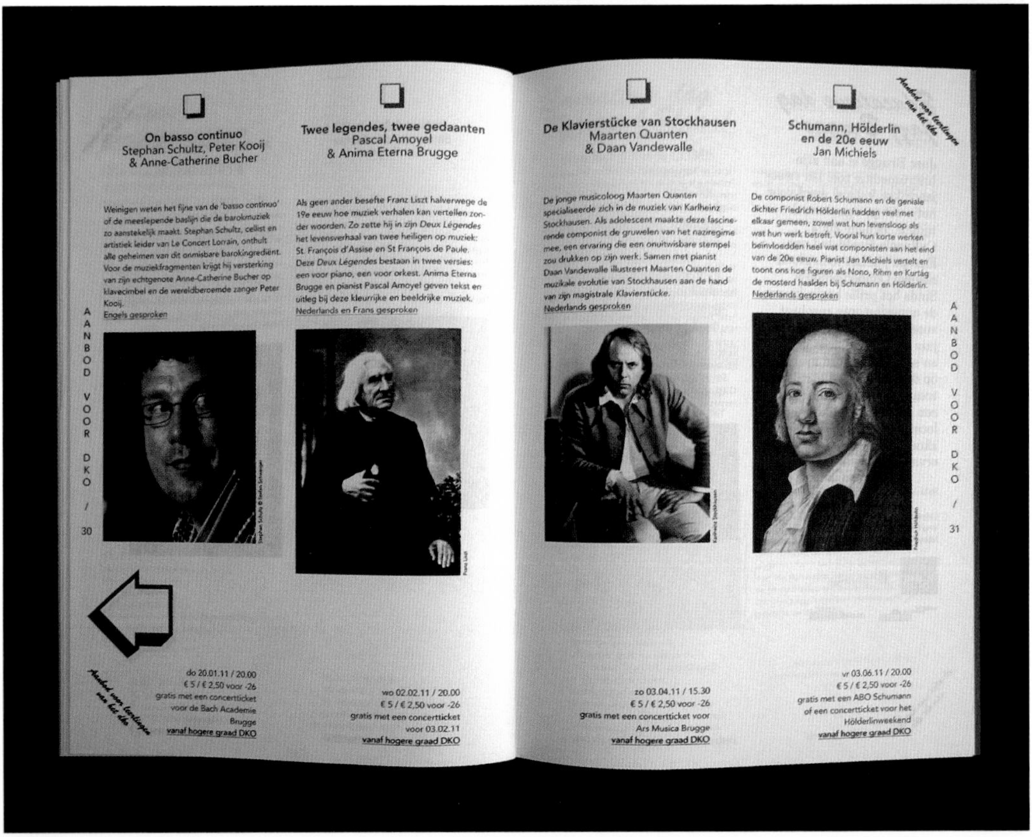

O

Jurgen Maelfeyt's Favorite Gill Sans Letter is "O".

Discovery
2010 — Brochure
Client Concertgebouw Brugge
Design Jurgen Maelfeyt

Brochure for educational program.

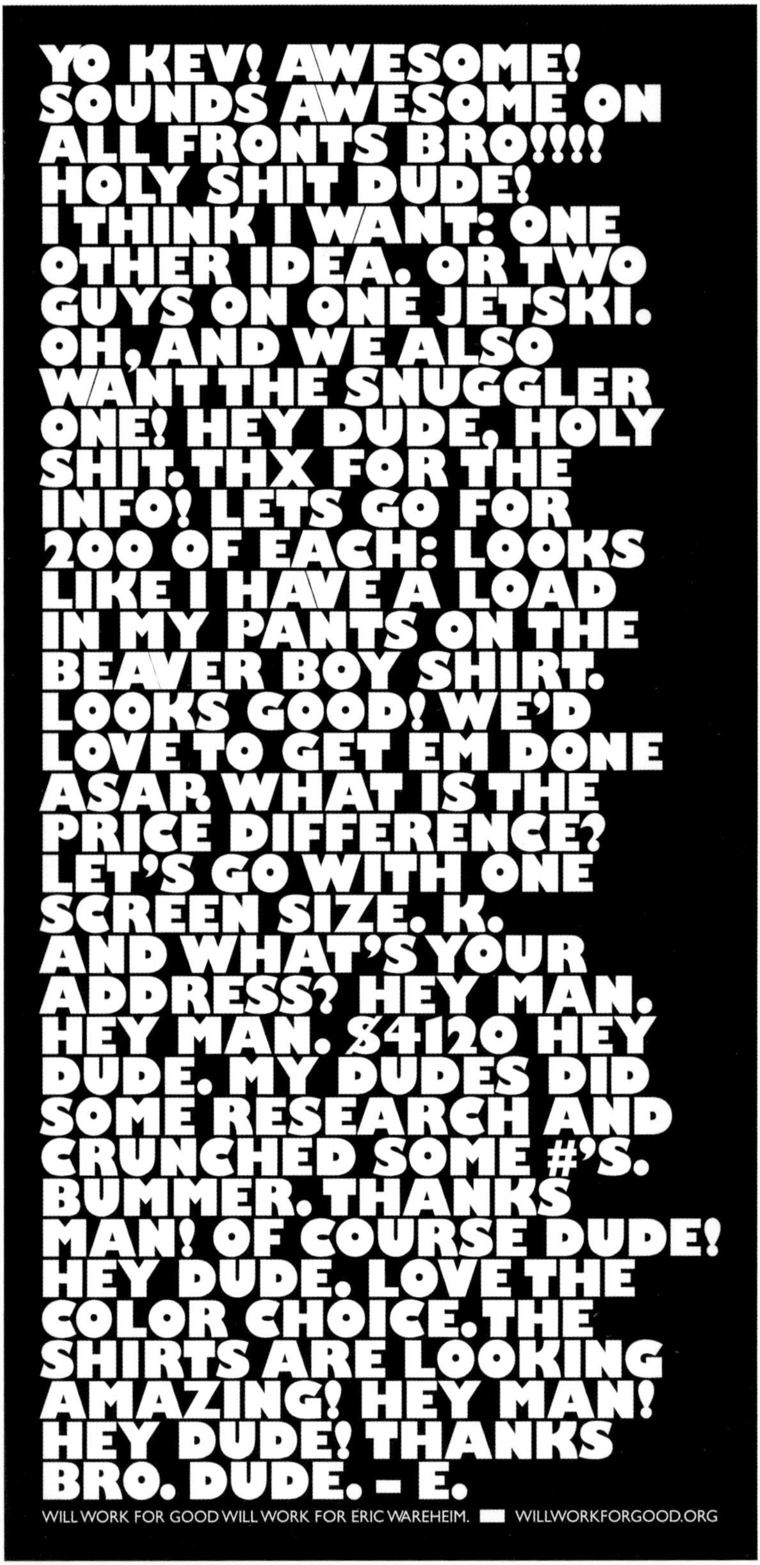

YO KEV! AWESOME!
SOUNDS AWESOME ON
ALL FRONTS BRO!!!!
HOLY SHIT DUDE!
I THINK I WANT: ONE
OTHER IDEA. OR TWO
GUYS ON ONE JETSKI.
OH, AND WE ALSO
WANT THE SNUGGLER
ONE! HEY DUDE, HOLY
SHIT. THX FOR THE
INFO! LETS GO FOR
200 OF EACH: LOOKS
LIKE I HAVE A LOAD
IN MY PANTS ON THE
BEAVER BOY SHIRT.
LOOKS GOOD! WE'D
LOVE TO GET EM DONE
ASAP. WHAT IS THE
PRICE DIFFERENCE?
LET'S GO WITH ONE
SCREEN SIZE. K.
AND WHAT'S YOUR
ADDRESS? HEY MAN.
HEY MAN. $4120 HEY
DUDE. MY DUDES DID
SOME RESEARCH AND
CRUNCHED SOME #'S.
BUMMER. THANKS
MAN! OF COURSE DUDE!
HEY DUDE. LOVE THE
COLOR CHOICE. THE
SHIRTS ARE LOOKING
AMAZING! HEY MAN!
HEY DUDE! THANKS
BRO. DUDE. – E.
WILL WORK FOR GOOD WILL WORK FOR ERIC WAREHEIM.
WILLWORKFORGOOD.ORG

Yo Kev!
2009 — Poster
Design Will Work for Good

Our work process revealed through the first line of every email from a selection of client for the duration of a single project.

Typeface in Use
Gill Sans Regular, Ultra Bold

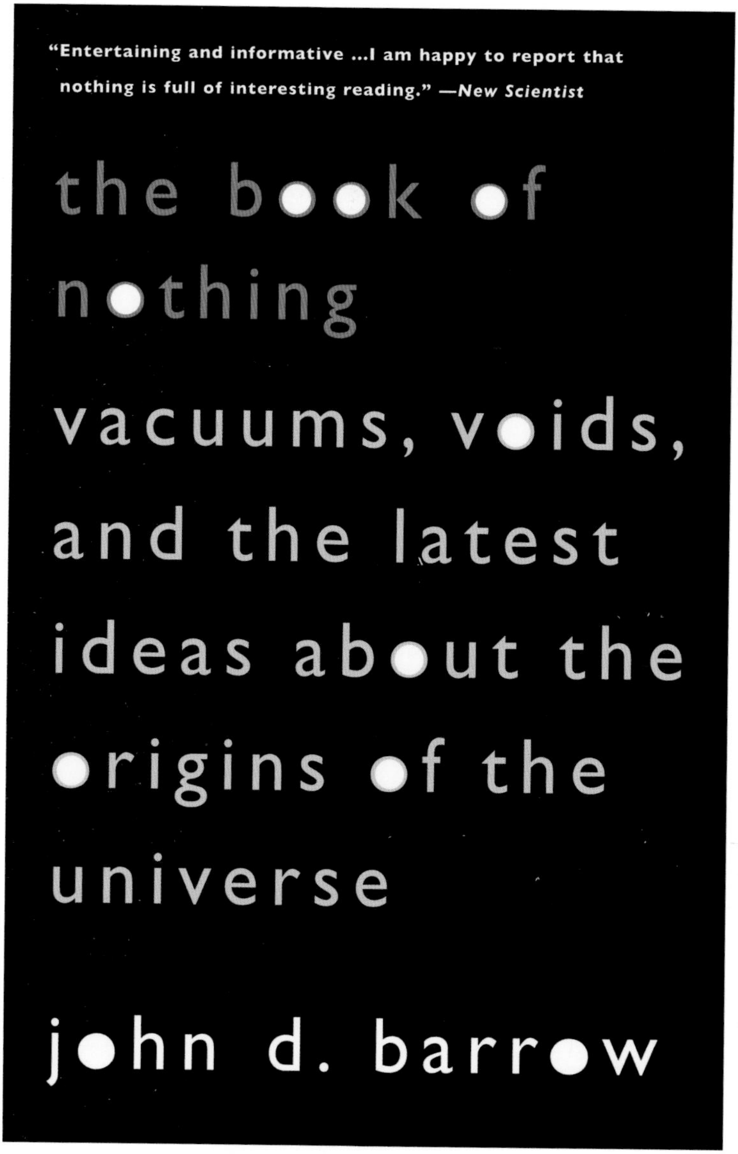

"Entertaining and informative ...I am happy to report that nothing is full of interesting reading." —New Scientist
the book of nothing
vacuums, voids, and the latest ideas about the origins of the universe
john d. barrow

The Book of Nothing by John D. Barrow
2002 — Book Cover
Client Vintage Books USA
Design Jamie Keenan

A play on the letter "O" and the number "0".

g

Jamie Keenan's Favorite Gill Sans Letter is "g".

Typeface in Use
Monotype Gill

"I used Gill because of its lovely letter 'O'."

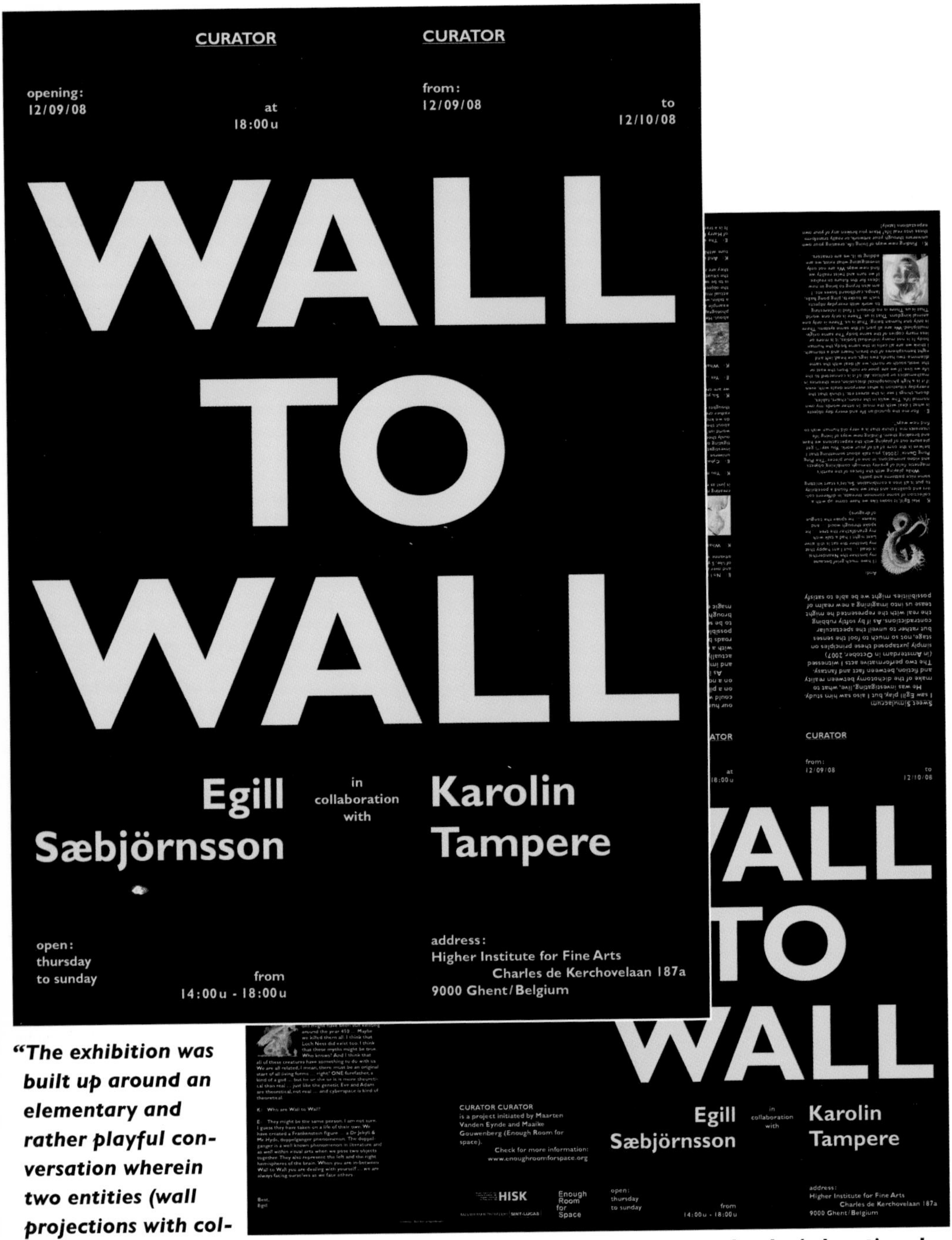
CURATOR
CURATOR
opening: 12/09/08
at 18:00u
from: 12/09/08
to 12/10/08
WALL TO WALL
Egill Sæbjörnsson
in collaboration with
Karolin Tampere
open: thursday to sunday
from 14:00u - 18:00u
address: Higher Institute for Fine Arts Charles de Kerchovelaan 187a 9000 Ghent/Belgium
CURATOR CURATOR is a project initiated by Maarten Vanden Eynde and Maaike Gouwenberg (Enough Room for space).
Check for more information: www.enoughroomforspace.org
HISK
Enough Room for Space

"The exhibition was built up around an elementary and rather playful conversation wherein two entities (wall projections with collaged faces) go into dialog about their perception of life and art. They start from the basics, looking at life and art again as children would do, questioning and wondering how art and our perception of it works. Bearing this content in mind, it was an obvious choice to set the text (dialog in the booklet) in Gill Sans, referring to the loads of children's books (educational and/or narrative) that were and are still being set in Gill Sans."

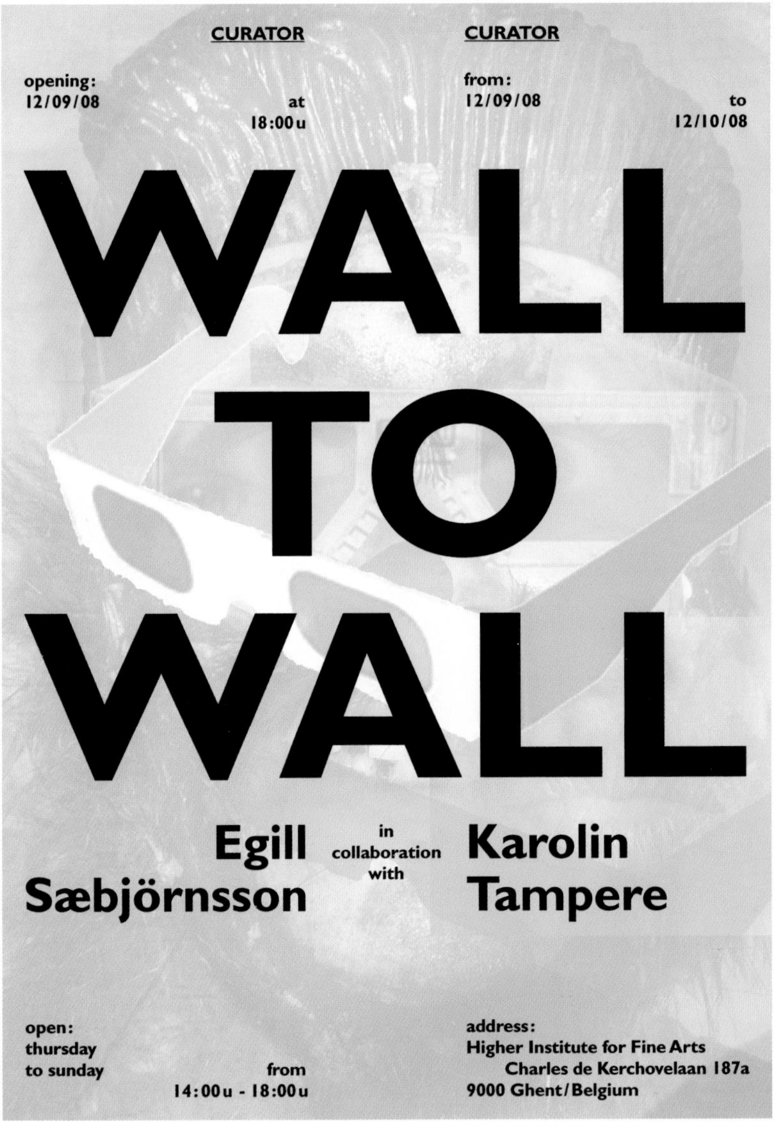
CURATOR
CURATOR
opening:
12/09/08
at
18:00u
from:
12/09/08
to
12/10/08
WALL
TO
WALL
Egill
Sæbjörnsson
in collaboration with
Karolin
Tampere
open:
thursday
to sunday
from
14:00u - 18:00u
address:
Higher Institute for Fine Arts
Charles de Kerchovelaan 187a
9000 Ghent/Belgium

k

Raf Vancampenhoudt's Favorite Gill Sans Letter is "k".

Curator Curator #1: Wall to Wall
2008 — Folder, Poster
Client HISK (Curator: Karolin Tampere)
Design Raf Vancampenhoudt

Typeface in Use
Gill Sans Std Bold

Design of the invitation and poster for the first edition of "Curator Curator", a project initiated by Maarten Vanden Eynde and Maaike Gouwenberg at the HISK (2008), Ghent. This edition "Wall To Wall" is a collaboration between Egill Saebjörnsson and Karoline Tampere.

"Gill Sans was the perfect type to materialize the formal bridge between the 1968's mood of why man creates and the nowadays use of typography in movie titles. Gill Sans also have this timeless visual sense of humor fitting very much with the sillyness of that movie."

Tell Me What You See (TMWYS)
2010 — Poster
Design Killian Loddo

S

Killian Loddo's Favorite Gill Sans Letter is "S".

TELL ME WHAT YOU SEE is a project that aims to replay movies in different contexts. Thoses movies are chosen for their unique aesthetic choices of direction, and their formal features first. The movies are highlighted by a series of posters who question the relevance and the adequacy between movie titles and raw images taken from the movies. Designing those posters again give a new look at the broadcast, questioning their appearance and recontextualization with a fresh look in tune with their time.

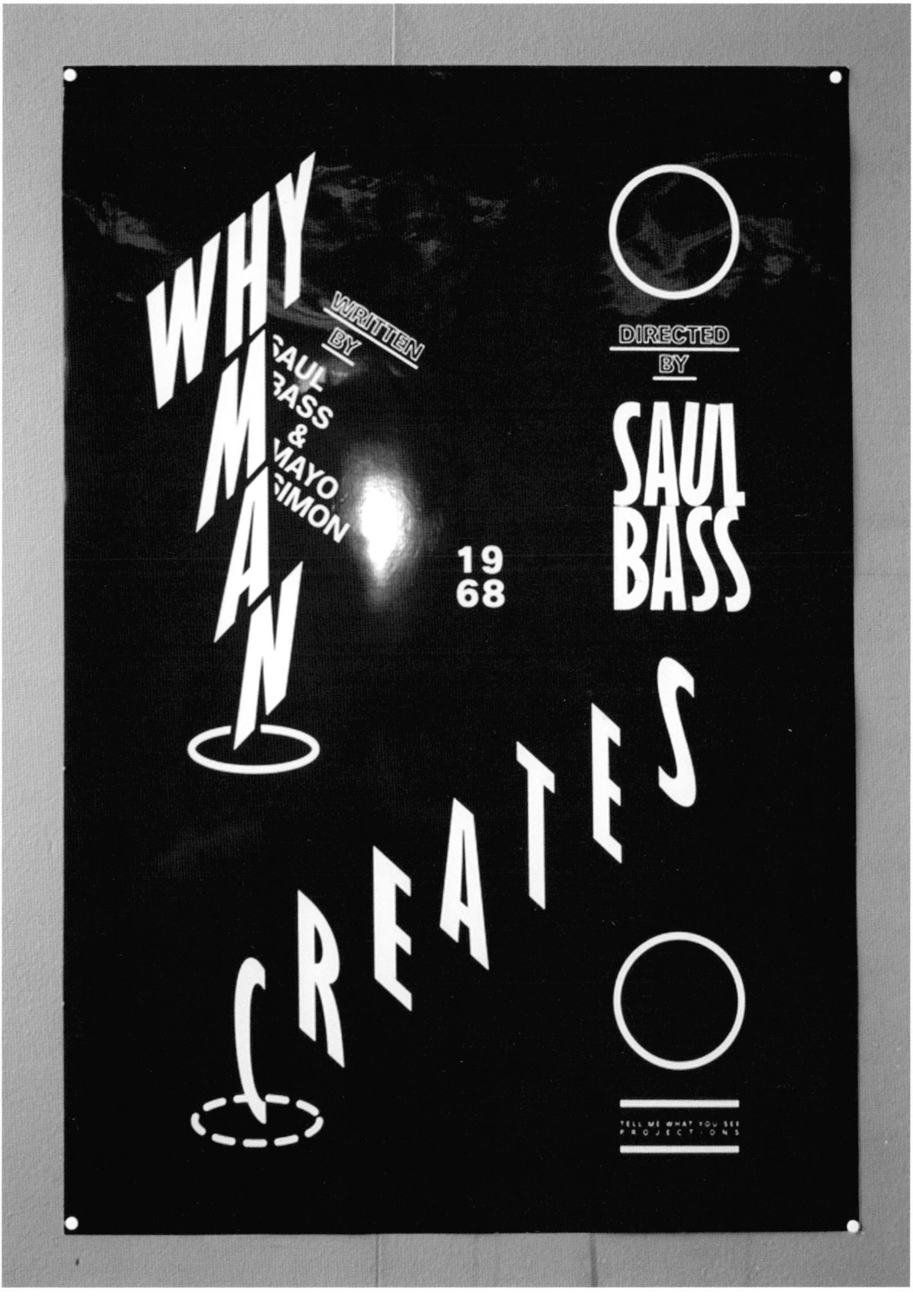
WHY
MAN
CREATES
WRITTEN BY
SAUL BASS & MAYO SIMON
19
68
DIRECTED BY
SAUL BASS

LE COMPA – CONSERVATOIRE DE L'AGRICULTURE
25 JUIN — 31 OCTOBRE 2009
CHARTRES
3 OCTOBRE 2009 — 28 FÉVRIER 2010
MUSÉE CHÂTEAU
NOGENT SAINT-JEAN
LE ROTROU
19 SEPTEMBRE 2009 — 28 FÉVRIER 2010
MUSÉE DE VENDÔME
VENDÔME
MUSÉE DES BEAUX-ARTS
ORLÉANS
3 MARS — 30 AOÛT 2009
11 MARS — 20 SEPTEMBRE 2009
CHÂTEAU ROYAL
BLOIS
MUSÉE DE L'OBJET
COLLECTION D'ART CONTEMPORAIN
11 MARS — 30 NOVEMBRE 2009
MARS 2009 — JUIN 2010
MUSÉE DES BEAUX-ARTS
TOURS
1ER OCTOBRE 2009 — 3 JANVIER 2010
MUSÉE MAURICE ESTÈVE
BOURGES
LA BOX 1ER OCTOBRE — 1ER NOVEMBRE 2009
31 MARS — 6 SEPTEMBRE 2009
SAVIGNY EN VÉRON
ÉCOMUSÉE DU VÉRON
MUSÉE DE L'HOSPICE SAINT-ROCH
ISSOUDUN
16 OCTOBRE 2009 — 24 MAI 2010
13 JUIN — 31 DÉCEMBRE 2009
LE BLANC
ÉCOMUSÉE DE LA BRENNE
DE MARS 2009 À MARS 2010
11 MUSÉES SE RASSEMBLENT AUTOUR DE L'ART CONTEMPORAIN
ŒUVRES DU CENTRE NATIONAL DES ARTS PLASTIQUES EN RÉGION CENTRE
www.musees.regioncentre.fr
Région Centre
design graphique : deValence

Typeface in Use
Gill Sans BQ

Tilt. Œuvres du Centre national des arts plastiques en région centre
2009 — Poster, Program
Client Centre National des Arts Plastiques
Design deValence (Alexandre Dimos, Gaël Étienne, Ghislain Triboulet)

We have been commissioned to design the poster, the program and the press kit for a series of exhibitions of the French national collection of contemporary art in the center region. We had to deal with lots of information on the documents (title, places, cities, and a long subtitle). That's why we decided to design a kind of typographic kit to use on the different objects. We played with the juxtaposition of our title design and the complexity of the infos of the exhibition.

"An elegant sans serif font that is easily recognizable. Several weights and lots of contrasts that we can play with."

t

deValence's Favorite Gill Sans Letter is "t".

Tuesday Lectures
2007 — Poster
Client Oslo National Academy of the Arts
Design Christian Brandt

A series of posters for Tuesday lectures at Oslo National Academy of the Arts.

t

Christian Brandt's Favorite Gill Sans Letter is "t".

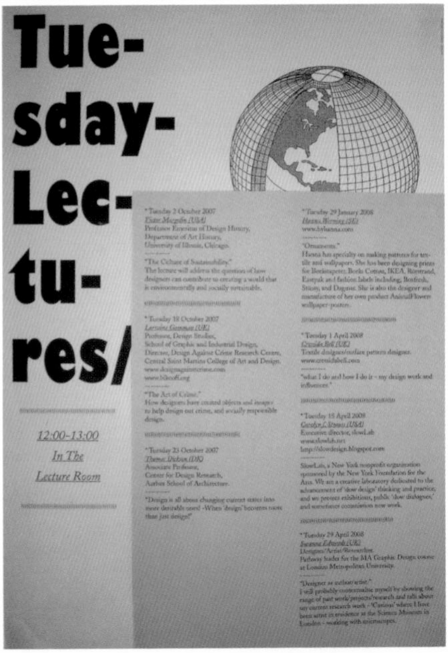

Typeface in Use
Gill Sans Ultra Bold

"The typeface has a lot of attitude and character"

Eric Gill, Un essai sur la typographie
2011 — Book
Client Ypsilon Éditeur, Paris
Author Eric Gill, translated by Boris Donné and Patricia Menay
Design Pauline Nuñez

The Bibliothèque typographique is a series directed by Sébastien Morlighem for the Paris publisher Ypsilon. Besides new monographs on type designers, such as the books on Roger Excoffon and José Mendoza y Almeida brought out in 2010, the Bibliothèque publishes French translations of classic texts on typography and type design. This translation of Gill's most celebrated essay is the first ever French edition since the book came out in 1931. The design tries to be faithful to the spirit of the original design of the second edition, adapted to the overall character of the Bibliothèque typographique. As in Gill's original, the cover uses Gill Sans and the interior is set in Joanna MT.

REVI-
SITING
THE
COM-
MUNITY
SHED
DESIGNED FROM
THE MEMORY OF
THE PLOT OWNERS
AT MANOR GARDENS
ALLOTMENTS
EAST LONDON
ROYAL COLLEGE OF ART
LONDON 2008
LIFEISLAND.ORG / THOMAS PAUSZ

G

Geoffroy Tobé's Favorite Gill Sans Letter is "G".

Revisiting the Community Shed
2008 — Identity
Author Thomas Pausz
Design Geoffroy Tobé

"I used Gill Sans Ultra Bold as a reflection of the generosity of the people who made the project possible — larger than life."

Revisiting the Community Shed is the reconstruction of a lost space. The reconstruction process became one with the making of the archive book. RCS aimed at regenerating links within a dislocated community of east London gardeners and collect/print their unique history. RCS is a celebration of memory, the transmission of design know-how between generations and cultures and of community survival against the odds. The handmade publication used recycled card, mirroring the allotment's practice of material re-use. The low manufacturing cost of the publication allowed the books to be distributed through exhibitions: another nod to the generous culture of knowledge shared by the protagonists.

LETRA
LT001
info@letra.com.pt
letra
LT001
Letra

Letra's Business Cards and Letterhead
2008 — Business Cards, Letterhead
Design Letra (Marco Balesteros)

Playful use of business cards and letterheads.

Typeface in Use
Gill Sans Ultra Bold Condensed

"In this case Gill Sans adds a cinematographic quality."

Zabriskie Point
2009 — Poster
Design Marco Balesteros

At the Werkplaats Typografie there are usually movie nights organized by the participants. My choice was Antonioni's *Zabriskie Point*. This poster was designed to announce the event.

Philharmoniker Hamburg Abonnement-Plakate
2010 — Poster
Client Philharmoniker Hamburg
Design Bureau Mirko Borsche

Poster for the *Philharmoniker Hamburg*.

Aargh!
2009 — Poster
Client Aargh Collective
Design Poststudio (Velina Stoykova)

Typeface in Use
Gill Sans Ultra Bold

SEMINÁRIO:
ARTE
CONTEMPORÂNEA
EM DEBATE
Participantes
Fabio Cypriano (Folha de S. Paulo e PUC/SP)
Lenora de Barros (Poeta e Artista Visual)
Marcia Fortes (Galeria Fortes Villaça)
Priscila Arantes (Paço das Artes e PUC/SP)
Mediadora
Profª Elaine Caramella (PUC/SP)
Data
16.08.2010
19h – 22h
Tucarena
Rua Monte Alegre 1024
Perdizes/São Paulo
Promoção
Curso de Graduação em Arte: História Crítica e Curadoria
Faculdade de Filosofia, Comunicação, Letras e Artes PUC/SP.
Curso de Pós-Graduação em Arte: Crítica e Curadoria
(ênfase em Arte Contemporânea) - COGEAE/PUC/SP.
Globo Universidade.
Realização
PUC-SP
PUC-SP
GLOBOUNIVERSIDADE
design: guilherme falcão
foto: mario ladeira

Typeface in Use
Gill Sans Ultra Bold, Amplitude

"Gill Sans Ultra Bold was used to create an attractive and recognizable signature to the event, that has a long and overly descriptive title. This particular weight of Gill Sans works well in contrast with Amplitude, since its shape becomes very geometric and angular (specially in letters such as 'O', 'N' and 'M'), while Amplitude has more of a humanist design."

Seminário:
Arte Contemporânea em Debate
2010 — Event Identity
Client PUC/SP (Pontifícia Universidade Católica de São Paulo), Globo Universidade
Design Guilherme Falcão
Photography Mario Ladeira

Identity, poster and flyer for a seminar/debate on Contemporary Art held at the PUC University in São Paulo, Brasil. As a means of representing the idea of spoken voice and different discourses, the double quotes were used as the main element of the pieces. The design intentionally articulates the title, set in Gill Sans Ultra Bold, the photograph of a microphone and other information together with heavy horizontal bars. This is meant to give the poster a sense of rhythm and a strange play on asymmetry — such as different opinions being voiced — but also to echo metal typesetting.

Typeface in Use
Gill Sans Light Shadowed, Pump

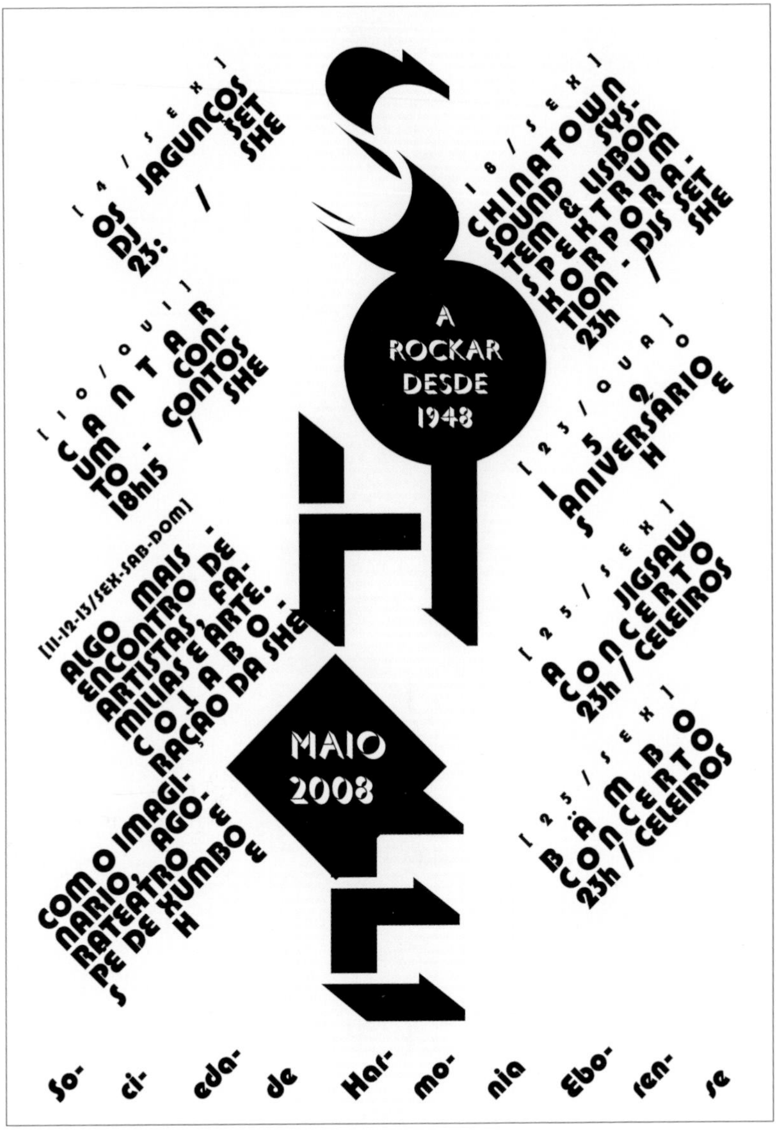

SHE — A rockar desde 1948.
2008 — Poster
Client SHE
Design Marco Balesteros

Poster developed for a cultural association (SHE). This poster aimed to promote cultural events within the association.

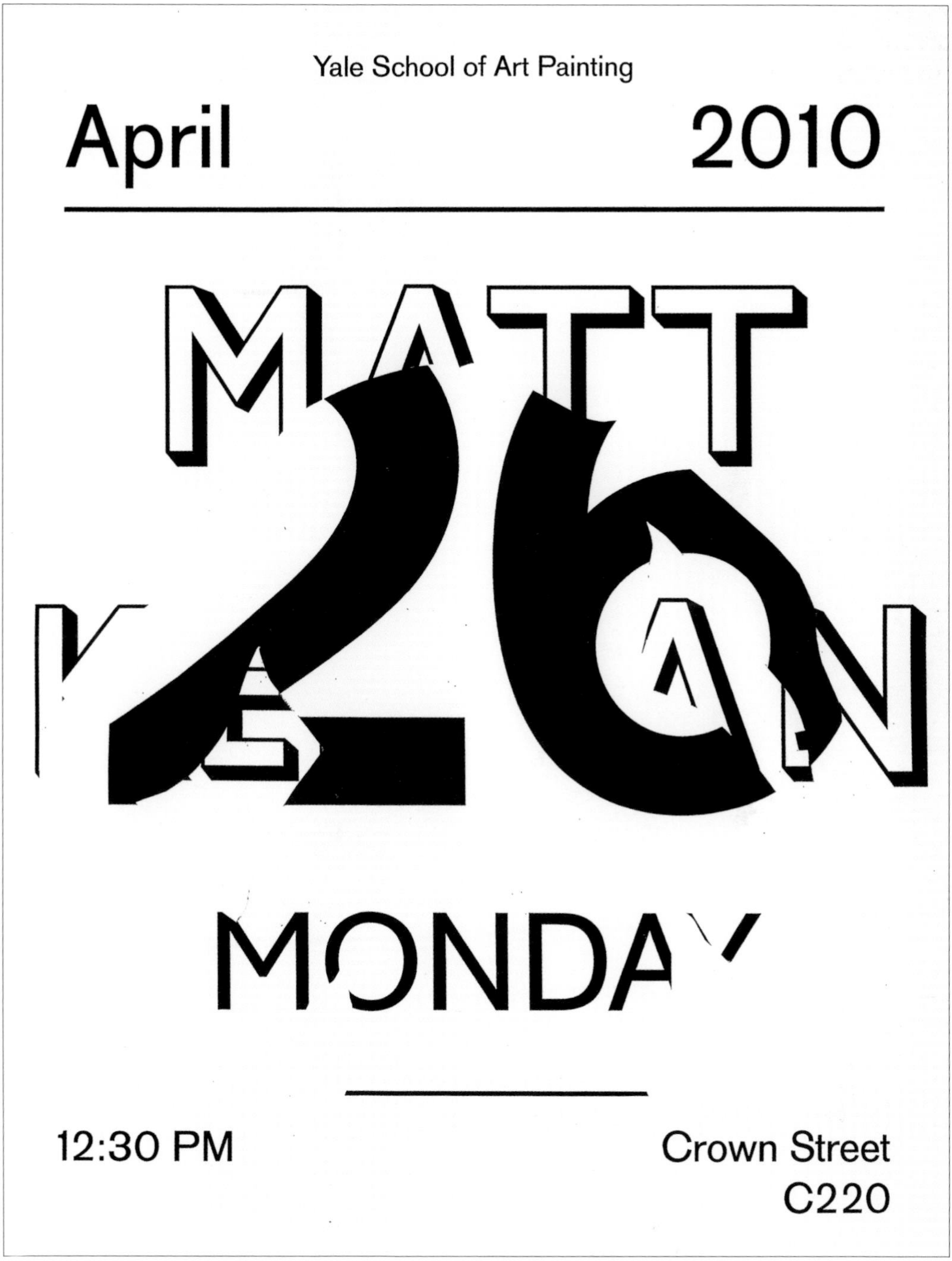

Matt Keegan
2010 — Poster
Design Mylinh Trieu Nguyen

Poster announcing a talk with Matt Keegan at Yale University.

"Much of Matt Keegan's work references time and space. I used this version of Gill Sans because it alludes to the same ideas with light and shadow guiding our temporal and spacial perception."

Fake Depth
2010 — Zine
Design Charlie Berendsen

"Fake Depth" explores the idea of depth on a 2D surface. Does a z-axis exist for the eye?

"The reason why 'Gill Sans' fitted for this project, was because the creator, Eric Gill, was first a stone sculpturer. Some of his sculptures to play with a 3D object which tends to be seen as a 2D image. Therefore, this typeface choice can be seen as a purely conceptual one."

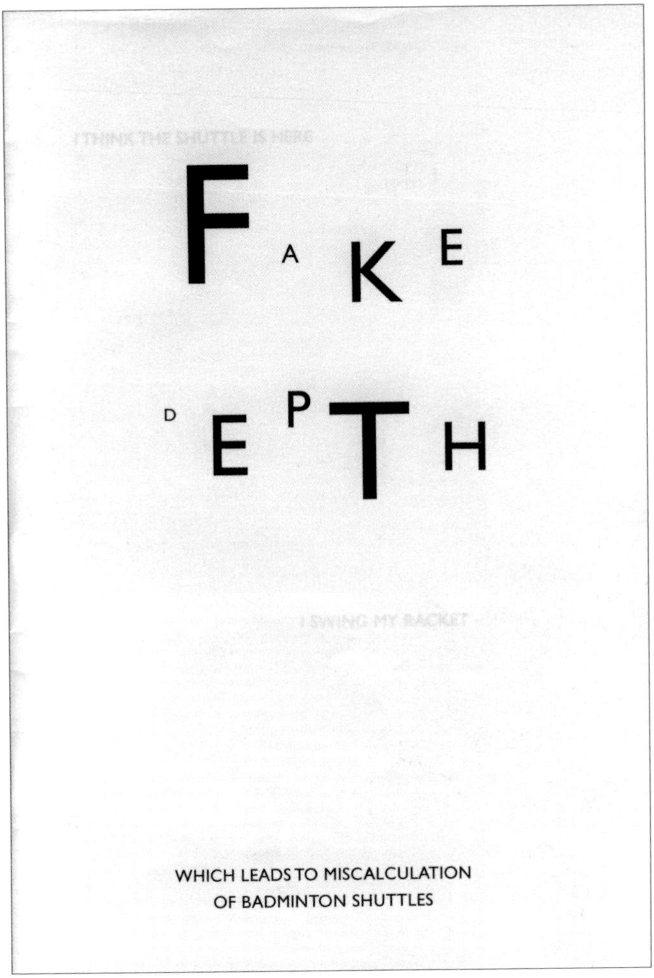

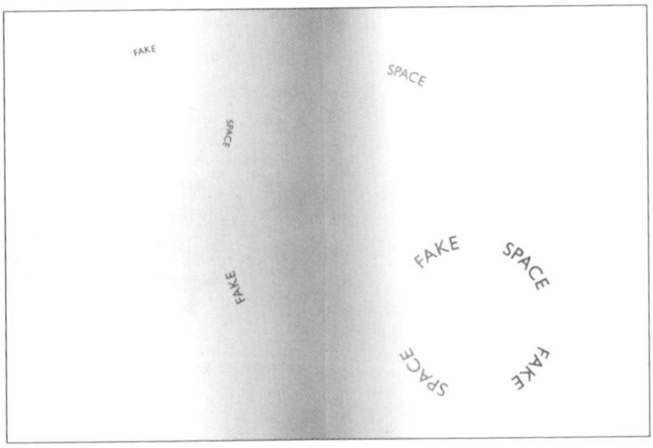

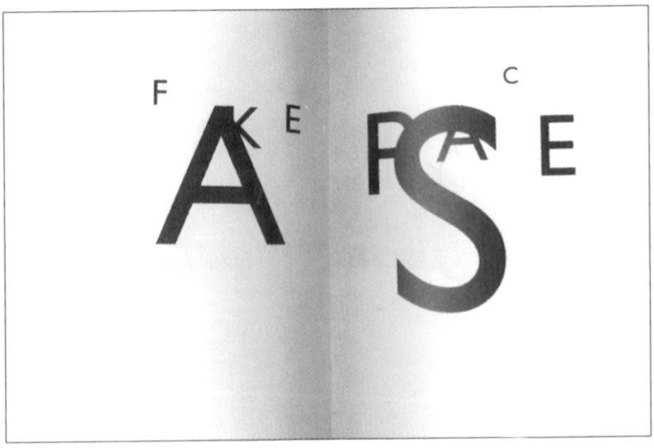

Typeface in Use
Gill Sans

Typeface in Use
Gill Sans Regular, Light

Gill Sans
is the
Helvetica
of England.
Designed by Eric Gill in 1927 and used by many British establishments.

Gill Sans is the Helvetica of England

"Gill Sans is truly British."

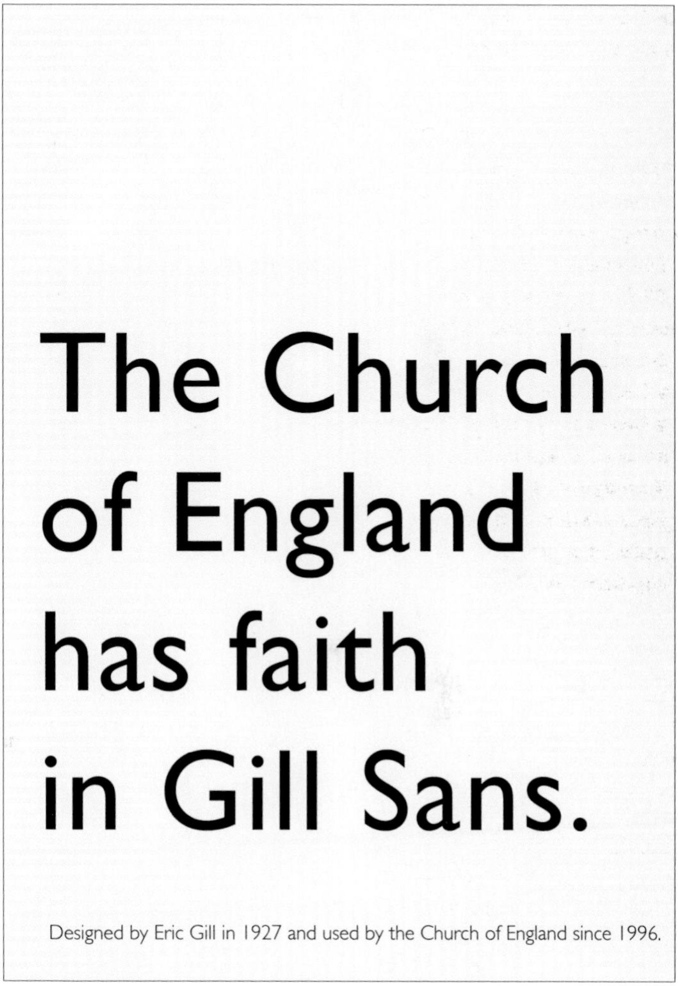

The Church
of England
has faith
in Gill Sans.
Designed by Eric Gill in 1927 and used by the Church of England since 1996.

The Church of England has faith in Gill Sans
2010 — Poster
Design Carolina Andreoli

Typographic posters celebrating the font Gill Sans.

Typeface in Use
Gill Sans Bold, Regular, handmade Labyrinth Type

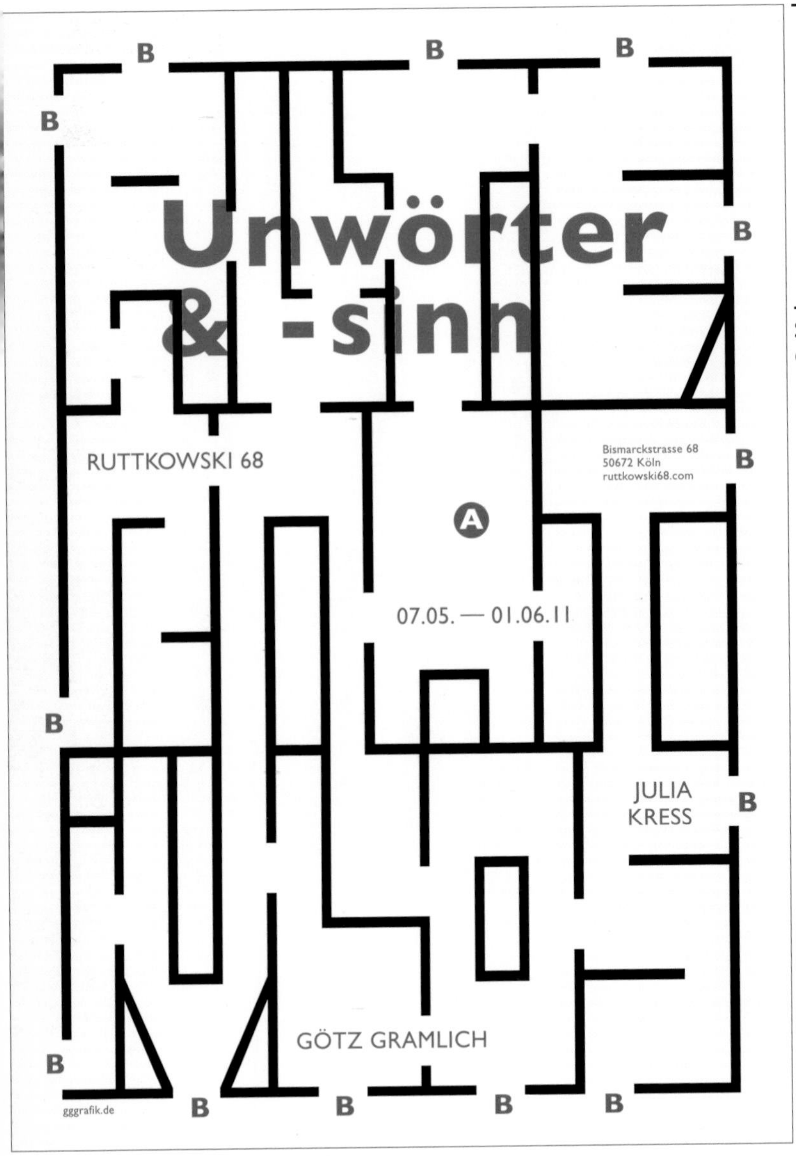

gggrafik's Favorite Gill Sans Sign is "?".

Unwörter & -sinn
2011 — Poster
Client Ruttkowski 68 Gallery
Design gggrafik design (Götz Gramlich)

"Because it's just beautiful, timeless and a good contrast to the handmade, angled type."

Poster for an exhibition with illustrated German faux pas words and lyrics in Cologne. Julia Kress and I showed illustrated German faux pas words and home-made prosa (typo) graphics.

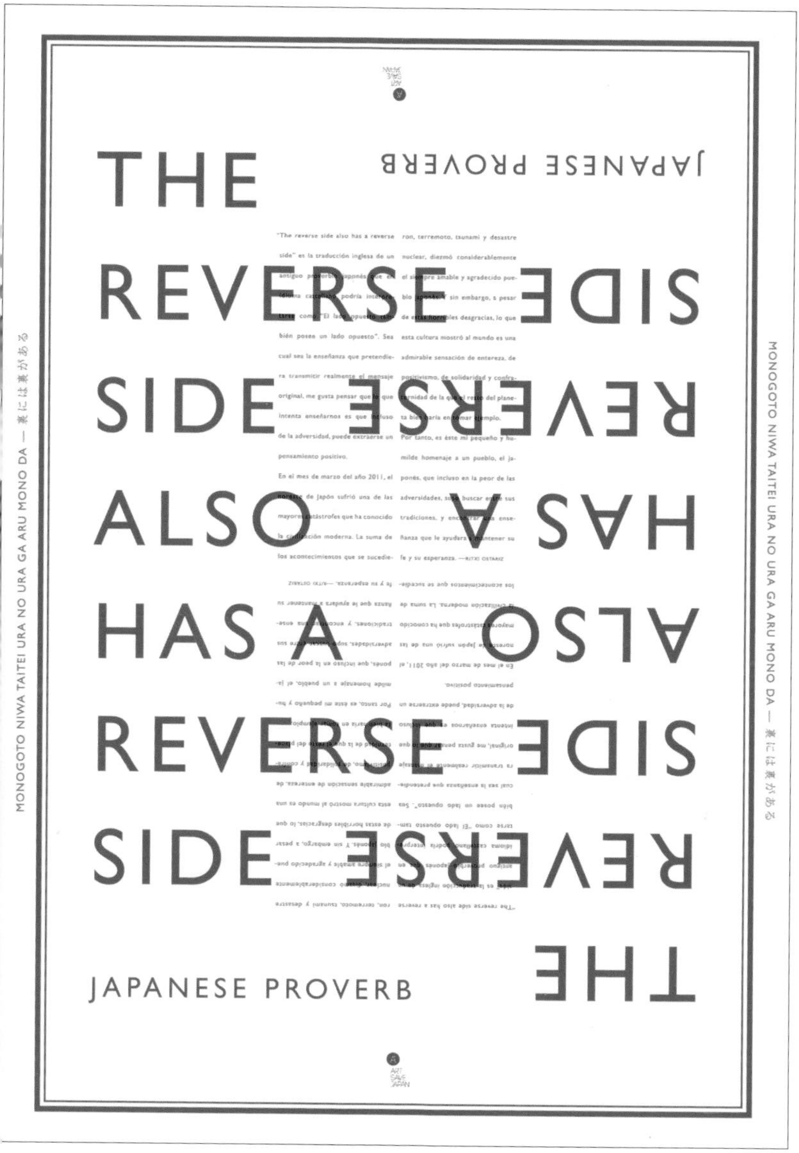

The Reverse Side
2011 — Poster
Client Art Save Japan exhibition
Design Estudio Ritxi Ostáriz

Poster for the "Art Save Japan" exhibition curated by IED Madrid in April 2011, in solidarity with Japan. "The reverse side also has a reverse side" is an old Japanese proverb.

R

Ritxi Ostáriz's Favorite Gill Sans Letter is "R".

Typeface in
Gill Sans MT
Ultra Bold C

The Great Gatsby
2010 — Poster
Client Deutsches Filmmuseum
Design Oliver Daxenbichler

Creating a teaser type poster referring to The Great Gatsby's summer party.

The famous quote was changed to the number of weeks till the party begins. As the design was reduced to a single typeface, the font had to reflect the look from the time being portrayed onscreen.

"The different varieties of letters make this font always a good choice for a characterful statement."

Change of address
2011 — Poster
Client showarchitekten
Design Oliver Daxenbichler
Photography Oliver Daxenbichler, Vanessa Fuentes

Typeface in Use
Gill Sans MT Ultra Bold Cond

Creating a visual language concept with a powerful impact to inform clients about the new address of the company. The new building consolidates different creative companies. The idea: creating a sculpture of different sizes of moving boxes building the keyvisual of the image. Each box itself stands for one of the companies residing at the new building. The 3 dimensional street number combines all companies in a visual way to a common statement.

I AM
EXPAT

WWW.IAMEXPAT.NL
IAMEXPAT.NL
FOR EXPATS OF ALL COLOURS, SHAPES & SIZES
IAMEXPAT.NL FOR EXPATS OF ALL COLOURS, SHAPES & SIZES
WWW.IAMEXPAT.NL

IamExpat.nl
2010 — Identity
Client Projekt 45
Design G Design Studio
Photography Alexandros Gavrilakis
Copywriting Katerina Roussou

IamExpat is a community-driven, online media platform aiming at covering the local needs of the expatriate population, who wish to socialize, share ideas and information as well as create and evaluate business opportunities. With the launch of the new website, IamExpat.nl is ready to become the most popular media platform for "internationals" in the Netherlands and even further. The IamExpat identity is a mixture of different colors, shapes and sizes. It accurately depicts the multiple segments of the Dutch expatriate community and the local multicultural society; the Netherland's social melting pot. The five-color palette, inspired by the different skin colors, is used in random order to create unique mosaics, while the “cut-out” letters portray the multicultural background of the international expatriate population. It also visualizes the commitment of IamExpat to every new coming expatriate regardless of race, ethnicity or appearance.

Typeface in Use
Gill Sans

"Gill Sans was the best match with the IamExpat concept."

Always and Forever
2009 — Framed Paper-cut
Design Helen Musselwhite

"I wanted to cut the type from paper so I choose the Ultra Bold version because the letters can be joined together and they don't loose their definition."

---

a

Helen Musselwhite's Favorite Gill Sans Letter is "a".

We Are Family
2009 — Framed Paper-cut
Design Helen Musselwhite

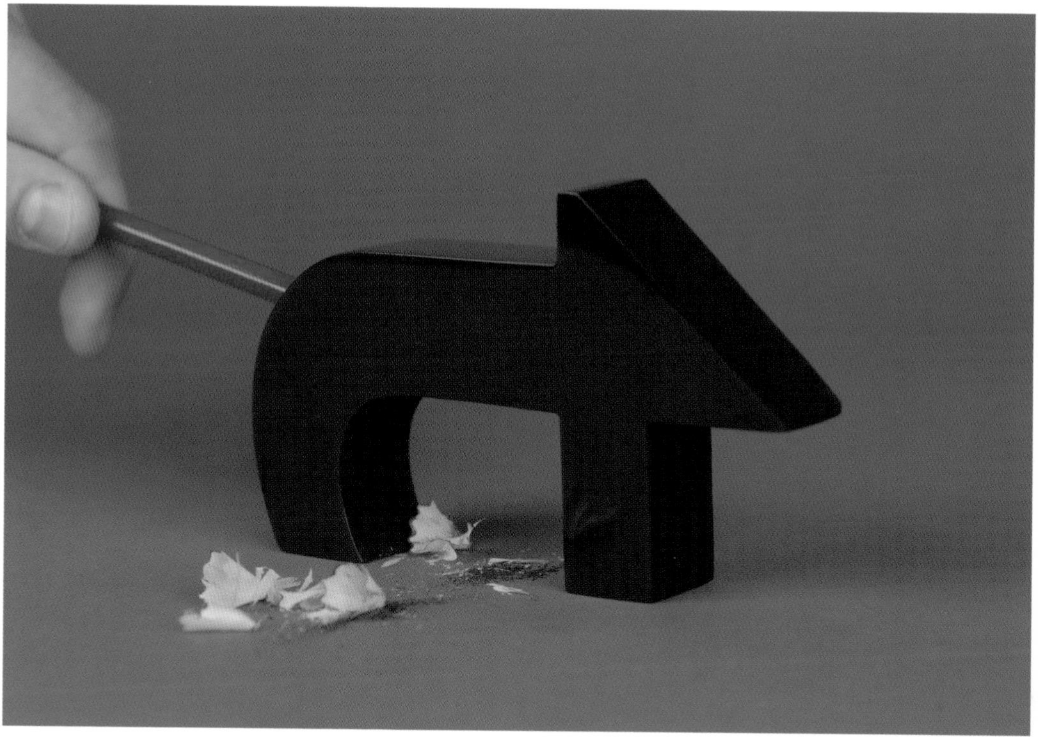

Gill t
2010 — Product
Design Jack Maxwell

Gill t tries to bring to light the suspected truths of Eric Gill's private life. Gill was believed to have had illicit sexual relationships, including one with his dog.

"Gill Sans for me is interesting as in my opinion the regular weight is beautiful, but the bold can be ugly."

t

Jack Maxwell's Favorite Gill Sans Letter is "t".

14 april -
12 augustus
2007
Genesis
Het leven aan het eind van het informatie-tijdperk
Centraal Museum Utrecht
centraal museum utrecht
centraal museum Utrecht
NWO

Genesis
2007 — Poster
Client Centraal Museum Utrecht
Design Lesley Moore
Photography Lard Buurman

The exhibition "Genesis — life at the end of the information age" in Centraal Museum Utrecht focuses on the development of art and science in relation to gene-technology. Central themes in the exhibition are order versus chaos and natural versus artificial.

The poster, seen from a distance, depicts an image which resembles a butterfly. As the viewer gets closer to the poster, the image dissolves into loose graphic objects and fragments of information.

e

Lesley Moore's Favorite Gill Sans Letter is "e".

"The Gill Sans family is a collection of characters with great personality. As opposed to more constructed sans serif typefaces like the Futura or Helvetica, one can feel that Gill Sans has its roots in the writing of the human hand."

a

Lars Amundsen's Favorite Gill Sans Letter is "a".

Euphorium Bakery
2001-03 — Corporate Identity, Packaging
Client Euphorium Bakery
Design Simon and Lars (Lars Amundsen & Simon Reed)

"At the end of the 90's, it was still unusual to see this kind of bakery in the center of London. Most of the products from Euphorium had their origins in France so we decided to use Gill Sans, the Brits favorite typeface, as a door-opener but in a non traditional way."

To set the new bakery apart from the previous Euphorium restaurant, our idea was to use typography in b/w with content from the world of baking, instead of the usual product photos. We felt the product looked really good displayed on the premises. Whenever the client opened a new bakery, we printed a new set of promotional postcards. 1st print-run: "bread world-records", 2nd: "bread superstitions", 3rd: "bread jokes". The jam jar labels are laser printed on the premises (containing random information about the ingredients.)

Typeface in Use
Gill Sans

"For me, no other typeface quite conjures the same nostalgic sense of what it is to be British."

MORTON
&
PEPLOW

Morton & Peplow
2009 — Identity
Client Morton & Peplow
Design Magpie Studio (Creative Direction: David Azurdia, Ben Christie, Jamie Ellul; Design: David Azurdia)

Serving up British food in style, Morton & Peplow is a Munich deli that specializes in British cuisine. The identity brings together two national icons — the bowler hat and the domed silver service platter — to create a mark that evokes a sense of heritage and style. A candy color palette and classic typography serve to continue this quintessentially British feel, tipping its hat to a lost era of elegant simplicity.

Typeface in Use
Gill Sans

Bodega Matador — Sol Lewitt Wine
2003 — Packaging
Client La Fábrica, Madrid, Spain
Design Fernando Gutierrez
Photography Nick Turner

Limited edition wine packaging for Bodega Matador. Wine label printed with artwork from artist Sol Lewitt.

"Gill Sans is an elegant sans serif font that has endured, it's timeless and has a nice link to Anglo Saxon type design and has a perfect balance of the modern and the classic. These values seemed to me have captured perfectly the spirit of the Matador project and where we wanted to position it."

g

Fernando Gutiérrez's Favorite Gill Sans Letter is "g".

Blue Boar Quad
→ Staircase 1
← Staircases 2, 3 & 4
← Lecture Theatre
← Exhibition Space
← Archive & Brewhouse

Staircase 4
Lecture Theatre
Exhibition Space

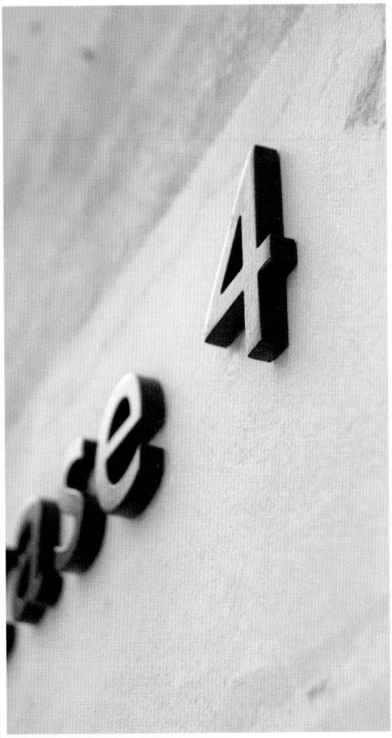
ase 4

Blue Boar Quad
2009 — Signage Design
Client Christ Church, Oxford
Design Maddison Graphic

Typeface in Use
Gill Sans

Blue Boar Quad was designed by renowned British architects Powell & Moya. It was recently listed grade II* and has undergone a complete refurbishment, its first since the building was completed in 1968. Maddison Graphic were commissioned to design the new signage scheme. It is a mixture of water cut steel lettering applied directly to the stone walls and white vinyl applied to powder coated steel tray signs.

"Gill Sans is a good typeface for signage. It is very clear from a distance, especially when widely spaced and although the building was designed 30 years after the Gill Sans, they are both distinctly modernist."

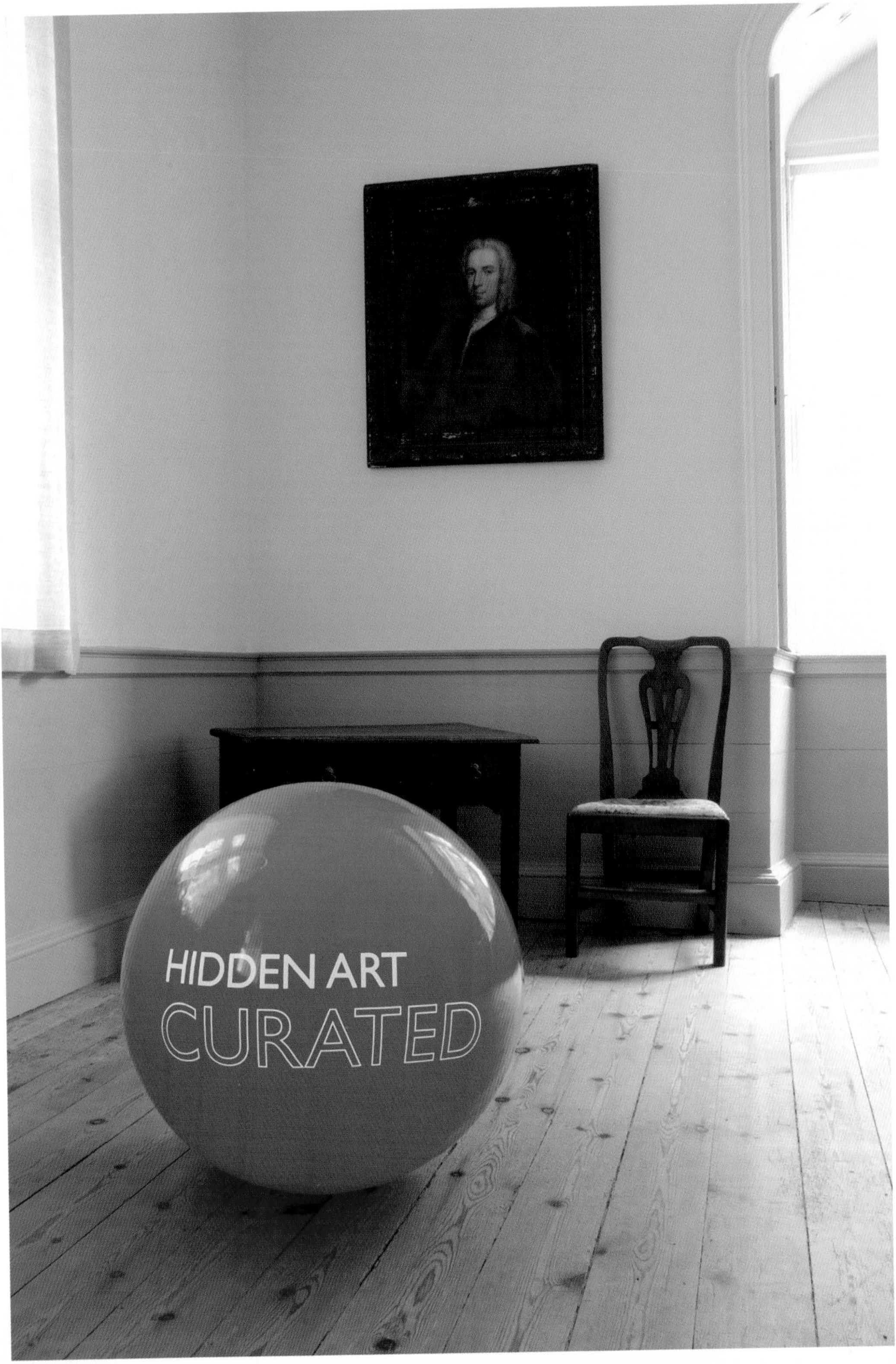
HIDDEN ART
CURATED

Typeface in Use
Gill Sans

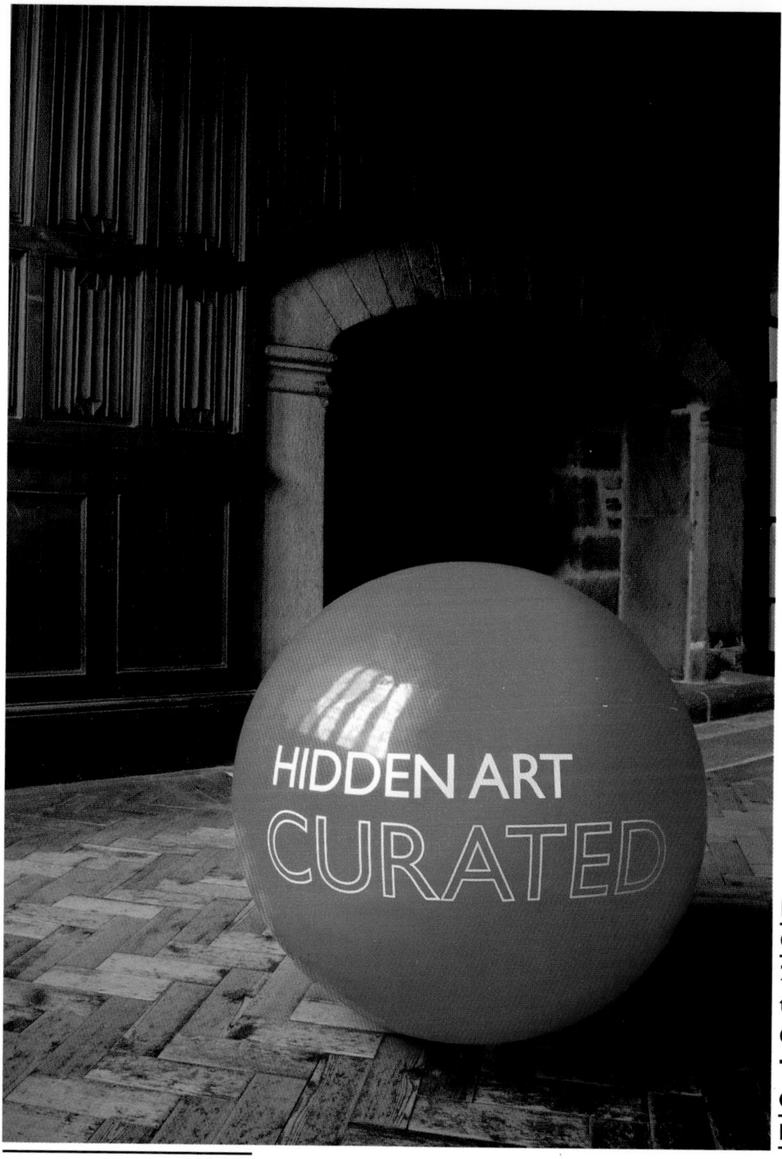

Hidden Art
Cornwall Design Fair
2008 — Event Identity, Poster, Leaflet, Catalog, Advertising, Tickets
Client Hidden Art
Design Two

k

Two's Favorite Gill Sans Letter is "k".

This annual three day event gives the public an opportunity to buy contemporary work directed from over 100 designer-makers in the unique setting of Godolphin House. Key to our approach, in designing the identity for the event, was to represent the unique mix of the organization, the event and the venue. The overlaid red circle, referencing the sold sticker from the Hidden Art logotype adds an easily recognisable device providing a united identity that is clear, confident and cohesive.

We also created the identity for Hidden Art Curated, a showcase of contemporary design within the context of the house itself.

"The mix of upper and lower case type settings of Gill Sans perfectly represented the balance of contemporary design presented in this historic setting."

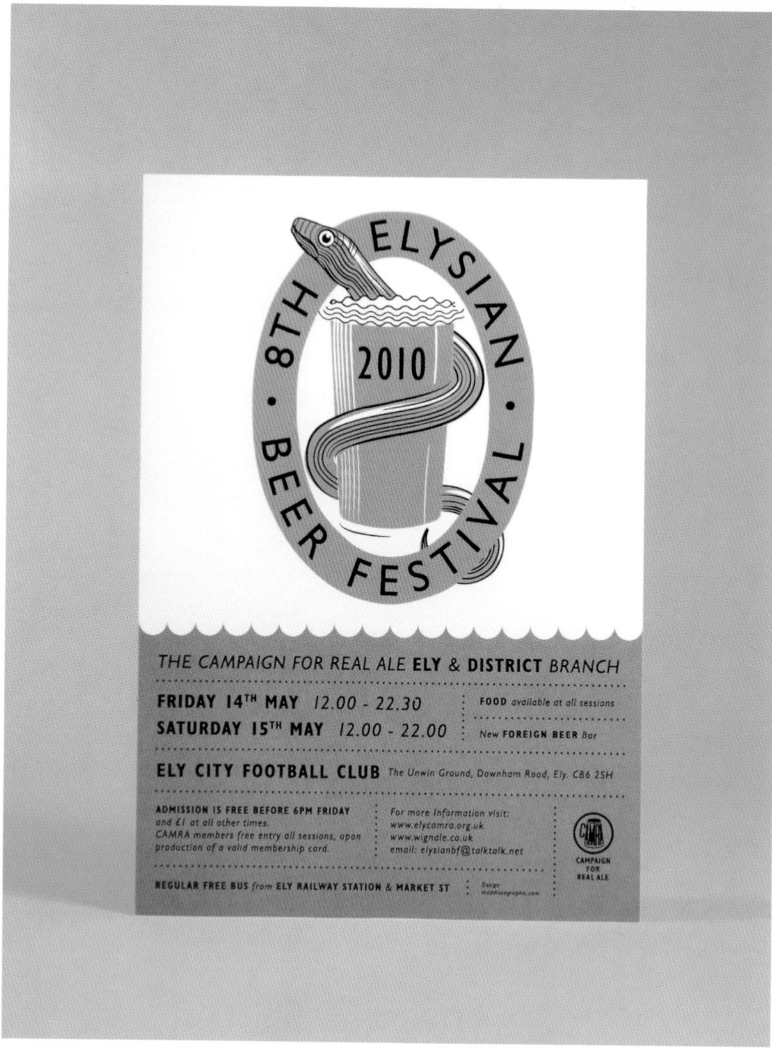

Typeface in Use
Gill Sans

"The style of the poster and logo reference mid 20th century design such as the publicity for the Festival of Britain. Gill Sans capital letters and in particular their italics look distinctly of this period."

Ely Summer Beer Festival
2010 — Logo, Glass, Poster
Client Ely Camra
Design Maddison Graphic

We were asked by a friend who is involved in the Ely Camra branch if we would like to do the design for the summer beer festival. We agreed because it was an opportunity to do something a bit different from our normal work and in exchange for the design work we were given free entry and beer at the festival.

g

Maddison Graphic's Favorite Gill Sans Letter is "g".

Typeface in Use
Gill Sans MT, Caslon 540

I.J. Mellis
2011 — Brochure
Client I.J. Mellis Cheesemonger
Design El Studio (Pete Rossi, Kenny Allan)
Photography Reuben Paris

G

El Studio's Favorite Gill Sans Letter is "G".

"Gill Sans and Caslon 540 was used for this project to give the feel of a timeless yet crafted brochure in keeping with the ethos of the I.J. Mellis brand and artisan approach. Thus mixing traditional craftsmanship with an air of modernity."

WRITERS'
CENTRE
NORWICH

Writers' Centre Norwich Rebrand
2009 — Identity, Literature, Website
Client Writers' Centre Norwich
Art Direction Bobby Burrage
Design The Click Design Consultants
Account Management Fiona Smillie

"Gill Sans is a classic English Sans Serif font, well suited to the credentials and aspirations of Writers' Centre Norwich. We wanted to create a brand identity with an intellectual, established air, something that the literary connotations of the font encapsulate perfectly. Penguin Books provide clear inspiration for this project and Gill Sans makes reference to this, it being the typeface used by the publisher on many of its jacket designs."

Writers' Centre Norwich, previously New Writing Partnership, required an entirely new brand identity with corresponding printed literature and website. We created a new name and visual identity to better reflect the newly streamlined structure of the charity and their creative plans for the future. We remain brand guardians of Writers' Centre Norwich to this day, designing regular publications, event literature and other products.

N
TEN NEW VOICES
FROM THE EAST OF
ENGLAND
ESCALATOR
LITERATURE 2009/10
N
TEN NEW VOICES
FROM THE EAST OF
ENGLAND
ESCALATOR
LITERATURE 2009/10

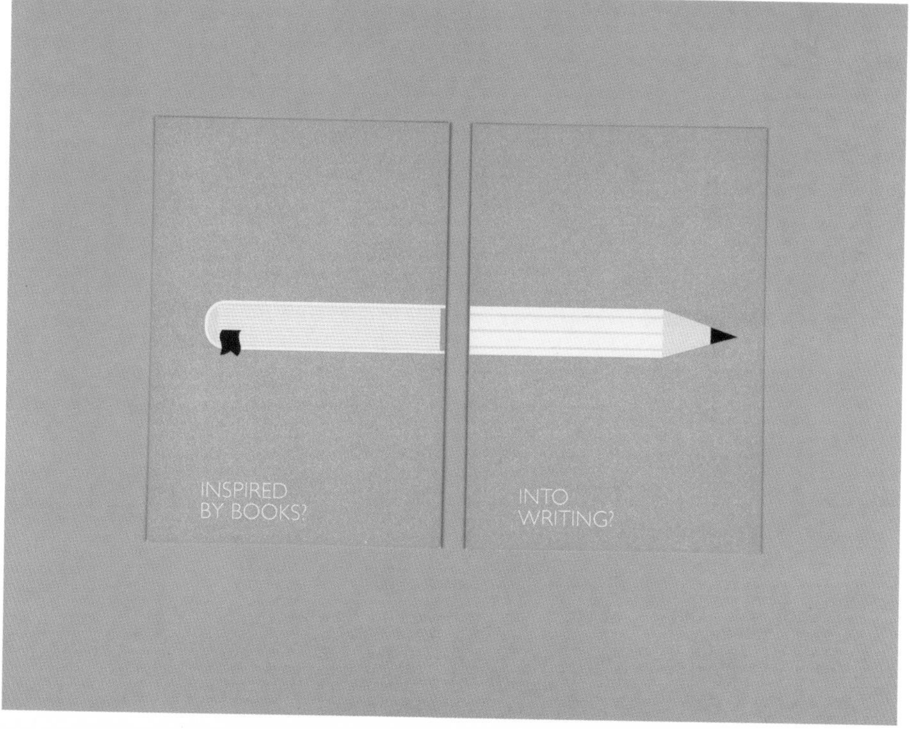
INSPIRED
BY BOOKS?
INTO
WRITING?

Typeface in Use
Gill Sans

Teixidors
2009 — Identity
Client Teixidors
Design Clase bcn
Photography Daniel Riera
Set Design Koen Meersman
Copywriting Carlos Serrat

A project for a very special cooperative, National Award for Craftwork, that is committed to the legitimacy of being different. The refined simplicity of the products provided the inspiration for our approach to the design. Clear forms, warm and simple colors and a very clean and fine typeface. The logotype refers to the basic component of weaving and also accents the most notable letter in the company's name.

"It's fantastic equilibrium and simplicity reminded us Teixidors's products character: clean, atemporary and elegant."

R

Uriah Gray's Favorite Gill Sans Letter is "R".

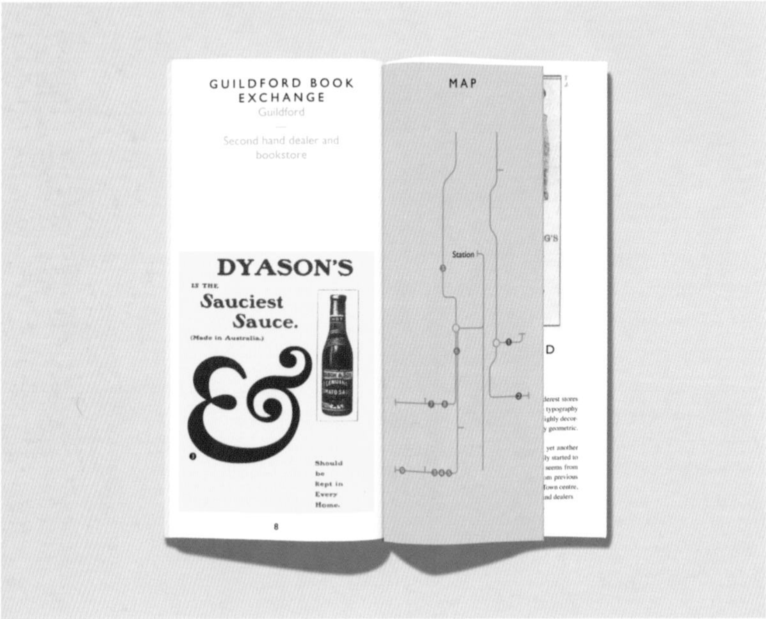

TYPE T TRACKS

Type Tracks
2009 — Identity, Book
Design Uriah Gray

Responding to a brief set by Vince Frost, which asked if the environment creates typography or typography creates the environment. A series of guidebooks explore this relationship, with a guided tour of vernacular typography surrounding Western Australian train stations.

Gill Sans Shadow, Gill Sans Medium

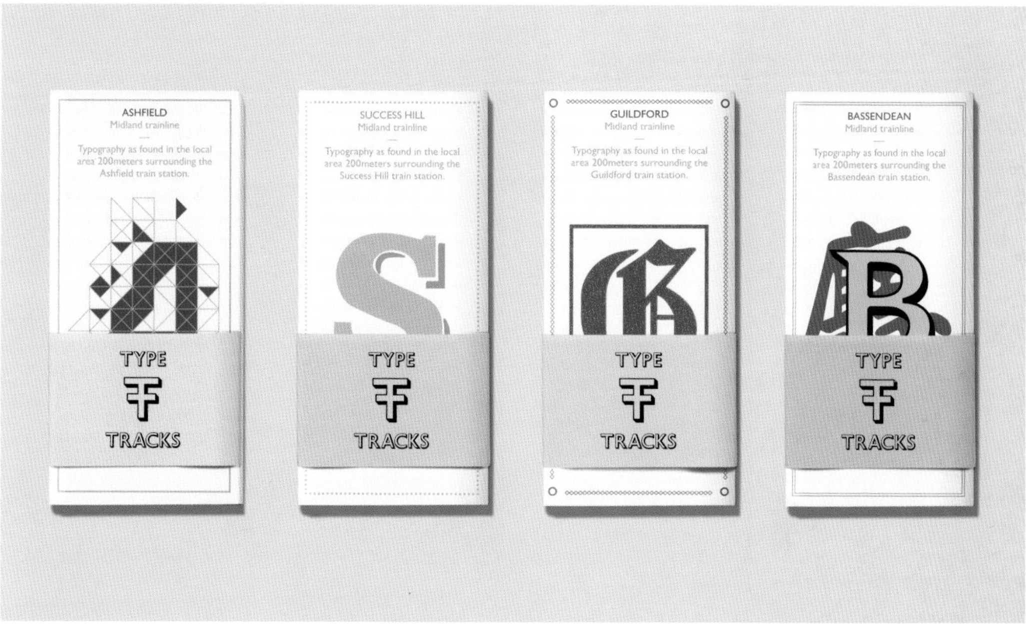

"The guidebooks used Gill Sans to reproduce the Perth train station identity and history. The train stations form the anchor and neutral starting point for exploring the typography in the suburbs. Gill Sans was used throughout the train stations from its early inception. It was used as a reference to the London Underground, an example of how English typography still influences Western Australia."

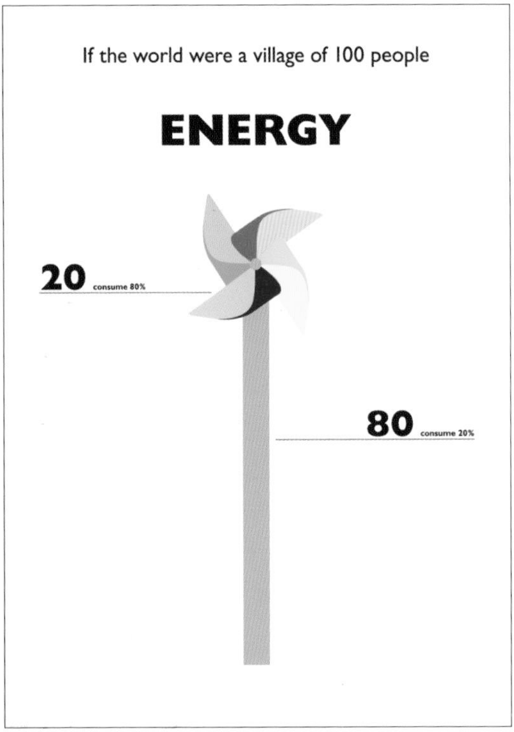
If the world were a village of 100 people
ENERGY
20 consume 80%
80 consume 20%

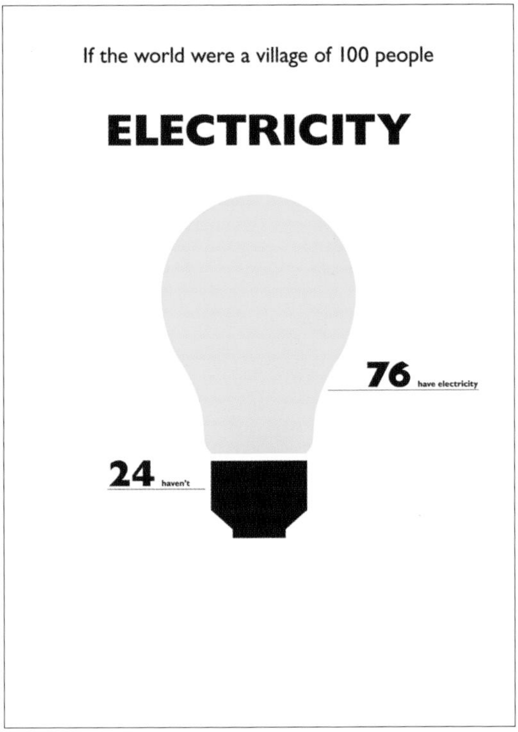
If the world were a village of 100 people
ELECTRICITY
76 have electricity
24 haven't

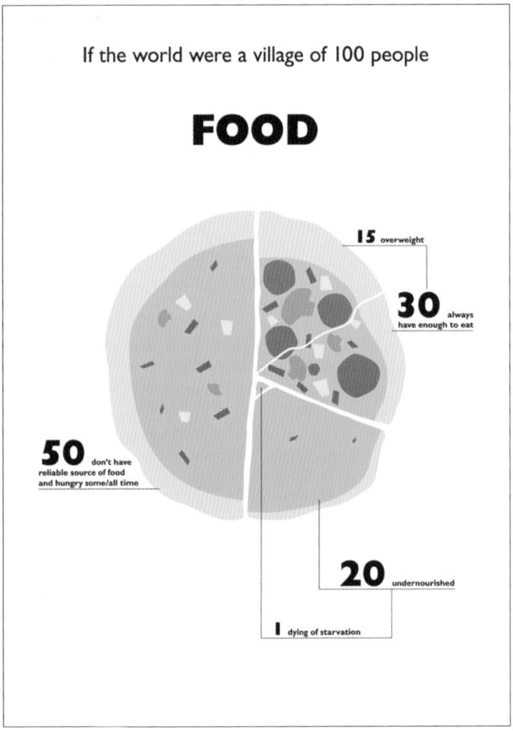
If the world were a village of 100 people
FOOD
15 overweight
30 always have enough to eat
50 don't have reliable source of food and hungry some/all time
20 undernourished
1 dying of starvation

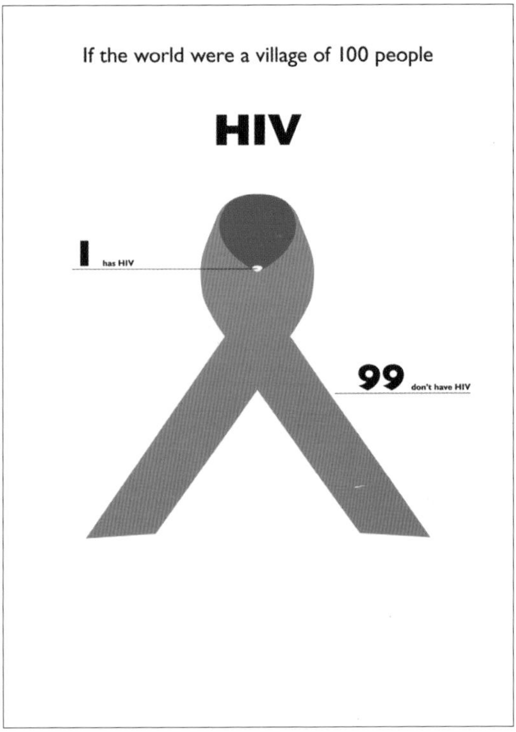
If the world were a village of 100 people
HIV
1 has HIV
99 don't have HIV

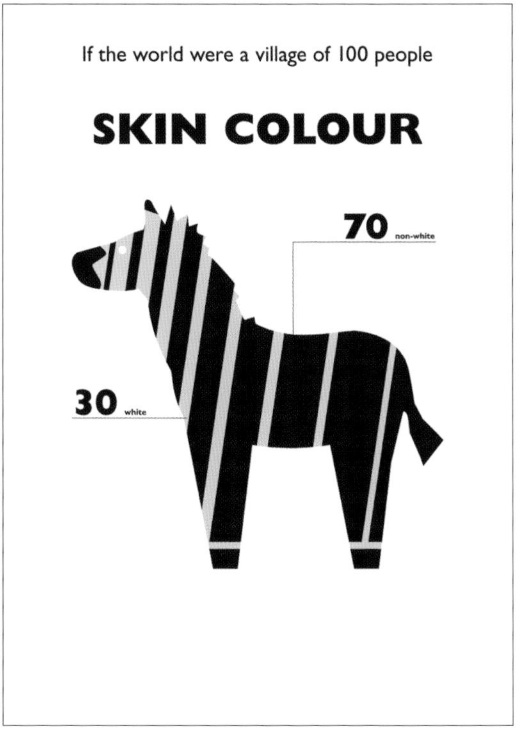

If the world were a village of 100 people
SKIN COLOUR
70 non-white
30 white

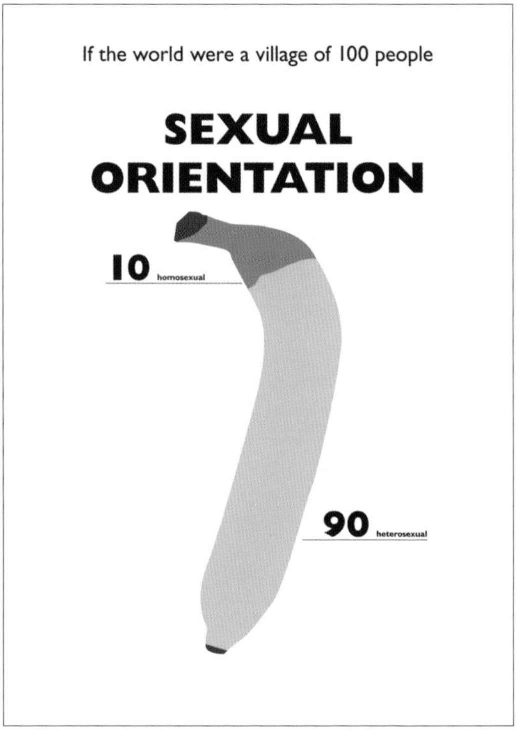

If the world were a village of 100 people
SEXUAL ORIENTATION
10 homosexual
90 heterosexual

The World of 100
2008 — Poster
Design Toby Ng

If the world were a village of 100 people, how would the composition be? This set of 20 posters is built on statistics about the spread of population around the world under various classifications. The numbers are turned into graphics to give the information another touch – Look, this is the world we are living in.

t

Typeface in Use
Gill Sans

Toby Ng's Favorite Gill Sans Letter is "t".

"The sense of humor matches perfectly with the illustration of this project."

HURRICANE
We have everything we had, and life's not so bad · 'Cos love's alive and lying living · Breathing lungs full-up and I'm giving nothing away am I? · I'm fifty feet high in the sky ·
It's gonna hit you hard, sure · Gonna make your head feel sore · It's gonna feel like stone inside of you · Just wait and see, see
See liar · It's me liar · Believe me liar
We leave everything we love, and that was enough · To pay the price for lying you're living · Breathing lungs full-up and I'm giving nothing away am I? · I'm fifty feet high in the sky
It's gonna hit you hard, sure · Gonna make your head feel sore · It's gonna feel like stone inside of you · Just wait and see, see
See liar · It's me liar · Believe me liar
I miss you so much · And I'm feeling the crush · Of the limits we reached · When we blocked all the leaks · In the buildings and towers · Emotion and power · I've been here for hours · But I'm still locked out
See liar · It's me liar · Believe me liar
BATTLE FOR HEARTS & MINDS
I cannot fight, I haven't got a sword or a gun · Even if I did, I'm not sure whose side I'd be on · 'Cos love battles harder than the hate that we possess · And the battles get harder, when you · Start saying no when you mean yes
Here in my bed, I'm something you both agreed on · I'd up and leave, but I'm not sure how fast I could run · 'Cos love is the metre, by which we work play and rest · So leave this 'til morning, 'til the sun comes up again
I can't fight because I'm unarmed · Even if I did, I'm not sure who I'm with, or what would give · Hearts and minds play with equal strength · I sit on the fence · Whilst my father lies, and mother cries
I can't fight because I'm unarmed · even if I did, I'm not sure who I'm with, or what would give · Hearts and minds play with equal strength · On this battle ground, yeah which we call home, but we can't stay here
PARK SLOPEY
All this I've been saving · For what I can't decide · I'm here and I'm still waiting · This love's for no one else
This year I've been stealing from my brother · This year I'm alone · This year I've been stealing from my brother · But I'll make this alone
On this I'm undecided · It's a tale I'm scared to tell · I'm here and I'm still stupid · With a love for no one else
This year I've been stealing from my brother · This year I'm alone · This year I've been stealing from my brother · But I'll make this alone
Don't worry, I know I lean on you · Don't worry, I know I need to leave · Don't worry, I know I lean on you · Don't worry, I know I need to leave

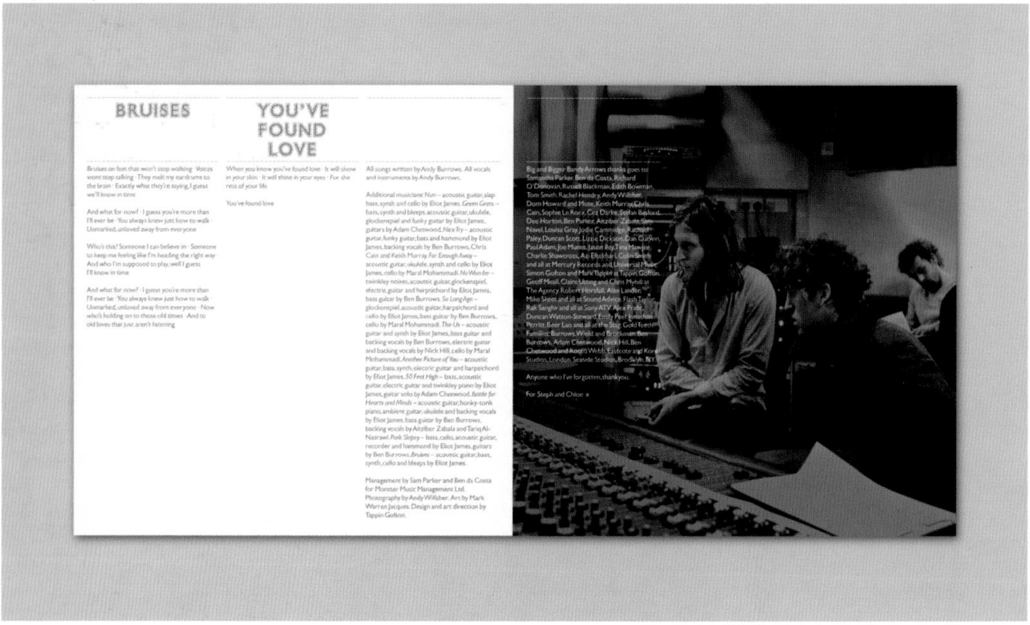
BRUISES
Bruises on feet that won't stop walking · Voices wont stop talking · They melt my eardrums to the brain · Exactly what they're saying, I guess we'll know in time
And what for now? · I guess you're more than I'll ever be · You always knew just how to walk · Unmarked, unloved away from everyone
Who's this? Someone I can believe in · Someone to keep me feeling like I'm heading the right way · And who I'm supposed to play, well I guess I'll know in time
And what for now? · I guess you're more than I'll ever be · You always knew just how to walk · Unmarked, unloved away from everyone · Now who's holding on to those old times · And to old loves that just aren't listening
YOU'VE FOUND LOVE
When you know you've found love · It will show in your skin · It will shine in your eyes · For the rest of your life
You've found love
All songs written by Andy Burrows. All vocals and instruments by Andy Burrows.
Additional musicians: Nun – acoustic guitar, slap bass, synth and cello by Eliot James. Green Grass – bass, synth and bleeps, acoustic guitar, ukulele, glockenspiel and funky guitar by Eliot James, guitars by Adam Chetwood. Nice Try – acoustic guitar, funky guitar, bass and hammond by Eliot James, backing vocals by Ben Burrows, Chris Cain and Keith Murray. Far Enough Away – acoustic guitar, ukulele, synth and cello by Eliot James, cello by Maral Mohammadi. No Wonder – twinkley noises, acoustic guitar, glockenspiel, electric guitar and harpsichord by Eliot James, bass guitar by Ben Burrows. So Long Ago – glockenspiel, acoustic guitar, harpsichord and cello by Eliot James, bass guitar by Ben Burrows, cello by Maral Mohammadi. The Us – acoustic guitar and synth by Eliot James, bass guitar and backing vocals by Ben Burrows, electric guitar and backing vocals by Nick Hill, cello by Maral Mohammadi. Another Picture of You – acoustic guitar, bass, synth, electric guitar and harpsichord by Eliot James. 50 Feet High – bass, acoustic guitar, electric guitar and twinkley piano by Eliot James, guitar solo by Adam Chetwood. Battle for Hearts and Minds – acoustic guitar, honky-tonk piano, ambient guitar, ukulele and backing vocals by Eliot James, bass guitar by Ben Burrows, backing vocals by Aitziber Zabala and Tariq Al-Nasrawi. Park Slopey – bass, cello, acoustic guitar, recorder and hammond by Eliot James, guitars by Ben Burrows. Bruises – acoustic guitar, bass, synth, cello and bleeps by Eliot James.
Management by Sam Parker and Ben da Costa for Monster Music Management Ltd. Photography by Andy Willsher. Art by Mark Warren Jacques. Design and art direction by Tappin Gofton.

Big and Bigger Bandy Burrows thanks goes to: Samantha Parker, Ben da Costa, Richard O'Donovan, Russell Boardman, Edith Bowman, Tom Smith, Rachel Hendry, Andy Willsher, Dom Howard and Mole, Keith Murray, Chris Cain, Sophie La Roca, Cris Clarke, Stefan Balsusz, Doc Horton, Ben Parker, Altzber, Zabala, Sam Nowel, Louisa Gray, Jodie Cammidge, Richard Paley, Duncan Scott, Lizzie Dickson, Dan Glasser, Paul Adam, Joe Martin, Jason Roy, Tim Hawkins, Charlie Shoesmith, Az Chadha, Chris Mynott at The Agency, Robert Horsfall, Alan Lawfler, Mike Steen and all at Sound Advice, Flash Taylor, Rak Singhr and all at Sony ATV, Alex Pattj, Duncan Watson Stewart, Emily Peel Productions, Merritt, Bert Lan and all at the Box, Gold Furniture Furniture, Burrows, Wreck and Buckethead, Ben Burrows, Adam Chetwood, Nick Hill, Ben Chetwood and Keith Webb, Eastcote and Konk Studios, London, Seaside Studios, Brooklyn, NY.

Anyone who I've forgotten, thankyou.
For Steph and Chloe x

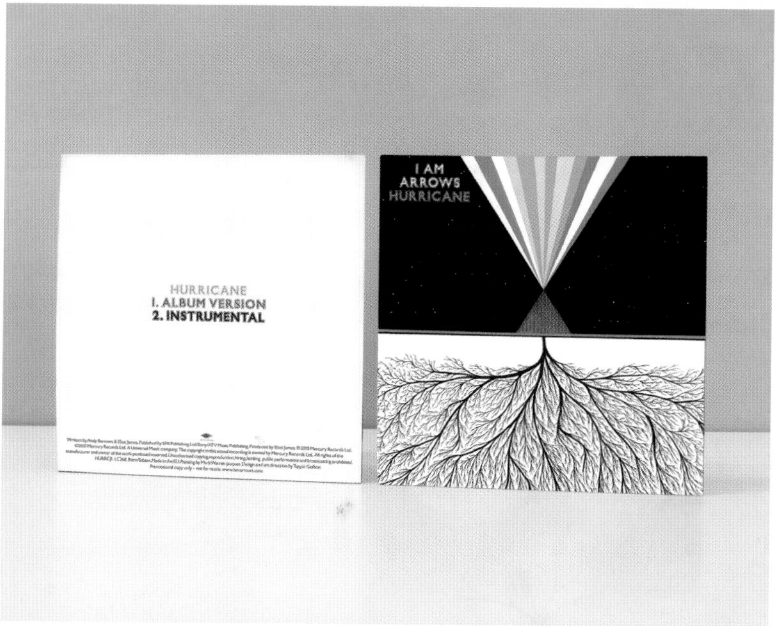

I Am Arrows
"Sun Comes Up Again"
2010 — CD Packaging
Client Mercury Records
Design Tappin Gofton (Simon Gofton)
Illustration Mark Warren Jacques

Design and art direction for I Am Arrows debut album "Sun Comes Up Again". The artwork features paintings by the American artist and "optimistic amateur philosopher", Mark Warren Jacques. The humanist sans-serif typeface Gill Sans, forms the basis for the band's typographic identity.

Typeface in Use
Gill Sans

I AM
ARROWS
SUN COMES
UP AGAIN

NUN
GREEN GRASS
NICE TRY
FAR ENOUGH AWAY
MONSTERS DASH
NO WONDER
SO LONG AGO
THE US
ANOTHER PICTURE OF YOU
HURRICANE
BATTLE FOR HEARTS & MINDS
PARK SLOPEY
BRUISES
YOU'VE FOUND LOVE
Produced by Eliot James for Audio Authority Management. Engineered by Eliot James and Samuel Navel. Mixed by Eliot James at Kore studios, assisted by Tariq Al-Nasrawi and George Apsion. Executive Producer Richard O'Donovan. Mastered by Geoff Peshe at Abbey Road Studios, London. Recorded at Eastcote Studios, London. Published by Sony/ATV Music Publishing. ℗2010 Mercury Records Ltd. ©2010 Mercury Records Ltd. A Universal Music company. The copyright in this sound recording is owned by Mercury Records Ltd. All rights of the manufacturer and owner of the work produced reserved. Unauthorised copying, reproduction, hiring, lending, public performance and broadcasting prohibited. 2738002. LC268. Biem/Sabam. Made in the EU.
I AM ARROWS
SUN COMES UP AGAIN

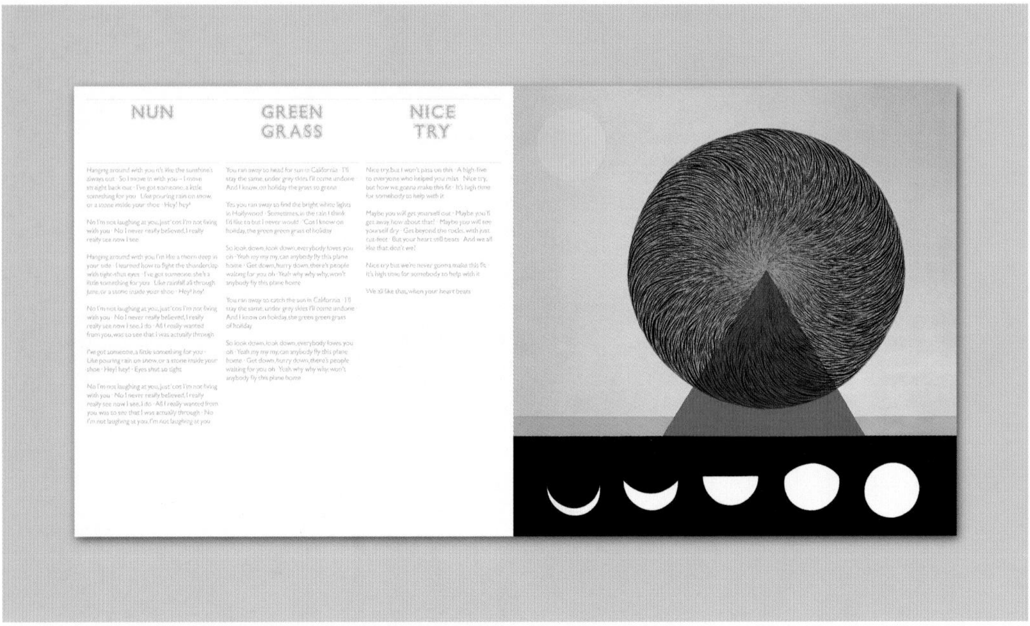
NUN
GREEN GRASS
NICE TRY

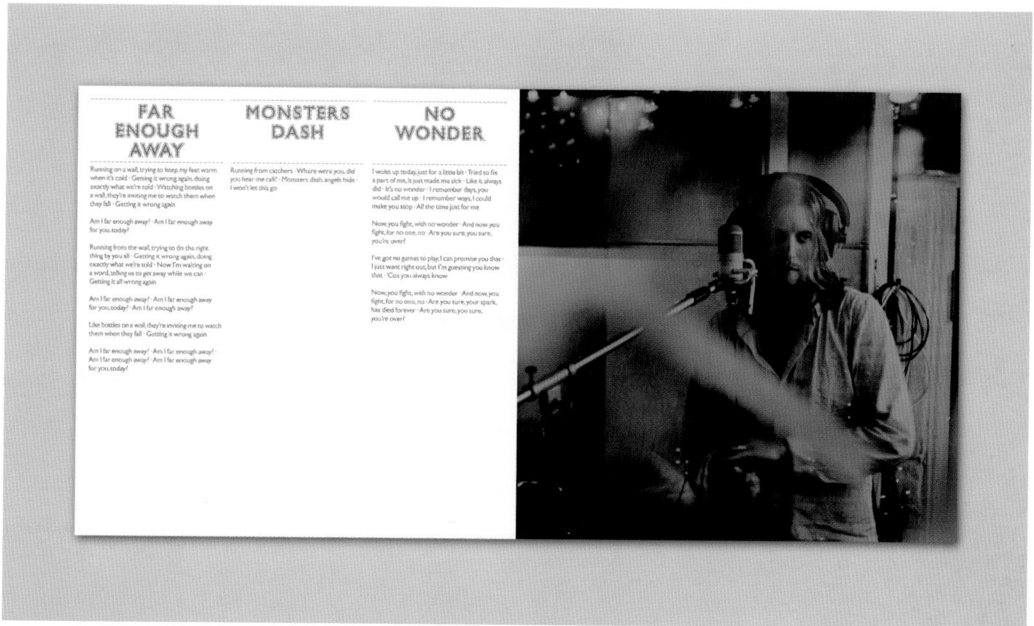

FAR ENOUGH AWAY

Running on a wall, trying to keep my feet warm when it's cold · Getting it wrong again, doing exactly what we're told · Watching bottles on a wall, they're inviting me to watch them when they fall · Getting it wrong again

Am I far enough away? · Am I far enough away for you, today?

Running from the wall, trying to do the right thing by you all · Getting it wrong again, doing exactly what we're told · Now I'm waiting on a word, telling us to get away while we can · Getting it all wrong again

Am I far enough away? · Am I far enough away for you, today? · Am I far enough away?

Like bottles on a wall, they're inviting me to watch them when they fall · Getting it wrong again

Am I far enough away? · Am I far enough away? · Am I far enough away? · Am I far enough away for you, today?

MONSTERS DASH

Running from catchers · Where were you, did you hear me call? · Monsters dash, angels hide · I won't let this go

NO WONDER

I woke up today, just for a little bit · Tried to fix a part of me, It just made me sick · Like it always did · It's no wonder · I remember days, you would call me up · I remember ways, I could make you stop · All the time just for me

Now, you fight, with no wonder · And now, you fight, for no one, no · Are you sure, you sure, you're over?

I've got no games to play, I can promise you that · I just want right out, but I'm guessing you know that · 'Cos you always know

Now, you fight, with no wonder · And now, you fight, for no one, no · Are you sure, your spark, has died forever · Are you sure, you sure, you're over?

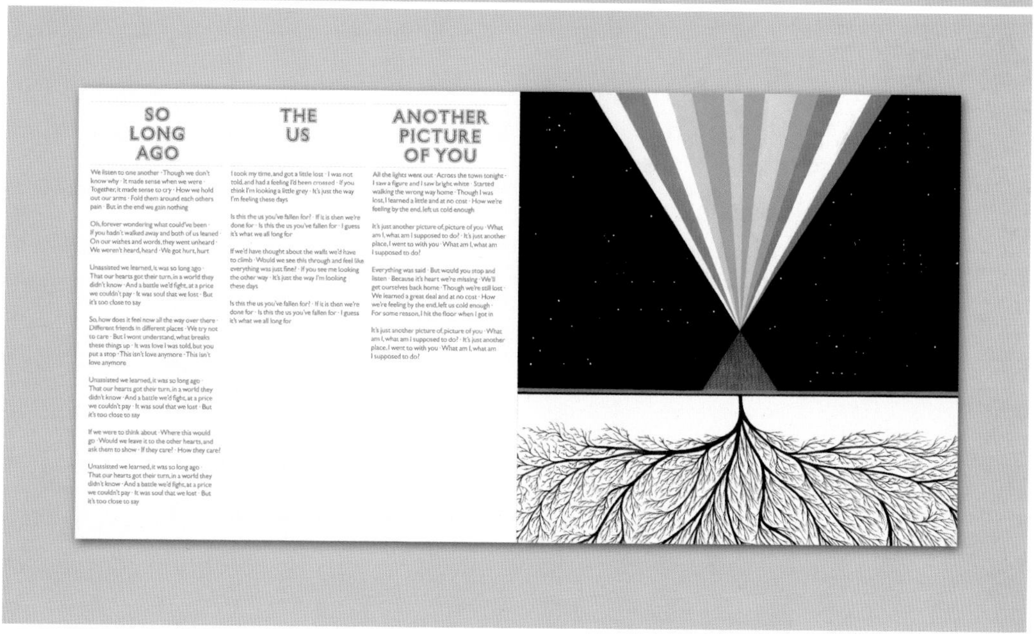

SO LONG AGO

We listen to one another · Though we don't know why · It made sense when we were · Together, it made sense to cry · How we hold out our arms · Fold them around each others pain · But in the end we gain nothing

Oh, forever wondering what could've been · If you hadn't walked away and both of us leaned · On our wishes and words, they went unheard · We weren't heard, heard · We got hurt, hurt

Unassisted we learned, it was so long ago · That our hearts got their turn, in a world they didn't know · And a battle we'd fight, at a price we couldn't pay · It was soul that we lost · But it's too close to say

So, how does it feel now all the way over there · Different friends in different places · We try not to care · But I wont understand, what breaks these things up · It was love I was told, but you put a stop · This isn't love anymore · This isn't love anymore

Unassisted we learned, it was so long ago · That our hearts got their turn, in a world they didn't know · And a battle we'd fight, at a price we couldn't pay · It was soul that we lost · But it's too close to say

If we were to think about · Where this would go · Would we leave it to the other hearts, and ask them to show · If they care! · How they care!

Unassisted we learned, it was so long ago · That our hearts got their turn, in a world they didn't know · And a battle we'd fight, at a price we couldn't pay · It was soul that we lost · But it's too close to say

THE US

I took my time, and got a little lost · I was not told, and had a feeling I'd been crossed · If you think I'm looking a little grey · It's just the way I'm feeling these days

Is this the us you've fallen for? · If it is then we're done for · Is this the us you've fallen for · I guess it's what we all long for

If we'd have thought about the walls we'd have to climb · Would we see this through and feel like everything was just fine? · If you see me looking the other way · It's just the way I'm looking these days

Is this the us you've fallen for? · If it is then we're done for · Is this the us you've fallen for · I guess it's what we all long for

ANOTHER PICTURE OF YOU

All the lights went out · Across the town tonight · I saw a figure and I saw bright white · Started walking the wrong way home · Though I was lost, I learned a little and at no cost · How we're feeling by the end, left us cold enough

It's just another picture of, picture of you · What am I, what am I supposed to do? · It's just another place, I went to with you · What am I, what am I supposed to do?

Everything was said · But would you stop and listen · Because it's heart we're missing · We'll get ourselves back home · Though we're still lost · We learned a great deal and at no cost · How we're feeling by the end, left us cold enough · For some reason, I hit the floor when I got in

It's just another picture of, picture of you · What am I, what am I supposed to do? · It's just another place, I went to with you · What am I, what am I supposed to do?

t

Research and Development's Favorite Gill Sans Letter is "t".

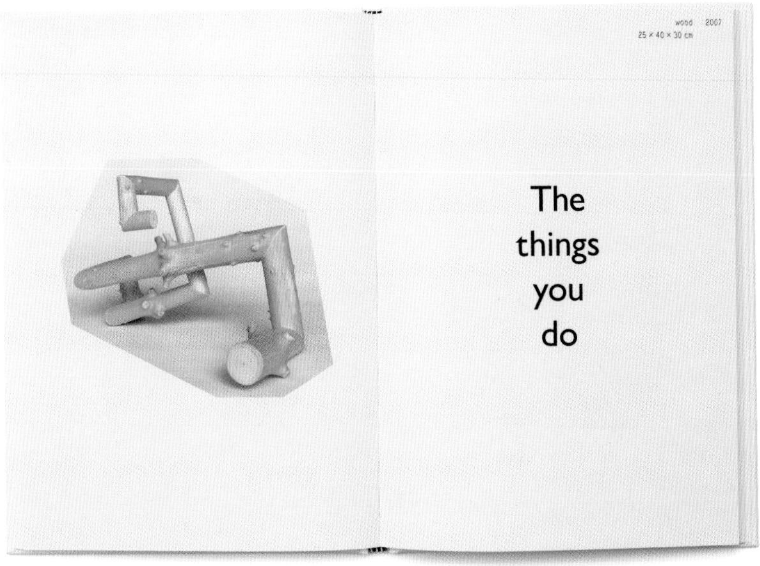

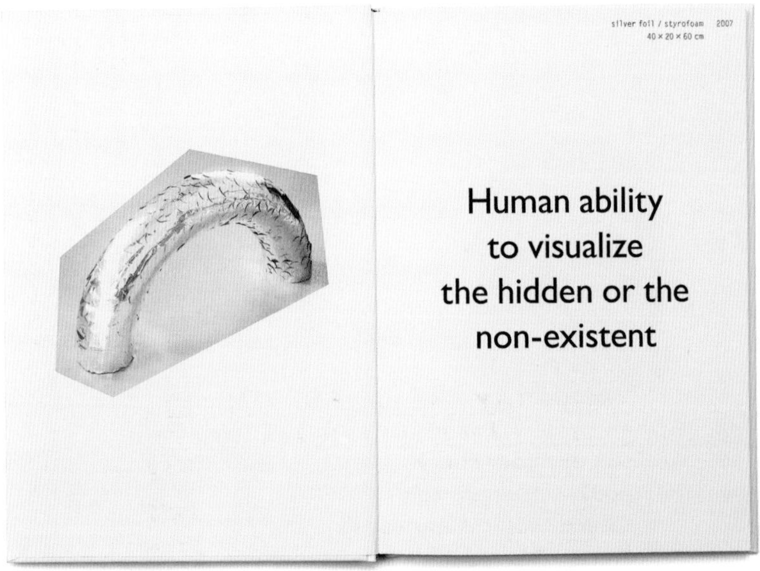

silver foil / styrofoam 2007
40 × 20 × 60 cm
Human ability to visualize the hidden or the non-existent

Typeface in Use
Gill Sans, Letter Gothic

"For us, it was challenging to use a typeface that for a long time has been badly treated."

ink on paper / cardboard / linen / glue 2007
17 × 24 × 1 cm
Jonas NOBEL
The memory
of this experience
will fade
and you will
eventually die
I'm sorry
I'm so very very
sorry

Jonas Nobel
The memory of this experience will fade and you will eventually die, I'm sorry, I'm so very very sorry
2007 — Monograph
Client Galleri Charlotte Lund
Design Research and Development

Hardcover with a selection of works by artist Jonas Nobel. The book is treated as the works described in it. Title, material and dimensions mentioned on front cover. Objects and titles are treated equally at the spreads as they are of equal importance in Nobel's work.

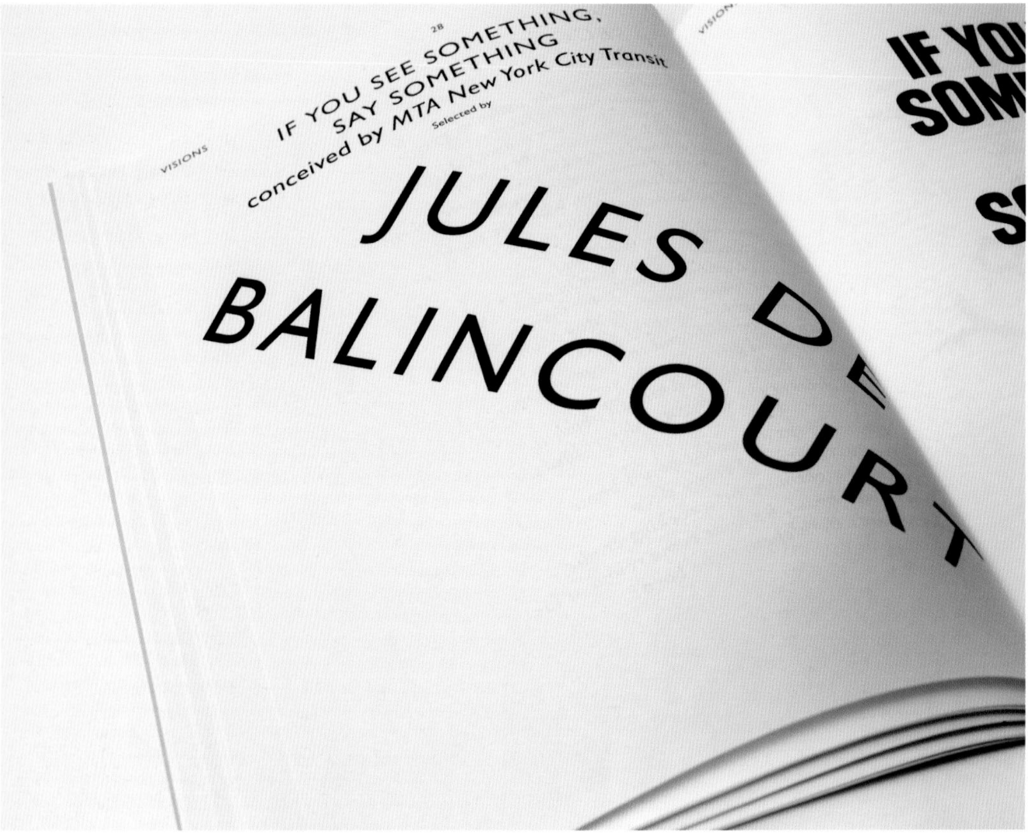

VISIONS
2011 — Exhibition Catalog
Client Monica de Cardenas Gallery
Design Studio Laucke Siebein

The catalog was designed on the occasion of the exhibition about visionary painting of five artists at Monica de Cardenas Gallery, Milan. The painters (Ali Banisadr, Jules de Balincourt, Tomory Dodge, Barnaby Furnas, Ryan Mosley) had chosen a piece of literature that complements their work — each is represented in a different typeface. The main typeface for the book is Gill Sans Regular, we used it with caps, italics, letter spacing and slightly oversized. The catalog starts with an image part on glossy paper, followed by the extensive text part.

Typeface in Use
Gill Sans Std Regular et al.

"Gill Sans is composed in a humanist as well as geometric manner that fitted best to the paintings in the book which are between figuration and abstraction."

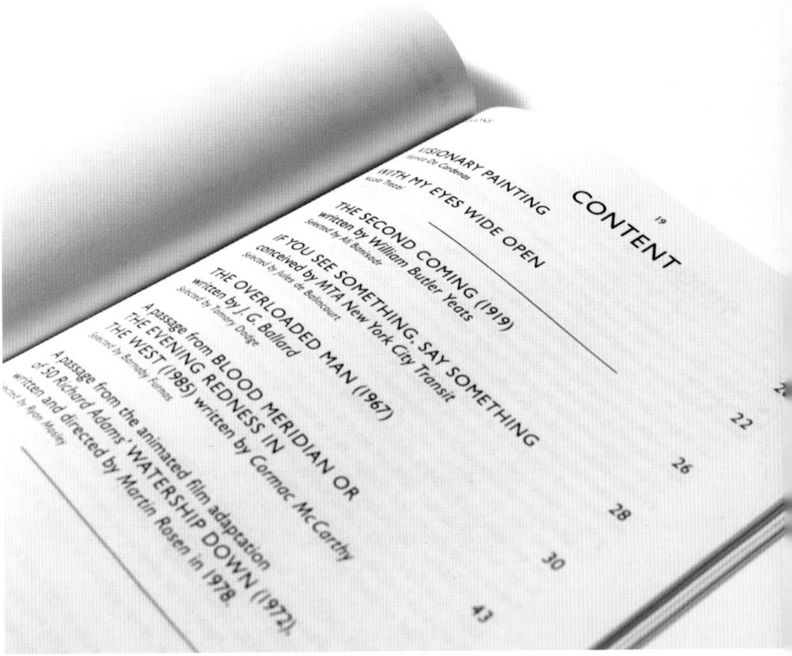

Jules de Balincourt — City Dwellers and Star Seekers, 2010
Oil on panel, 15 3/4 × 18 1/2 × 2 1/3 inches, 40 × 47 × 6 cm
Ali Banisadr — Jules de Balincourt — Tomory Dodge
— Barnaby Furnas — Ryan Mosley
VISIONS
MONICA DE CARDENAS GALLERIA

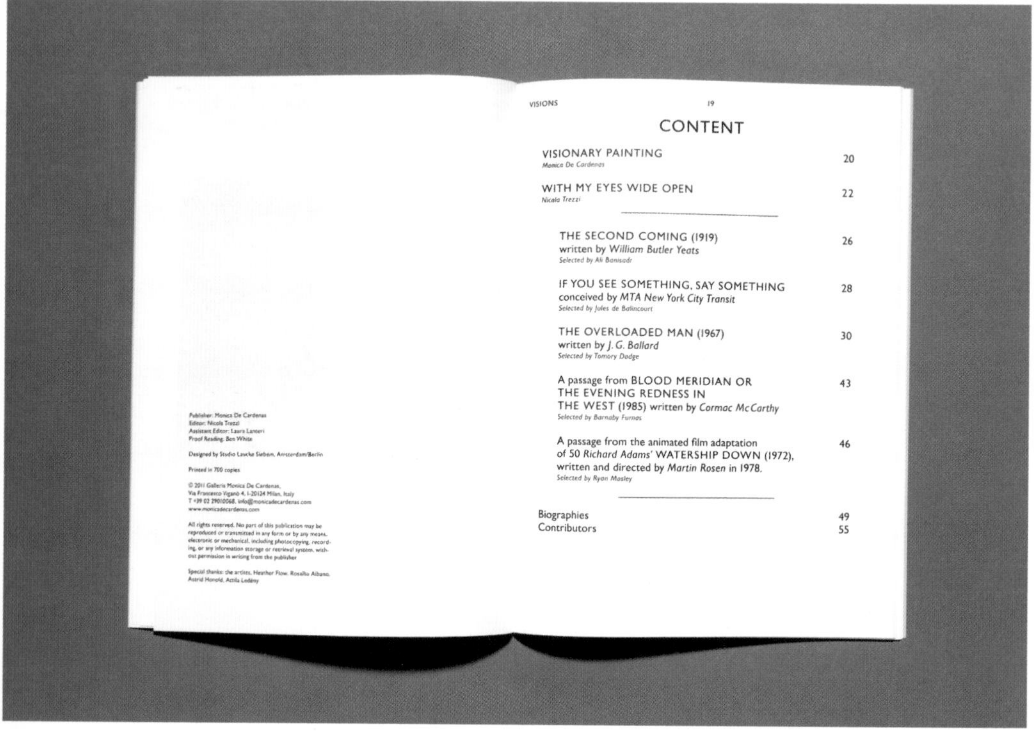
Publisher: Monica De Cardenas
Editor: Nicola Trezzi
Assistant Editor: Laura Lanteri
Proof Reading: Ben White
Designed by Studio Laucke Siebein, Amsterdam/Berlin
Printed in 700 copies
© 2011 Galleria Monica De Cardenas,
Via Francesco Viganò 4, I-20124 Milan, Italy
T +39 02 29010068, info@monicadecardenas.com
www.monicadecardenas.com
All rights reserved. No part of this publication may be reproduced or transmitted in any form or by any means, electronic or mechanical, including photocopying, recording, or any information storage or retrieval system, without permission in writing from the publisher
Special thanks: the artists, Heather Flow, Rosalba Albano, Astrid Honold, Attila Ledény
VISIONS 19
CONTENT
VISIONARY PAINTING 20
Monica De Cardenas
WITH MY EYES WIDE OPEN 22
Nicola Trezzi
THE SECOND COMING (1919) 26
written by William Butler Yeats
Selected by Ali Banisadr
IF YOU SEE SOMETHING, SAY SOMETHING 28
conceived by MTA New York City Transit
Selected by Jules de Balincourt
THE OVERLOADED MAN (1967) 30
written by J. G. Ballard
Selected by Tomory Dodge
A passage from BLOOD MERIDIAN OR THE EVENING REDNESS IN THE WEST (1985) written by Cormac McCarthy 43
Selected by Barnaby Furnas
A passage from the animated film adaptation of 50 Richard Adams' WATERSHIP DOWN (1972), written and directed by Martin Rosen in 1978. 46
Selected by Ryan Mosley
Biographies 49
Contributors 55

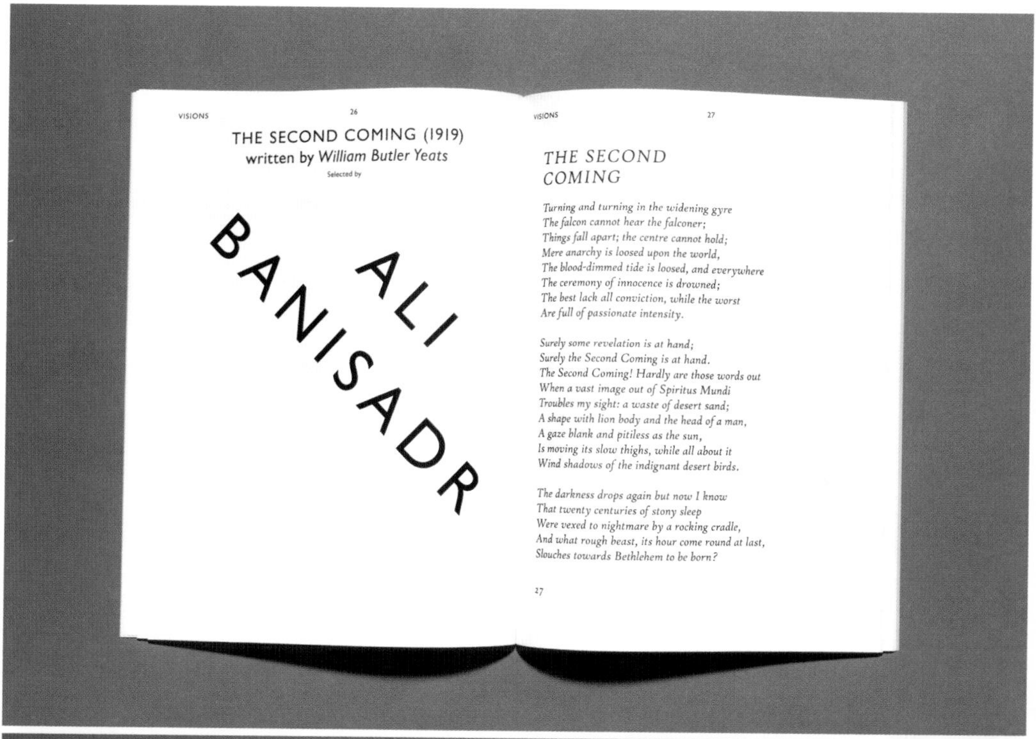

VISIONS 26

THE SECOND COMING (1919)

written by *William Butler Yeats*

Selected by

ALI BANISADR

VISIONS 27

THE SECOND COMING

Turning and turning in the widening gyre
The falcon cannot hear the falconer;
Things fall apart; the centre cannot hold;
Mere anarchy is loosed upon the world,
The blood-dimmed tide is loosed, and everywhere
The ceremony of innocence is drowned;
The best lack all conviction, while the worst
Are full of passionate intensity.

Surely some revelation is at hand;
Surely the Second Coming is at hand.
The Second Coming! Hardly are those words out
When a vast image out of Spiritus Mundi
Troubles my sight: a waste of desert sand;
A shape with lion body and the head of a man,
A gaze blank and pitiless as the sun,
Is moving its slow thighs, while all about it
Wind shadows of the indignant desert birds.

The darkness drops again but now I know
That twenty centuries of stony sleep
Were vexed to nightmare by a rocking cradle,
And what rough beast, its hour come round at last,
Slouches towards Bethlehem to be born?

27

VISIONS 22

WITH MY EYES WIDE OPEN

Nicola Trezzi

"Look wide, and even when you think you are looking wide – look wider still."
Robert Baden-Powell

At eight-year old and with my mother's guidance, I became a member of the local scout association, following in the footsteps of my older siblings who had already joined the club. Having learned about the movement's founder Robert Baden-Powell and his sociological theories and practice at school, my mother felt that Scoutism should be a very important aspect of our education. So, I joined at eight and left the movement at twenty-four – only because of my imminent move to the Unites States. Scoutism had a great impact on who I am and how I see and how I understand reality.

The most interesting twist happened when I applied to the Brera Academy of Fine Art in Milan and began to learn about the contemporary art scene. On one side I was doing social service with the scouts and on the other side I was learning about Joseph Beuys and his notion of "Social Sculpture," his direct engagement with political issues and with society. I was assisting scout leaders with kids or serve meals to the homeless and at the same time I was discovering the early works by Rirkrit Tiravanija in which he would serve Thai food to the visitors for the entire duration of a gallery show. I would experience long moments of absolute solitude, meditation and silent – "desert," that's how scouts call them. And during the explorers' camps eat frugal meals and wash in a freezing-cold river, something that generated a strange and amusing kind of déjà vu when I saw a clip featuring Marina Abramović's performance workshops.[1]

Since my time at the academy, I always tend to associate these two sides of my life, which apparently could not be more separate. I seek connections between the works by artists I admire and ideas generated by my sixteen-year experience as a scout in Italy. As strange as it may seem, while looking at the work, and thinking about the practices of Ali Banisadr, Jules de Balincourt, Tomory Dodge, Barnaby Furnas and Ryan Mosley, I have the same *epiphany*.[2] The skill I improved the most during my training as a scout was my *vision*. Good Scoutism teaches you to be visionary. Sometimes being visionary means that you have to pretend to be a character of Rudyard Kipling's *The Jungle Book*, an animal precisely.[3] No one can call you with your real name because you are Bagheera, the panther, or Akela, the wolf. During junior camps, time was suspended – like in many paintings of the aforementioned artists. Being a visionary meant sharing a meal with the parents and relatives of friends I have been playing with in the Serbian block of Sarajevo; "Paddle Your Own Canoe"[4] or walking under a hallucinating sun for hours with an enormous backpack, your tent in your hands while looking for the place where you will stay for the night. All of this is to say that Scoutism is about establishing a link between everyday life and an outer reality that is different, special and unique. The most important thing is not the other reality, but instead the *link* – the *vision*, in other words – between that reality and our everyday reality. This is why the scouts go very often outside metropolitan settings in order to embrace nature. This is not an exile, quite the opposite. The encounter with nature must begin and end because the real goal is to go back to the city so you can experience the city as a jungle, an adventurous and sometimes dangerous metropolitan jungle.

When I see the paintings of Ali Banisadr, Jules de Balincourt, Tomory Dodge, Barnaby Furnas and Ryan Mosley I have the feeling that these artists have been to a journey and brought us back visions from that journey. They are all *linked* to something we don't know about – their works are diaries from an outer reality and their attachment to reality is not under discussion. These artists need to go to this other world in

VISIONS 23

order to come back to normality and look at it through the filter of their vision. It is not about escaping, but rather about going out and coming in, building up and breaking down every moment of the everyday life. Banisadr, de Balinbourt, Dodge, Furnas, and Mosley open a window for the unexpected.

To some extent, the attitude through which I would like to approach their practices would be similar to that of Italian novelist Emilio Salgari. During his life, Salgari wrote more than 200 adventure tales set in exotic locations, with heroes from a wide variety of cultures. Without ever leaving Italy, he gained inspiration from foreign literature, newspapers, travel magazines and encyclopedias, which created a plethora of visions populated by pirates, outlaws and barbarians, fighting against greed, abuse of power, and corruption. In his books I see the elements present also in the works of the five artists I am about to explain: exoticism, poetry, history, fiction ... you name it!

The work of Ali Banisadr is not only poetic it is indeed pure poetry. A keen reader of poetry himself, Banisadr seems to invite viewers to a universe that is as quiet as it is chaotic. His paintings, often rendered with oil paint applied on linen canvas, are lyrical to a level that sometimes you forget the hints of figuration he injects within the composition and you just want to follow the rhythm and set your spirit free from any kind of constraint set by the rules of representation. For his show at Leslie Tonkonow in New York, Amanda Church writes: "In Iranian artist Ali Banisadr's show of explosive, exuberant canvases it's hard to pinpoint the exact nature of the action, but there's a lot of it, and it's compellingly allusive. The exhibition's title, "It Happened and It Never Did," suggests a sort of political machination that merges fact and fiction. With their amassing of so many small marks and strokes in a palette variously fiery or verdant, his paintings are riotous and chaotic, creating scenes of what could be either paradise or a battlefield."[5]

If for Banisadr poetry is the outer world, then for Jules de Balincourt[6] everything starts with images found online. These found images become the prime material – the starting point for his visionary paintings exclusively created with his unique and signature technique. American politics, tourism, war, an apocalyptic future, propaganda, security and labor: these are the themes of his paintings. Bob Nickas states: "Central to de Balincourt's project is the appearance of the work as immediate, graphic, making no claims to painted virtuosity and yet visually sophisticated in its execution. Painted on board, he often incises the surface to delineate simply rendered figures and scenes. He plays vibrant, keyed-up color against whites, grays, deep blues and black, or off of lightly stained or bare board. (...) De Balincourt's state of unease extends to the escapism of his own generation, as well as to the recent art which skims the surface of '60s/'70s art and culture and celebrates itself as 'radical' or 'free'."[7]

The more a viewer visually inspects the work of Tomory Dodge, the more he sees the near collapse of the border between abstraction and figuration. Brushstrokes applied freely and yet in a very disciplined fashion can be found in abstract compositions as well as in figurative imageries. Even the titles swings from being descriptive – *After Party, Delta, Inside Out* – to free associative and lyrical – *Siren Sound, Cloud Chamber, However*. According to Sarah Douglas: "Dodge is concerned with the intersection of nature and culture. In one, a forest floor is strewn with beer cans and sundry other detritus, and strings of Christmas light are draped from the trees – leftovers from revelry of some kind or another. Dodge paints a barren tree, its branches festooned with beer bottles, set against the sky of powdery Tiepolo blue. In another painting, a tree or shrub, set in a lush green landscape, seems to explode into parti-colored brushstrokes, and in yet another, the entire surface is taken by such energetic brushstrokes, to the point of near-total abstraction."[8]

History, political figures, images of disasters and war are the subjects around which Barnaby Furnas builds his complex and technically compelling works of art. Urethane and spirits on burnt calfskin vellum, urethane and dye on linen, urethane on burned goatskin are the almost alchemic techniques the artist uses to depict historical figures like John Brown, a radical abolitionist who waged a terror campaign on Southern slave owners, or effigies of symbolic figures

O

Yann Alary & Martin Selle's Favorite Gill Sans Letter is "O".

Typeface in Use
Gill Sans Bold, Ultra Bold

"For its strength and presence of the Gill Sans, and at the same time for a round, likeable and attractive side."

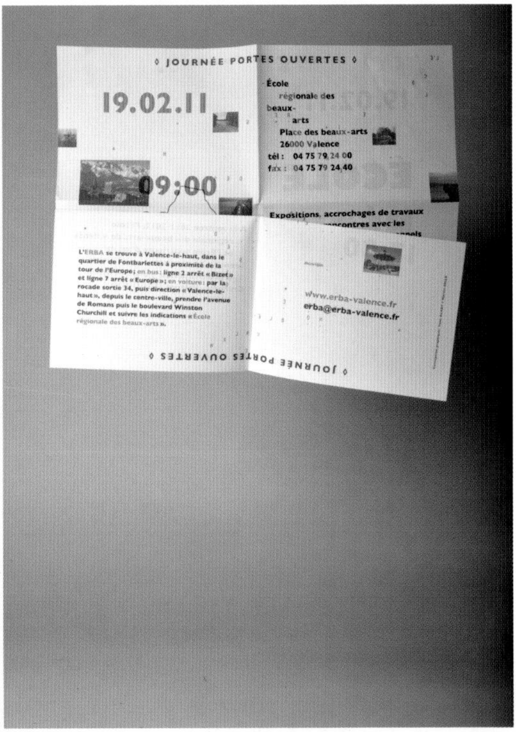

Portes Ouvertes
ERBA Valence 2011
2011 — Poster
Client ERBA Valence
Design Yann Alary, Martin Selle

The project evolved at the same time as the Beaux Arts in Valence was merging with the Beaux Arts in Grenoble to become one sole institution. There were tight guidelines to be considered a 400mm x 600mm folding brochure that became a poster as the user opened it out and began reading the information contained within. We tried to answer by a composition and a typographic calibrations which prioritizes information and make the reading easier. The iconographic choice highlighted the itinerary between the two schools as well as an interactive card on line even though only the name of Valence is used in this version. A screen application for web was developed and shows each time the user afresh, a different version of the poster with randomly treated images, typography, composition (size, position, layout). This process tries to question the place of poster in digital and more globally, digital evolutive identity.

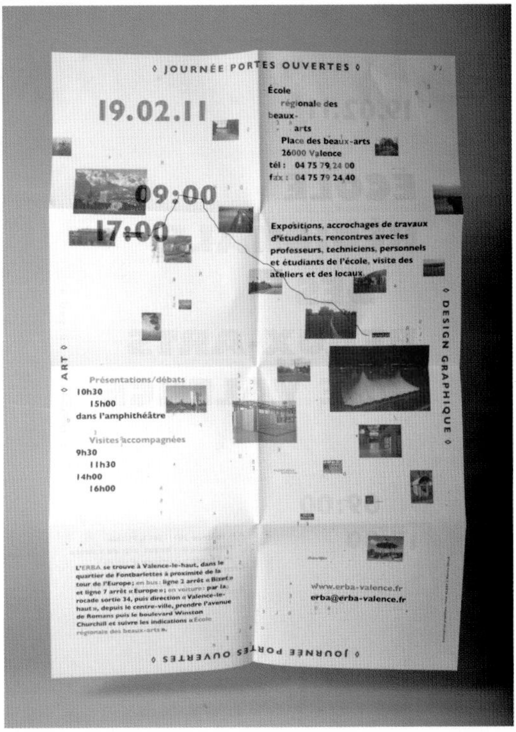

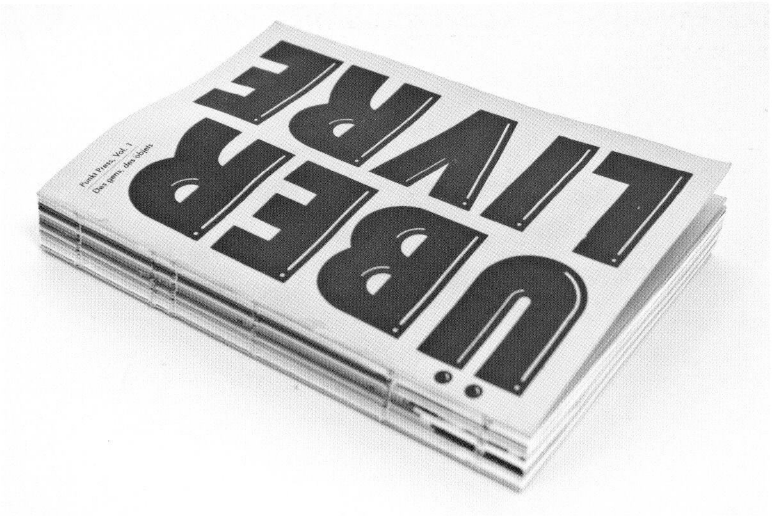

Punkt Press vol.1
2011 — Booklet
Client Atelier Punkt
Design Emmanuel Plougoulm, Château-vacant

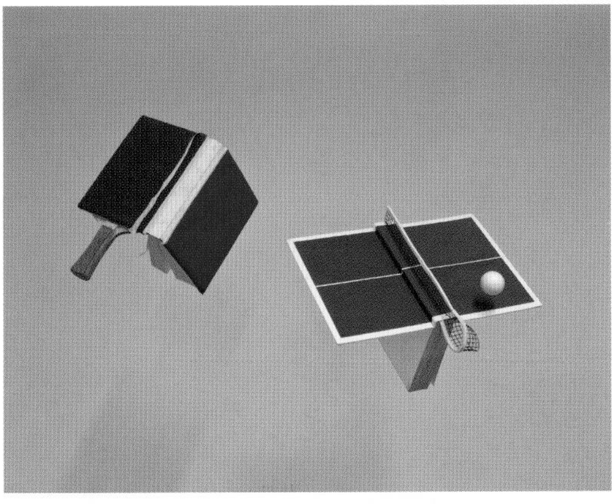

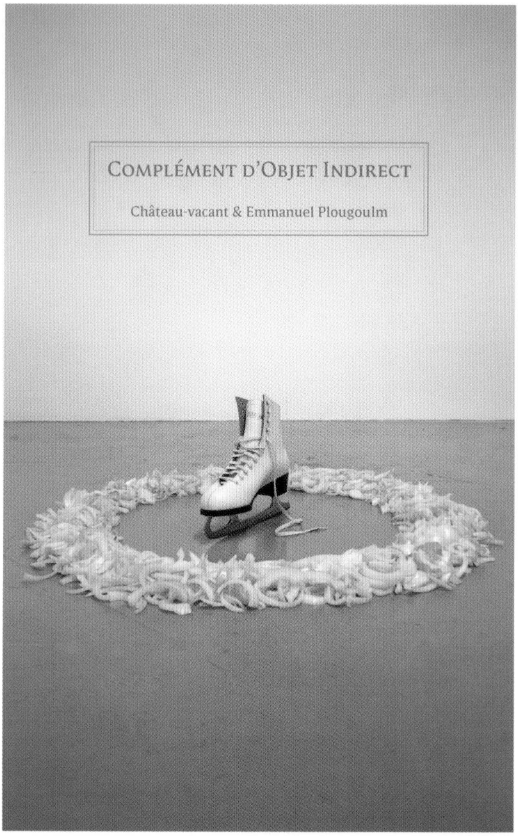
Complément d'Objet Indirect
Château-vacant & Emmanuel Plougoulm

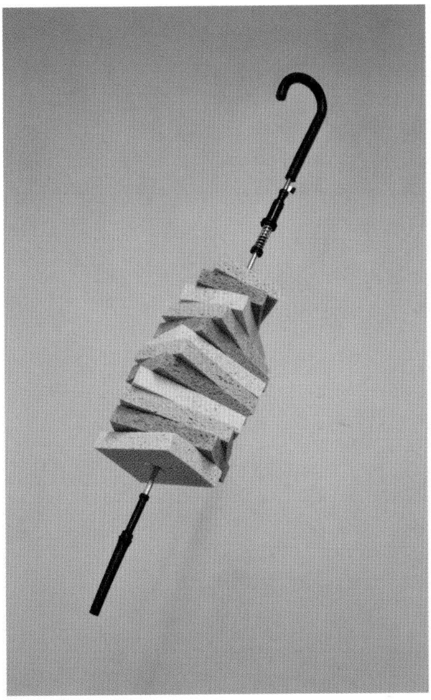

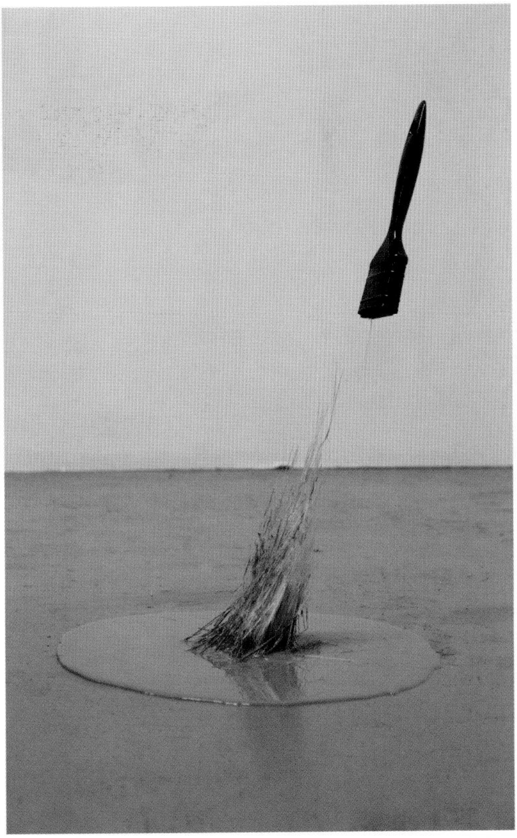

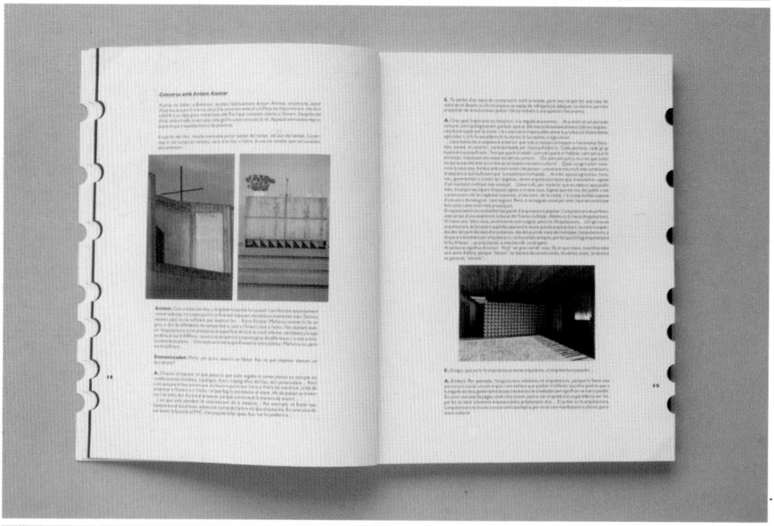

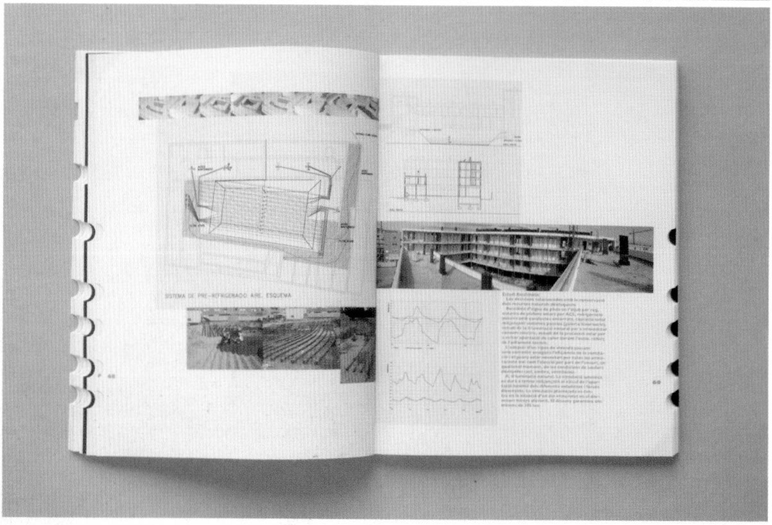

Premis d'Arquitectura de Mallorca 2004-06
2008 — Editorial Design
Client Col·legi Oficial d'Arquitectes de les Illes Balears
Design Folch Studio

This publication collects all the selected works in between 2004 and 2006 of architectural projects made by the architectural bureaus of the Balearic Island. The book pretends to be a useful publication. The index is shown on the cover and the "nail marks" guide the user straight from the cover to the content.

"We decided to use Gill Sans because of its rich family and the Extra Bold version. We were looking for a unique typeface which would help us to visualize all the hierarchies of the book."

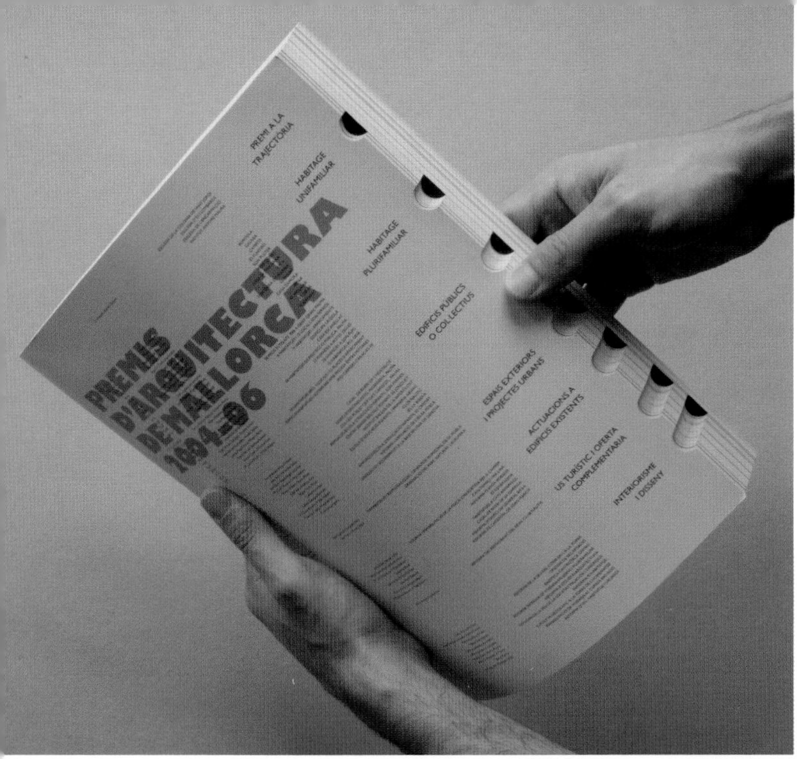

Typeface in Use
Gill Sans Ultra Bold, Extra Bold, Regular, Light, Italic

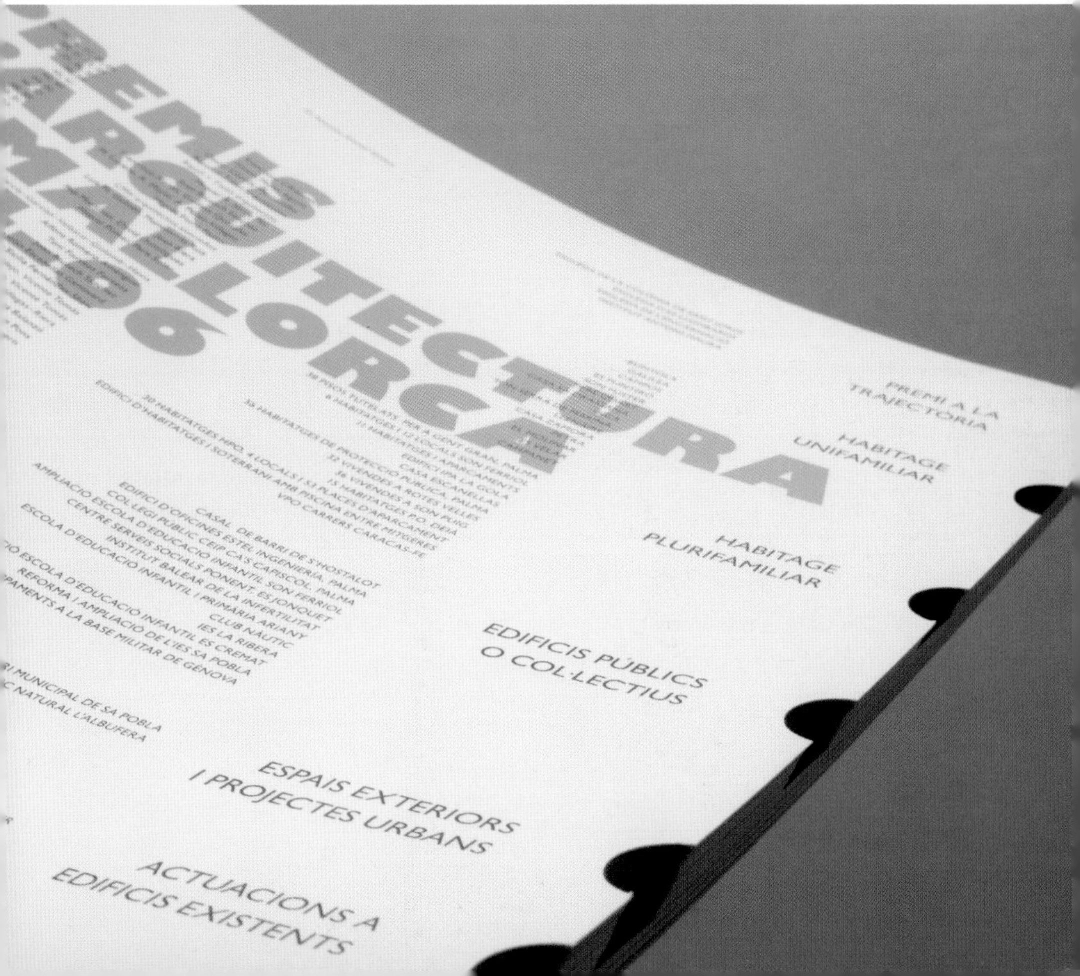

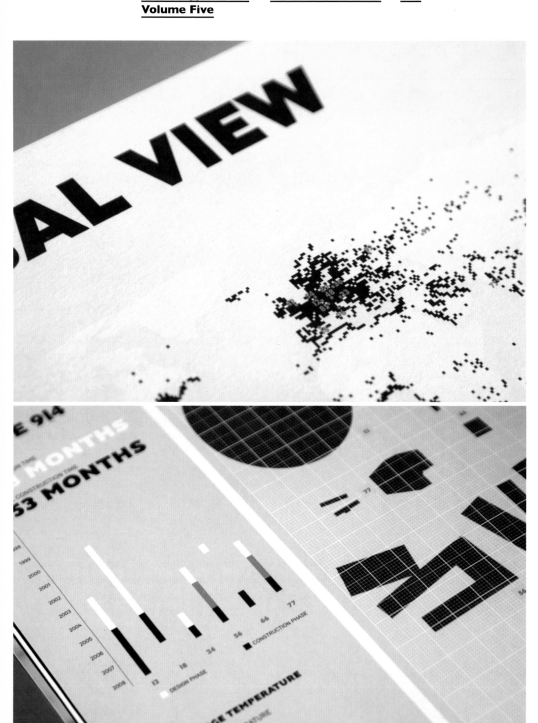

AL VIEW

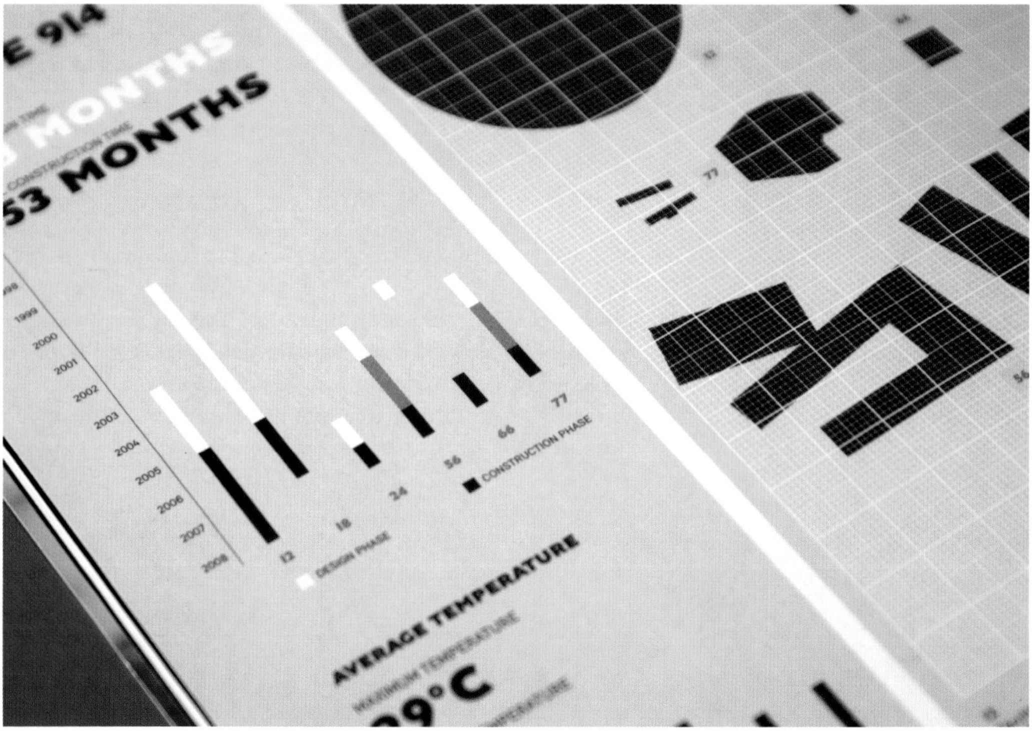
E 914
53 MONTHS
1999
2000
2001
2002
2003
2004
2005
2006
2007
2008
12
18
24
56
66
77
DESIGN PHASE
CONSTRUCTION PHASE
AVERAGE TEMPERATURE
°C

Domus Magazine
2008-10
— Magazine
Client Editorial Domus, Milan, Italy
Design Onlab (Nicolas Bourquin, Sven Ehmann, Linda Hintz, Thibaud Tissot)
Type Design Mika Mischler

Founded and edited by the Milanese architect Gio Ponti, the first issue of the monthly magazine *Domus* came out on 15 January 1928. Over the course of eighty years of history, the magazine changed regularly to reflect the demands and interest of the times but the aim of *Domus* has always remained that of creating a privileged insight into identifying the style of a particular age. Following the several redesigns (Ettore Sottsass, Alan Fletcher, Simon Esterson), onlab creates the new *Domus* starting with its April 2008 issue. As the magazine's editor-in-chief, Flavio Albanese, notes in the editorial, "With its new formal appearance, *Domus* has finally attained its objective of being a publication on the same wavelength as the Zeitgeist, the spirit of our times, that no longer accepts information and knowledge divided into water-tight compartments."

Typeface in Use
Gill Oroso, Relevant (Gill Oroso is based on Gill Sans Display Extra, that was created in the same year Domus was first published.)

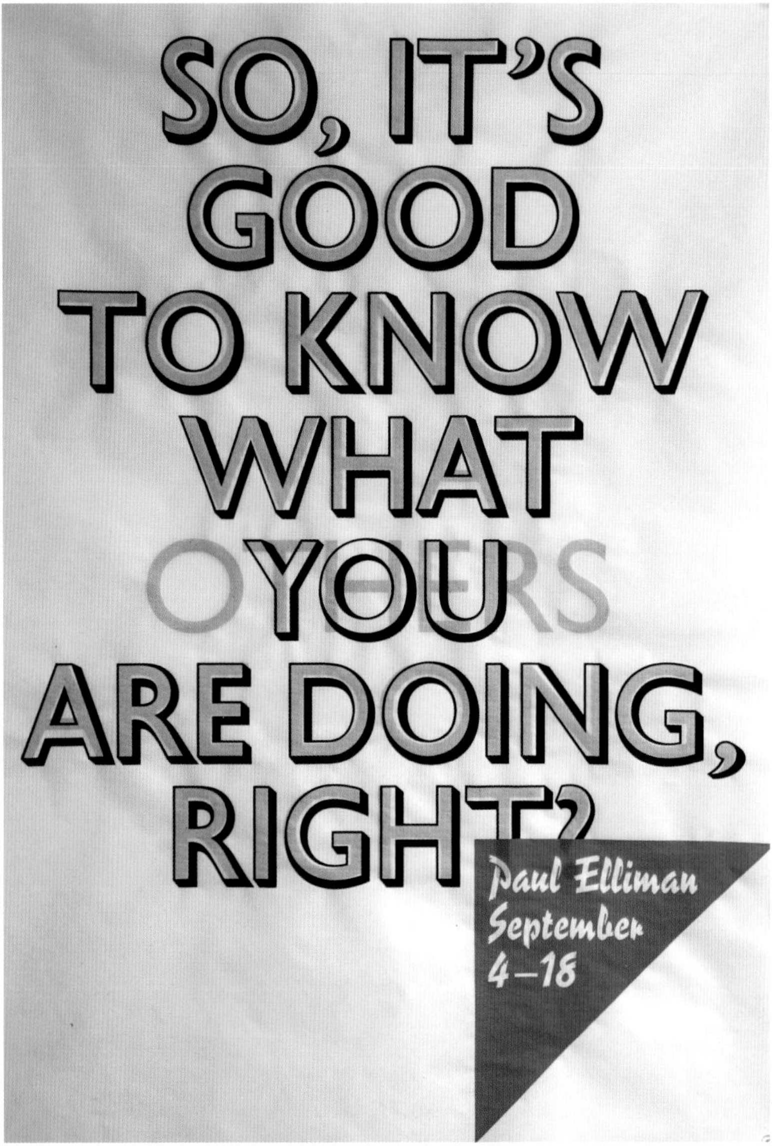
SO, IT'S
GOOD
TO KNOW
WHAT
OTHERS
YOU
ARE DOING,
RIGHT?
Paul Elliman
September
4–18

Paul Elliman Poster
2008 — Poster
Design Neil Donnelly

Paul Elliman's use of the same phrase with a pronoun replaced was a fitting encapsulation of his time at Yale, prompting us to consider the motivations behind both our own and others' work.

R

Neil Donnelly's Favorite Gill Sans Letter is "R".

Typeface in Use
Gill Sans Shadowed, Reporter

"I liked the correspondence between Gill Sans Regular and Shadowed, but also that they weren't meant to nest and don't fit perfectly together. There's an obvious relation, but the two are still a slightly awkward pair."

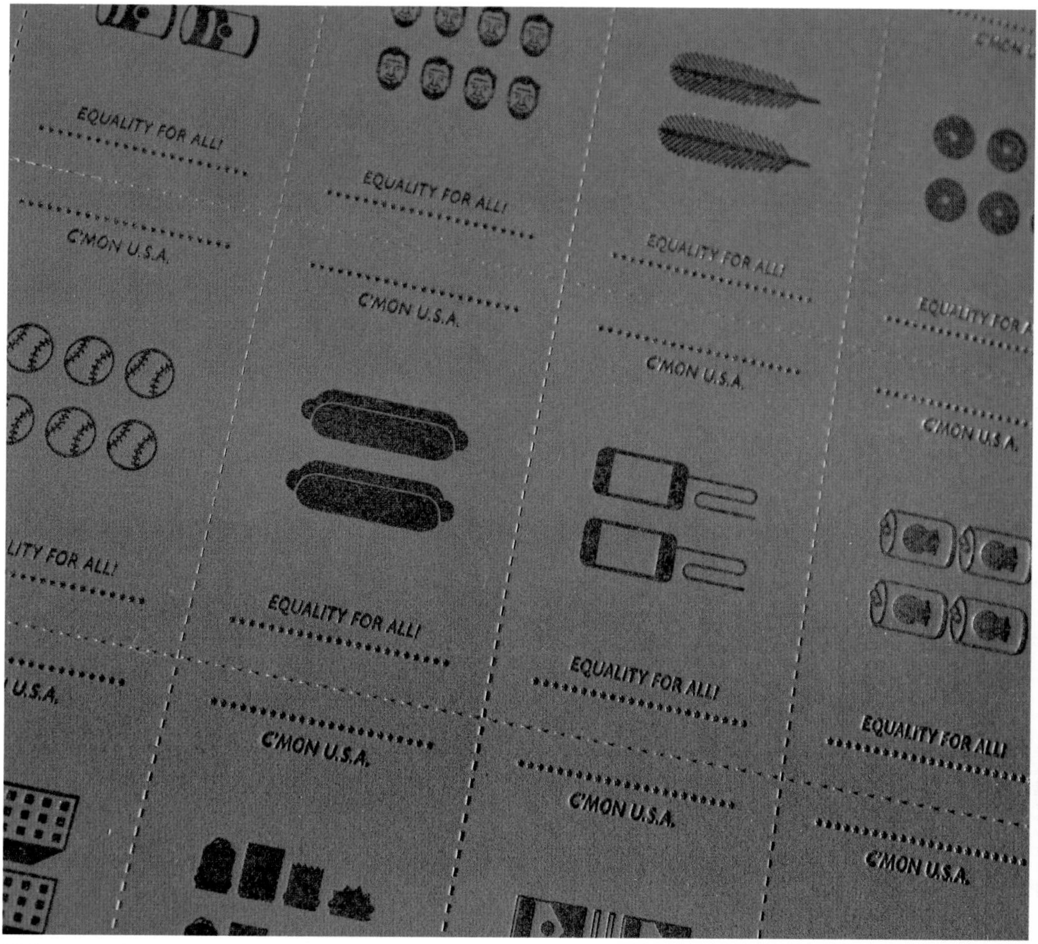

"The typeface was chosen for it's distinct character, its openness and its elegance."

C'mon USA
2010 — Poster
Design Susana Londoño

I was working under constraints, a one week assignment. The work is the response to a randomly assigned aesthetic and thematic criteria — color: Green, typeface: Gill Sans, concept: Gettysburg Address, format: poster. The poster was handsilkscreened green and letterpressed with black ink. Perforations allow the poster to be divided into individual pieces.

Q

Susana Londoño's Favorite Gill Sans Letter is "Q".

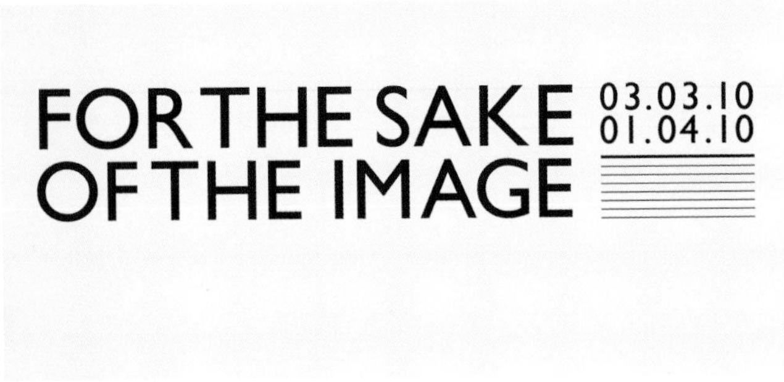

For the Sake of the Image
Client Jerwood Charitable Foundation
Design Teacake (Graham Sykes, Robert Walmsley)

"In this instance it was due to Gill Sans's open yet technical appearance. It looks great when widely kerned and manages to retain a classic non-obtrusive aesthetic without sacrificing style and impact which is essential for exhibition work of this nature. The variable weights also ensured we could use this typeface alone throughout building a much bigger impact in our promotion."

Curated by artist Suki Chan *For the Sake of the Image* investigated the reciprocal relationship between moving image and sound. With six artists all exhibiting very different pieces ranging from animated sculpture to documentary video installations, this body of work included invites, posters, gallery signage and a custom designed DVD package presenting a showreel of the collection on display.

FOR THE SAKE
OF THE IMAGE
FOR THE SAKE
OF THE IMAGE
ASNAT AUSTERLITZ
RICHARD BEVAN
SUKI CHAN
JUAN FONTANIVE
PAUL O'KANE
MARK RAIDPERE
DAN WALWIN

FOR THE SAKE
OF THE IMAGE
03.03.10
01.04.10

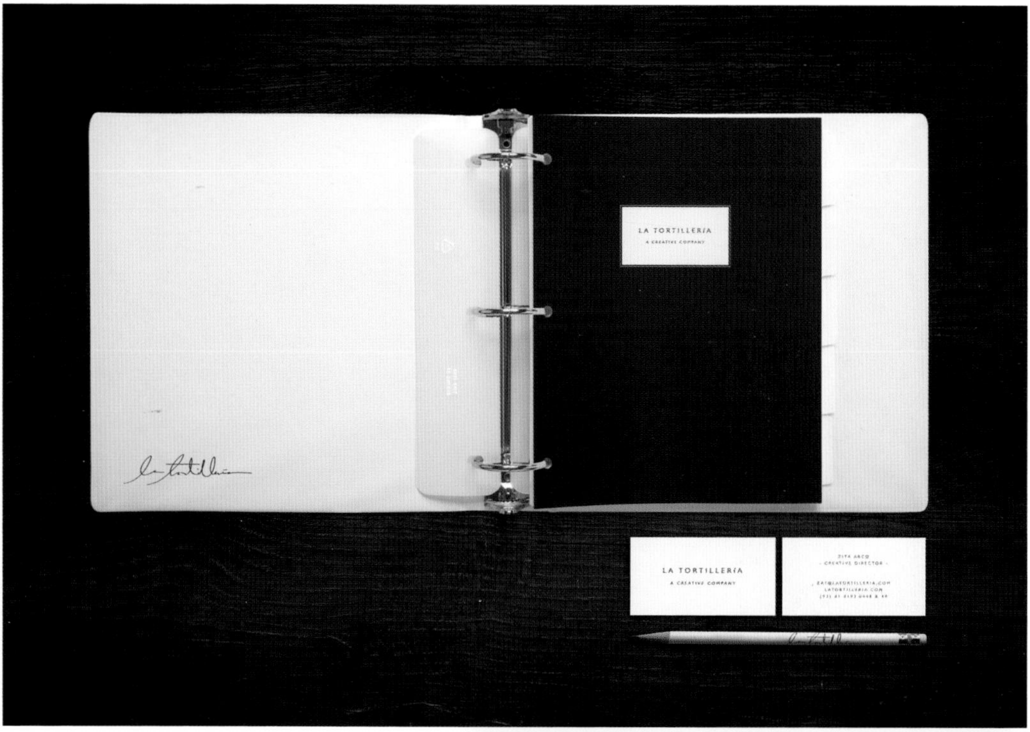

Typeface in Use
Gill Sans

"We fell in love with Gill Sans the moment we discovered typography itself."

La Tortillería
A Creative Company
2011 — Identity
Design La Tortillería (Zita Arcq, Sonia Saldaña, Carolina Díaz)

Our very simple identity.

R

La Tortillería's Favorite Gill Sans Letter is "R".

Gordon Millar Award
2011 — Award, Online Presence
Client SAE Foundation
Design moodley brand identity

The new Gordon Millar Award honours individuals and organizations that demonstrate philanthropic support of the SAE Foundation (Society of the Automotive Engineers) which promotes science students and young engineers. The design for this award created by moodley is a placard that is not only visual but also tactile representing the way young engineers learn (leather-like paper, sealing wax, foil embossed lettering). The font used for the logo is Gill Sans. The eclectic use of diverse other fonts creates a visual whole.

"I love the personality of Gill Sans — a Grotesque with a lot of characteristic."
Kurt Glänzer

G

moodley's Favorite Gill Sans Letter is "G".

THE GORDON MILLAR AWARD

Bureau Mirko Borsche
www.mirkoborsche.com

Bureau Mirko Borsche is a munich based graphic design studio founded by Mirko Borsche in 2007. The studio has been producing numerous projects such as magazines, catalogs, books, posters, typefaces, identities, industrial design, fashion design, exhibition design, movies and websites. Their clients are from the fields of culture and business.
-pp. 36-43, 52-55, 87

Carolina Andreoli
www.carolinaandreoli.com

A graphic designer made in Brazil but living in London.
-pp. 93

Charlie Berendsen
www.charlieberendsen.nl

The work of Charlie Berendsen (1990, the Netherlands) lies in the field of information design, where data (input) and poetics (output) meet after the link (design). Charlie studied at the Interaction Design department at ArtEZ Academy of Arts Arnhem.
-pp. 92

Chris Svensson
christophersvensson.org

Chris Svensson lives and works mostly in Los Angeles, California.
-pp. 34-35

Christian Brandt
www.christianbrandt.org

Christian Brandt works in different fields of graphic design and develops solutions for identities, posters packaging, book design, editorial design, typefaces etc. He believes in strong ideas and strive to push boundaries based on conceptual thinking.
-pp. 80

Clase bcn
www.clasebcn.com

Clase bcn is a graphic design and visual communication studio in Barcelona made of a team of ten young, international, multidisciplinary professionals whose work has won a number of awards. They work on all areas of design, but pay particular attention to typefaces and the element of surprise.
-pp. 122-123

David Pearson Design
davidpearsondesign.com

David previously worked in-house at Penguin Books as typographer and later, cover designer before leaving to set up his own studio in August 2007. He has won numerous awards for book design and has been listed as one of Britain's Top 50 Designers by the Guardian as well as being nominated for the Design Museum's Designer of the Year Award.
-pp. 58-63

deValence
www.devalence.net

deValence was established in 2001 by Alexandre Dimos and Gaël Etienne, who were joined by Ghislain Triboulet in 2007. The studio seeks to develop a distinctive approach to graphic design, visual communication and type design. Its output, structured by editorial content and a strong relationship with type, spans catalogues, artist book, posters and magazines, as well as visual identities and signage.
-pp. 78-79

Doeller & Satter
www.doeller-satter.com

Doeller & Satter is an independent graphic design studio based in Frankfurt am Main, Germany, runned by Sandra Doeller and Michael Satter who founded it in 2010. The studio mainly works in the field of printed matter such as books, art catalogs, magazines, and posters. It also develops logotypes, corporate design, branding, and websites. Doeller & Satter works both for customers and on self-initiated projects.
-pp. 12-13

El Studio / Pete Rossi
www.el-studio.co.uk
www.pgerossi.co.uk

El Studio is a creative graphic design studio which works in all aspects of brand identity. We partner companies and individuals that understand the importance of branding and embrace the true value of creative, effective design solutions. Our research, understanding, evaluation and creative processes aligns with strategical marketing objectives, visually communicating to our clients audiences. Our approach and expertise translates through all communication fields from print to digital. We are driven by a meticulously crafted attention to detail. Pete Rossi is a graphic designer, visual artist and maker of things. Pete was born just outside Glasgow, Scotland in 1981. His passions lie within Typography, Identity, Layout/Book design, Art and cultural issues. He is a firm believer in pushing boundaries within every creative avenue he seeks.
-pp. 118-119

Emmanuel Plougoulm & Château-vacant
emmanuelplougoulm.fr
www.château-vacant.com

Emmanuel is a french graphic designer especially interested in creating tangible materials. In November 2010, he got an one year scholarship at the Benetton's Research Center in Treviso, Italy. There he has been been working as a graphic designer and a videomaker for both COLORS magazine and the Video department. Lately, he has decided to extend this experience abroad by moving to Montreal.
Lémuel, Yannick and Baptiste, born in 1986,85,84 in France, built Château-vacant in march 2010 in Montréal, qc (Canada). They create images and videos thinking with objects & spaces. They are also involved in illustration, photography and graphic design.
-pp. 140-143

Estudio Ritxi Ostáriz
www.ritxiostariz.com

Estudio Ritxi Ostáriz is specialized in graphic and editorial design. Most of the projects are related with Culture and Music; art exhibitions catalogs, books, brochures, Cd artwork, posters, merchandise... This work also includes art direction and design for magazines and events, branding and identity, and websites.
-pp. 66, 95

Family / Daniel Westwood
www.designedbyfamily.com

Family is an award winning, multi-disciplinary design studio based in the UK, providing a unique and different approach to sectors such as music, fashion, culture and the arts.
-pp. 64-65

Folch Studio
www.folchstudio.com

Folch Studio was born in 2004 in the city of Barcelona, directed and managed by Albert Folch. The Studio specializes in editorial design, art direction, advertisement, corporative image, web design and video. FS works with national and international clients and projects. The studio has been featured in many national and international publications.
-pp. 144-145

G Design Studio
www.georgiougavrilakis.com

G is an award winning design studio located in the old city centre of Athens. A busy, noisy, dark, multinational scenery. They always seek to promote an idea. To create based on each project's specific and unique needs as assigned by our clients. The whole process is quite complicated as the final outcome should always facilitate public dialogue. They design for the public view.
-pp. 98-101

Geoffroy Tobé
www.geoffroytobe.com

Geoffroy Tobé graduated from the ESAG Penninghen, Paris and he's teaching graphic Design in the same school. He lives and works in Paris.
-pp. 82-83

gggrafik design
www.gggrafik.de

gggrafik was founded by Götz Gramlich in 2005. He was born in 1974. In 2005 he graduated from Communication Design at the University of Applied Arts Darmstadt. His thesis was "The typographical visualization of music" (Co-Professor Niklaus Troxler). From 2003 to 2005 he was an assistent in StudioTroxler in Willisau. Since 2005 he runs his own Studio in Heidelberg.
-pp. 94

Guilherme Falcão
www.guilhermefalcao.com

Guilherme Falcão Pelegrino is a graphic designer from São Paulo, Brazil. BA from the Senac College of Communication and Arts (2006) and currently a postgraduate student of Art: Critique and Curating at PUC/COGEAE (2011). His activities as a designer also include workshops, lectures, collaborations, self initiated projects such as the Parasite Zine and Pequeno Comitê, a think tank of cultural projects and ideas. His works have been featured in books and publications both inside and outside of Brazil.
-pp. 89

Helen Musselwhite
www.helenmusselwhite.com

Helen studied graphic design and illustration and has worked in the creative world ever since. Working with various paper types and nature as her muse Helen cuts, folds, scores and layers to create intriguing and intricate views into a fairytale world of flora and fauna.
-pp. 102

Hvass&Hannibal
www.hvasshannibal.dk

Hvass&Hannibal is a multidisciplinary arts and design studio based in Copenhagen. Since 2006, its founders, Nan Na Hvass & Sofie Hannibal have worked in close collaborative partnership with illustrative and conceptual design in a number of different fields for numerous clients in Europe, Asia and the US. Whether in the digital realm or on a three-dimensional scale, the studio takes projects from illustrative beginnings to a full art direction and graphic design solution, all in-house.
-pp. 68-69

Isabel Seiffert
www.isabelseiffert.com

Isabel Seiffert graduated from Merz Akademie in Stuttgart in early 2011 and started working for the BrandRetail Company LIGANOVA. She is now heading to Switzerland to start her Masters of Design at the Zurich University of Arts and concentrate on more integrated and interdisciplinary design projects.
-pp. 22-23

Jack Maxwell
www.jackmaxwell.co.uk

Jack Maxwell is a graphic Designer working and living in London. He works at an East London based user experience and product design studio designing interfaces for the worlds most successful brands.
-pp. 103

Jamie Keenan
www.keenandesign.com

Jamie Keenan set up his own studio in 1998 and has since worked mainly for European and American book publishers. His work has been recognised by the D&AD and AIGA among others, and he has talked about and exhibited his work at the School of Visual Arts in New York, for the BNO in the Netherlands, as part of the Gateways series in Portugal and at the British Library in London.
-pp. 73

Jenny Tondera
www.jennytondera.com

Jenny Tondera is a graphic designer and art director currently living and working in Philadelphia. Originally from the Detroit area, she received her BFA from the Minneapolis College of Art and Design. She has worked with such clients as: Urban Outfitters, Topman UK, photographer Alec Soth, University of Notre Dame, Mercedes-Benz USA, DePaul University, Philadelphia Photo Arts Center, and Adobe. Her work has been exhibited at the Walker Art Center and the Cranbrook Academy of Art.
-pp. 44-45

Josep Román
www. joseproman.com

Josep Román graduated in Technical Engineering in Industrial Design at Elisava design school in Barcelona in 2009. Afterwards he started to study a bachelor in graphic design, combining it with an student exchange at Écal, University of Arts and Design of Lausanne, Switzerland. His favourite fields are editorial design, art direction, typography, illustration, corporate identity and website.
-pp. 24-27

jungundwenig
www.jungundwenig.com

Christopher Jung and Tobias Wenig met at the Academy of Visual Arts (HGB) in Leipzig in 1999. Among their professors were Cyan and Günter Karl Bose. In 2004 they founded Jung + Wenig (jung = young, und = and, wenig = little). Their work includes books, magazines, CD covers, film and multimedia works for clients in the cultural sector. Above all, they want their design to relate to the project; and the result should look good and make the client, consumers and the designers themselves happier. Most of the time they get the greatest satisfaction out of very small things: a letter that looks like an animal, an almost empty page with two or three good placed basic elements on it, a nice color or surface. It can be anything.
-pp. 16-21, 28-33

Jurgen Maelfeyt
www.jurgenmaelfeyt.be

Jurgen Maelfeyt studied graphic design at Sint-Lucas in Ghent (Belgium). In 2005 he started his own studio and works for cultural organisations, artists and publishers. In 2010 he founded APE (Art Paper Editions), a small independent publishing studio specializing in art, photography, illustration and typography.
-pp. 70-71

Killian Loddo
www.killianloddo.fr

After finishing a DSAA (Higher Degree of Applied

Arts) in graphic design in Nevers in 2009, Killian Loddo joined the Gerrit Rietveld Academy in Amsterdam, where he finished a bachelor in graphic design. He developed a graphic design activity and initiates in parallel personnal projects questionning boundaries between autonomous art graphics and fashion, he works regularly with the graphic designer Laurent Fetis and collaborates on various projects with the studio OfficeABC or with Parallel School of Art which is an active member.
-pp. 76-77

La Tortillería
www.latortilleria.com

One Creative Company. Two story agency. Three driven partners. Four talented designers.
-pp. 152-153

Lesley Moore
www.lesley-moore.nl

Lesley Moore is an Amsterdam-based graphic design agency, founded in May 2004 by Karin van den Brandt (1975, Blerick, The Netherlands) and Alex Clay (1974, Lørenskog, Norway). Van den Brandt and Clay studied at the Arnhem Academy of the Arts (The Netherlands). Merits include: European Design Awards for best Magazine 2008, Official selection Chaumont 2008, European Design Awards Miscellaneous and Jury Award 2007, Art Directors Club Netherlands 2007 and Dutch Design Awards 2007.
-pp. 104-105

Letra
www.letra.com.pt
www.random-press.com

Marco Balesteros is a graphic designer and editor, founder of studio Letra. Masters in Design and Typography by the Werkplaats Typografie (werkplaatstypografie.org), ArtEZ Institute of Arts, Arnhem — NL, 2009. Simultaneously with studio work, develops editorial and educational projects concerning self-publishing, together with Sofia Gonçalves.
-pp. 84-86, 90

Maddison Graphic
www.maddisongraphic.com

Maddison Graphic is a small design studio formed by brothers Edward and Alfie Maddison in late 2006. Based in Ely, Cambridgeshire, their portfolio includes work for cathedrals, universities, artists and architects. Combining typography, photography and illustration, we work on projects of all shapes and sizes, including: posters, books, websites, signage, identities, and exhibitions.
-pp. 112-113, 117

Magpie Studio
www.magpie-studio.com

Magpie Studio was founded in 2008 by 3 like-minded creatives, David Azurdia, Ben Christie and Jamie Ellul. Their studio has a simple approach: listen to their clients; understand their audience; solve their problems. Based in London, they've answers communication problems for clients around the globe, ranging from one-man-bands to orchestras. Their colorful projects cross a broad spectrum of disciplines, taking in branding, digital and packaging. Appropriately enough, they also love typography.
-pp. 108-109

Meiré und Meiré
www.meireundmeire.de

Meiré und Meiré has been working for German and international brands and companies for 25 years at the interface between culture and design. The studio develops magazines, newspapers, corporate and brand literature, digital media and campaigns in a distinctive style.
-pp. 48-51

moodley brand identity
www.moodley.at

Moodley Brand Identity is one of Austria's leading design and branding agencies with offices in Vienna and Graz. The team currently consists of 33 employees from six different countries. For over 10 years, Moodley has contributed substantially to positioning a multitude of companies, brands and products in a clear, distinct and self-confident manner. Based on a positioning that has been developed together with the customer and subsequently carefully elaborated on, Moodley Brand Identity understands how to create visualised implementations and solutions effectively and strategically.
-pp. 154-155

Mylinh Trieu Nguyen
www.mylinhtrieu.com

Mylinh Trieu Nguyen is a designer and artist based in Miami, FL. Her work explores ideas of distribution, collaboration and curation through new and appropriated systems and frameworks. Her projects mediate the space between subjectivity and objectivity, while continually striving to recontextualize the familiar and mundane.
-pp. 91

Neil Donnelly
www.neildonnelly.net

Neil Donnelly is a graphic designer who makes printed matter, websites, exhibitions, videos, and typefaces. He has worked with the New Museum, Yale University, the Guggenheim Museum, The New York Times, and Storefront for Art and Architecture, among others. He teaches at Rutgers University and holds an MFA from Yale.
-pp. 148

Oliver Daxenbichler assoc.
oliverdaxenbichler.com

Oliver Daxenbichler, founder of Oliver Daxenbichler Design, Inc., is a 34 year old Art director and Graphic designer who lives and works currently in Frankfurt Main, Germany. Over the course of almost one decade he has been working on a large variety of print and new media based projects including conceptualizing and producing ad campaigns and catalogs, logos and brand identities and magazine design.
-pp. 96-97

onlab
www.onlab.ch

The Swiss graphic design agency Onlab—founded in 2001 and based in Berlin, Germany—works on commissioned, collaborative as well as self initiated design projects. The focus of the commissioned work lies in editorial design and visual communication projects.
-pp. 146-147

Pauline Nuñez
www.ypsilonediteur.com

Pauline Nuñez (b. 1983) learned Typography in École Estienne in Paris, began working as a freelance designer in 2007 and became Ypsilon Éditeur's Art Director in 2008. Her work is concentrated on book design, but she also ran museography projects and has a personal penchant for lettering.
-pp. 81

Research and Development
researchanddevelopment.se

Research and Development collaborates with artists, curators, critics, collectors, directors, museums and cultural institutions. They design books, catalogs, posters, exhibition graphics, identity programs and other kinds of printed matter. Occasionally they arrange film screenings and produce

or participate in exhibitions.
-pp. 132-133

Raf Vancampenhoudt
www.rafvancampenhoudt.be

A freelance graphic designer working and living in Gent, Belgium. The main focus in his work lies on typography, where in most cases the typography becomes a layered image on itself. One of the main goals within projects is to get a clear and unambiguous vision on the content in dialogue with commissioner, in order to be able to wield a no-nonsense (and to-the point) language that ensouls a publication in a logic and supportive way.
-pp. 74-75

Simon and Lars
www.designbylars.com

Simon Reed and Lars Amundsen met at the college Central Saint Martin´s in 1995. After graduation (MA Communication Design) in 2000 they set up their studio in north London developing the original graphic identity for Euphorium Restaurant and Bakery. In 2003 Lars moved to Spain while Simon remained in London. Currently Lars lives in Tenerife and develops projects for TEA (Tenerife Espacio de las Artes) and other clients.
-pp. 106-107

Studio Laucke Siebein
studio-laucke-siebein.com

Studio Laucke Siebein is a design studio based in Amsterdam and Berlin. Its focus is on creative strategy, dynamic identities, graphic, book and web design within the scope of cultural and commercial projects.
-pp. 134-137

Studio Fernando Gutiérrez
fernandogutierrez.co.uk

The Studio of Fernando Gutiérrez specializes in graphic design. They work as consultants and project leaders on branding and design challenges across all media. Studio Fernando Gutiérrez typically collaborate long-term with their clients, often leading or facilitating solutions that require partnership with other strategic and creative advisers. But they also take on smaller projects because they're interesting and they keep them grounded. To be as efficient as possible while also enjoying the journey, is their motto.
-pp. 46-47, 110-11

Susana Londoño
www.slondono.com
slondono.tumblr.com

Susana Londoño is a New York based artist and graphic designer. She studied fine arts and received an undergraduate degree from the Cooper Union in 2012.
-pp. 149

Tankboys
www.tankboys.biz
Tankboys are an independent graphic studio born in 2005 and based on the Island of Giudecca, Venice. The founders are Lorenzo Mason and Marco Campardo. They graduated at the Venice's Design Faculty of IUAV and they haven't stopped working together ever since. Tankboys deal with arts and communication, focusing mainly on print and editorial projects. In 2008 they cofounded XYZ, a non-profit gallery for the applied arts (graphics, photography, design) based in Treviso. In 2009 with Ilustrator Elena Xausa they gave birth to the independent publishing house Automatic Books.
-pp. 14-15

Teacake Design
www.teacakedesign.com

Teacake (Graham Sykes & Robert Walmsley) is something quintessentially British, inventive and conscientious. They love visual organization, people, places and the idea of creating a tangible interaction with those who see their work. This has subsequently led to them having a strong affiliation with design for print and a passion for typography inspired by time spent working in the design capital of the world, Amsterdam.
-pp. 1150-151

Tappin Gofton
www.tappingofton.com

Tappin Gofton is a multidisciplinary design studio based in London. They create thoughtful, inspired design and art direction for our clients. Their work is defined by innovative ideas that are unique to each commission, founded on a close working relationship with the clients and the creative collaborators they work with.
-pp. 128-131

The Click Design Consultants
www.theclickdesign.com

The Click Design Consultants is an award-winning, independent, multi-disciplined creative design consultancy. They create outstanding brands. It's their passion. Developing engaging, memorable and effective work audiences really click with – they focus on brand identity, advertising, print and digital communications.
-pp. 120-121

Toby Ng
www.toby-ng.com

Toby Ng graduated in Graphic Design from Central St. Martins, London and is now stationed in Hong Kong with Sandy Choi Associates. Ng previously associated with London design agencies such as Landor and Saatchi & Saatchi Design. Lately selected as one of the 36 Young Designers in Asia by Designnet magazine, Korea.
-pp. 126-127

Two
www.twodesign.co.uk

Two is an independent graphic design studio based in Cornwall, in the UK. They have extensive experience in creating brand identities, print and communications and website and online design for cultural and corporate clients. By working closely and openly with clients they believe in creating appropriate and distinctive graphic design that not only communicates but also engages audiences.
-pp. 114-116

Uriah Gray
www.uriahgray.com

Uriah Gray is a graphic designer who explores print and interactive design. He graduated with a BA in 2009 and is currently working at Coöp in Melbourne (co-oponline.net.au).
-pp. 124-125

Will Work for Good
www.willworkforgood.org

Will Work for Good is an art and design studio in Brooklyn NY working on projects that support creative endeavors of inspiring groups/individuals: independent record labels, musicians, artists, galleries, comedians, non-profit organizations, friends and neighbors.
-pp. 56-57, 72

Yann Alary & Martin Selle
yan.dn.free.fr

Yann Alary and Martin Selle are two french students of ESAD Valence school, France. After a diploma obtained with honors in 2011, they continue to develop graphic design questions around print and digital, in order to start a multidisciplinary studio.
-pp. 138-139

First published and distributed by
viction:workshop ltd.

viction:ary™

Unit C, 7th Floor, Seabright Plaza,
9-23 Shell Street, North Point, Hong Kong
URL: www.victionary.com
Email: we@victionary.com
www.facebook.com/victionworkshop
www.weibo.com/victionary

Designed & Edited by TwoPoints.Net

Preface by Jan Middendorp

Typeface in Use:
Gill Sans Bold, Bold Italic

Kindly supplied by Allan Haley of Monotype Imaging.

©2012 viction:workshop ltd.
The copyright on the individual text and design work is held by the respective designers and contributors.

ISBN 978-988-19438-7-3

All rights reserved. No part of this publication may be reproduced, stored in retrieval systems or transmitted in any form or by any means, electronic or mechanical, including photocopying, recording or any information storage and retrieval systems, without permission in writing from the copyright owner(s).

The captions and artwork in this book are based on material supplied by the designers whose work is included. While every effort has been made to ensure their accuracy, viction:workshop does not under any circumstances accept any responsibility for any errors or omissions.

Printed and bound in China

We would like to thank all the designers and companies who made significant contribution to the compilation of this book. Without them this project would not be able to accomplish. We would also like to thank all the producers for their invaluable assistance throughout this entire proposal. The successful completion also owes a great deal to many professionals in the creative industry who have given us precious insights and comments. We are also very grateful to many other people whose names did not appear on the credits but have made specific input and continuous support the whole time.